# Novel

## EDUCATION

# Studies in the
# Postmodern Theory of Education

Joe L. Kincheloe and Shirley R. Steinberg
*General Editors*

Vol. 300

PETER LANG
New York • Washington, D.C./Baltimore • Bern
Frankfurt am Main • Berlin • Brussels • Vienna • Oxford

Deborah P. Britzman

# Novel

## EDUCATION

Psychoanalytic Studies of Learning
and Not Learning

PETER LANG
New York • Washington, D.C./Baltimore • Bern
Frankfurt am Main • Berlin • Brussels • Vienna • Oxford

Library of Congress Cataloging-in-Publication Data

Britzman, Deborah P.
Novel education: psychoanalytic studies of learning and not learning /
Deborah P. Britzman.
p. cm. — (Counterpoints; v. 300)
Includes bibliographical references and index.
1. Psychoanalysis and education. 2. Learning, Psychology of.
I. Title. II. Series: Counterpoints (New York, N.Y.); v. 300.
LB1092.B753   370.15'23—dc22   2005035612
ISBN 0-8204-8148-3 paperback
ISBN 0-8204-8666-3 hardcover
ISSN 1058-1634


Bibliographic information published by **Die Deutsche Bibliothek**.
**Die Deutsche Bibliothek** lists this publication in the "Deutsche
Nationalbibliografie"; detailed bibliographic data is available
on the Internet at http://dnb.ddb.de/.

Cover design by Lisa Barfield

Cover art by Yukari Yoshimoto


The paper in this book meets the guidelines for permanence and durability
of the Committee on Production Guidelines for Book Longevity
of the Council of Library Resources.

© 2006 Peter Lang Publishing, Inc., New York
29 Broadway, New York, NY 10006
www.peterlang.com

Printed in the United States of America

# contents

# Preface

The title of this book came to me while taking notes in a psychoanalytic workshop devoted to the writing of clinical case studies and, so, to the question of narrative. Panelists came to disagree over what seemed to be an economic problem: How much narrative play may analysts have in representing their clinical work? Should the case study be able to note its unconscious dynamics and the drafts of its free association? Beyond the ordinary disguises and needed distortions created to protect the privacy of the analysand, the disagreement toppled into the dynamic tension of fiction as both figment of imagination and the runaway story. If the case study reads like fiction, like metapsychology, what can we say is represented? Far from being an exercise in the death of the author, that day the author of the case study exhibited too much life. I cannot pinpoint where my thoughts began to stray, but along with the doodles that crowded my notes, I began to sketch my own pedagogical and existential concerns. From a pedagogical side, what is it to report, to one's colleagues and students, the experience of one's work and remark upon how the ideas made and sometimes discarded there resist and instruct the narrative? How is a case study an encounter with learning and not learning? Existentially, what form of life do words create? What are the psychodynamic tensions within interpretation, the ones analysts create in the analytic time and those that constitute the afterwardness of treatment, that is, the writing of the case study? What is it to write therapeutically?

These questions touch on the conflict of hermeneutics, the study of the interpretation of interpretation, or interpretation's historicity. We mean something beyond what is said, and this excess returns to unsettle meaning. In his study of Freud, Ricoeur (1970) suggests two disparate meanings or functions of the psychoanalytic interpretation: An interpretation may restore meaning and be made to destroy illusions that are also meaning. Yet how does one tell the difference if the case study may be working at both levels and if the very nature of narrative requires and involves this double action? There also emerged the question of (and what some in the workshop saw as) the analyst's "flights of fantasy"—wild associations taken through the playground of theory and also the audience's transference. How different can the analyst's understanding be from the analysand's own understanding? And would this difference be then seen as either reparative or destructive? Second thoughts on these matters may bring us to the literary problem of representing the work of affect. Here we encounter the noncoincidence of experience to the vicissitudes of its meanings. Here, too, we may glimpse a remarkable, runaway, affected subjectivity. Perhaps the case is that when writing, reading, or listening to the case study, there is no such thing as innocent bystanders; we find ourselves on the side of otherness, the affect.

When we read between its lines and listen for how we are affected by the case study's theory of learning and not learning, clinical writing alters its purpose. Yet it is precisely in this excess of meaning that loyalties divide. Is the psychoanalytic case study on the side of empiricism and its proof, merely recording what happened? Or, is there an aesthetic, therapeutic consideration that structures both the work and its writing and so therefore presents the excess of what the analytic event cannot contain? What would it mean for a case study to be a study of its own affected divide? Can the case study be affected by the literary qualities of both the subjective world and the act of representing it again in writing? And, if we claim we are writing novels, must that cancel the question of the truth effects of psychoanalysis or even destroy what it can mean to generalize processes of psychical life as now posing an interminable, unruly human condition?

Many of these problems between knowledge and truth, I believe, alter the work of education. There, researchers are asked to settle the best practices, confirm effective methods, and service social adaptation. With governmental pressure for what is known as "evidence-based research," the researcher is required to demonstrate, before it can be carried out, the value of the research. Under the crushing assumption that education can and must be knowable in advance, the uses of research have been reduced to standardized application. On this view, there is no such thing as unrepeatable research. These demands for certainty, stability, and transparency of method place research close to the procedures of an assembly line and defend against the overwhelming anxiety that mass education also presents. And yet, the hegemony of certainty leaves us with is pitiful products: zero tolerance, fear of failure, and technocratic language. On this view, unruly subjectivity becomes an improper study. I say to make a novel education we need to stay close to this affected improper study. Then, research itself can be conceptualized as a thought experiment, as a note of counter-discourse. Let us return research to what it does not know, to let this ignorance come out, and so become our novel education.

What can fiction mean in the helping professions? I bring this question to many of my current learning situations: university professor of education, researcher, candidate in a psychoanalytic institute, analysand, and in my clinical practice as therapist. The studies of learning and not learning gathered here represent my uneasy dialogue between the clinic of education and the clinic of psychoanalysis. Throughout this book, I put pressure on education with psychoanalytic views but also press psychoanalysis to express its theories of learning. I pose these disparate contexts as clinics because they are rare places the mind may take refuge. They can be places to freely wonder over the purpose of both reparation and destruction. They are clinics in the sense that strangers meet to affect ideas and each other. Allowing these sites their fictions, that is, their alienation from taken-for-granted sense—allowing these sites their adventure and disappointment with meaning and their anxieties over significance not yet reached, but still demanding form—creates a transitional space for subjectivity to be without justification, to be an improper study. These are the needed conditions for psychological significance to be risked and for thinking to be made anew.

The chapters that follow are psychoanalytic studies of the value of, and objections to, fiction in conceptualizing and representing the delegates, object relations and history of learning and not learning. Fiction will be a shorthand for the problem of understanding the reach of history, with what becomes of actual events, with what we make happen from signs. Sometimes I use fiction to signify literary design, as in the writing of novels. At other times, fiction will take its place only in confrontation with trying to know, through the affect, reality as such. Then, fiction will reach into the sublime, into that which both alienates and fascinates. I will associate with the movements of fiction to understand why we split success from failure, fact from fiction, subjectivity from objectivity, and literature from life. Fiction will cross wires with anxiety, even as it telegraphs its own anxiety. The unreal reality of psychical life will also go under this name, as will discussions of dependency, the transference, and the activity of writing. The Freudian fiction of the drives will be given free reign as will their work of animating its representational vicissitudes. Dreams, too, will be models, as will dream-work, free association, and interpretation.

An underlying question that brings these chapters together begins not with what is novel about education but rather with what a novel education is like. This question invites comparative efforts across the human professions and the humanities, but it also turns on a particular dilemma of how knowing self/other relations affect the nature of the relation, with how, through an interest in psychical reality, object relations, and the literary, knowledge is expressed and its history enlivened. It turns out that there is a literary school concerned with education. Good and bad novels of education are carried out through the genre of the *bildungsroman*; there bringing up culture prepares the lines for the plot of bringing up of a life. Obstacles will come in the form of characters but also will be the condition for subjective events to affect our narrator. In this literary genre, the narrators, usually at first unwittingly, come to arrange arbitrary life into lessons on learning to live. These are novels of affected psychology and affected education; they may be read as narratives on the passions of learning and not learning but also as points of entry into understanding the work of trying to know the self and the Other. These novels play between the lines of making fiction from life and making life from fiction. How different is this from what we do in learning, from gathering our objects, obstacles, and events to sketch the studies for representing—taking note of—our own novel education?

To ask what a novel education is like will take us into the problem of narrating the emotional experience of learning and not learning and into the question of how the emotions are to be noted and used. There will always be others involved, yet their hands may be invisible. The first half of this book analyzes the history of education in psychoanalytic theory and practice, while the second half narrates contemporary education and its history of trying to know its narrative acts. A theme developed in Chapter One turns on Freud's double problem of presenting psychoanalysis to the general public and experiencing the surprise of being affected by both theory and practice. The history of Freud's accidental pedagogy will introduce to readers the aesthetic and theraputic preoccupations of this book, perhaps the key one being how we come to know our representatives of education, then and now. Psychoanalysis gathers objections against its technique to make from these its technique and theory. One of its methods, perhaps the only one that distinguishes psychoanalysis from other therapeutic practices, is the free association, the topic of Chapter Two. There, fiction accepts its accidental qualities only to become a problem of association. The question of narrative freedom may then be noticed. Automatic writing and free writing also take a turn in this second chapter, as will its history of advice from the poets and mythology.

The gathering of objections, now from the vantage of self-alienation and creation will take us into a study of an ego defense known as "identification with the aggressor," the topic of Chapter Three. This chapter stages learning and not learning within the world of object relations. Here, fiction takes on the qualities of identification, linking itself to the problem of love and hate. The painful fiction concerns what the ego will do to sustain a needed relationship that does not satisfy, and that takes the ego into conditions of oppressive love. The pleasurable fiction is that aggression may well be one way the ego sets itself loose from the confines of compliance to make its own demands. The chapter has a further purpose in that this psychoanalytic concept has migrated into discussions of postcoloniality and anti-racist pedagogy, used there as a lens to consider self/other relations. At times, when brought to social theory, we are apt to disengage this ego defense from its relation to phantasy. The place of the unconscious will also make agency insecure. As with most psychoanalytic language, the concept of "identification with the aggressor" I argue, cannot be understood as an explanatory device, but can be used to imagine mundane development as involving tenderness, passion, aggression, and alienation.

Chapters Four and Five turn to problems in education as they are played out in the history of analytic relations between children and adults. These chapters play in the psychoanalytic archive, rummaging for the problems it leaves us to think. Education will appear through its most fantastic qualities: as wishes, anxieties, magical learning, and as questions that cannot be answered. In Chapter Four, readers meet the early case studies of Sigmund Freud and Melanie Klein as these analysts work through the improbable question, what is sexual enlightenment? I argue that the eighteenth-century question of what enlightenment is became, in the twentieth century a failed project of determining what sexual enlightenment is. There, theories of existence between the adult and the child write their own private novels. Learning will take on magical qualities, but so, too, will this magic be disillusioned with the analyst's attempt to interpret the affects of love and hate. Chapter Five continues a study of the psychoanalytic archive, now focusing on the question of inhibition through Melanie Klein's work with Little Richard at the height of World War II. Richard's symptoms tell a novel story of psychoanalytic education and love: He used his psychoanalysis to explore the meaning of existence, aggression, and forgiveness. But Klein also narrates this story as one of being affected by Richard. In both chapters, the novel education emerges from how the analyst and analysand transform their respective questions.

Chapters Six, Seven, and Eight continue with the theme of being affected by representing the felt experiences of learning and not learning. Chapter Six analyzes two disturbances of memory and problems in recollection. The first disturbance is contained in a birthday greeting Freud wrote to the author Romain Rolland. The second falls under the auspices of how the problem of teaching fiction turned out to be a story of remembering the fictions of teaching. The teacher's memory is disturbed when narrating a story of trying to remember learning to teach. Chapter Seven takes a different view of disturbances, with notes on the teacher's depression. There, I consider the fictions that defend against encountering the teacher's illness. I arrange this chapter as a series of notes to convey something of the chaos of representing illness and to suggest the incompleteness of my sketches. I draw upon psychoanalytic discussions of the analyst's education, and the idea that the analyst's education invites the analyst's madness that is already there. What can it mean for education to contain the teacher's madness when the teacher's history of education may be a part of the story of illness? Fiction appears differently in this chapter through Freud's idea of the transference in the analytic setting and how, as an artificial illness, it may be interpreted. I suggest that the term "teacher burn out" is cover for the teacher's depression, but also that illness—rather than be confined to the discourse of attributes—can be conceived as a substitute to a missing or broken relation. Objections to conceptualizing the teacher's illness come from many sources, including the profession of education.

In the last chapter, contemporary questions of knowing education are raised. I consider a persistent problem in psychoanalytic practice that also may animate our sense of education and what can be imagined from our fact of natality and existence as such. In psychoanalysis, the ongoing debate is born from the interminable question: What is a clinical fact? This question was raised in Chapter Six, from the vantage of memory. In Chapter Eight, two dilemmas are brought into tension. One emerges from representing clinical practice. This is the tension between being addressed by the idiomatic aspects of intersubjectivity and constructing a theory from what is particular and perhaps unrepeatable in intersubjective practice. A second dilemma follows. It concerns the relation between objectivity and subjectivity and what each perspective means for representing the emotional world of teaching and learning. Both suggest a constitutive problem with subjective practices in the human professions, where analysts and teachers must depend upon their subjectivity in order to practice at all but in doing so experience epistemological uncertainty, anxiety, and the transference. So stretching this clinical question to education I ask, "What is a pedagogical fact?" How do we characterize our work as mediating reality and as affecting the self's perception of mediation? Can a fact keep company with subjectivity as a relation? This chapter, too, considers the playground of fiction, now from the vantage of understanding the actions of what is so subjective and so accidental about our work.

Throughout this book, I take note of education's likeness to problems in philosophy and literature, to practices and theories of psychoanalysis, and to debates in clinical and educational research, taking as my objects narratives of learning and not learning. And because these elusive objects are those that contain histories of relationships and our wishes for them, I ask, how does narrative affect the narrator? How does a field of a thought and practice present and affect its aesthetic difficulties and promises? More intimately, how do words make a form of life? How, in our work and in our writing, do we encounter the Other, including there, one's own Otherness?

Contemporary psychoanalysis is contentious, complex, and alive. It may also be the case that we need to ask, "Which psychoanalysis?" This, too, is a large debate for the differences between schools of thought at times can seem to cancel each other out. Sometimes these debates are characterized as a problem of updating psychoanalytic knowledge, as if we could reset the clock of theory to keep time with its object. As I see it, the perennial problem psychoanalysis presents, and one that it shares with education, is how we think while being affected by affected theory and practice. More often than not, there is pressure to choose sides, to be loyal to schools of thought, to declare which psychoanalytic school one follows. But here, too, one may find divided loyalties and ambivalence, specifically because this contentious field also respects the experience of being theoretically right and practically wrong, of needing the gap between theory and practice, of respecting uncertainty and the promiscuity of words. Throughout these studies, I work with theories that do argue with each other. The crisis of representation, so discussed in the Humanities and Social Sciences, touches psychoanalytic and educational practices. Symbolizing and associating with this crisis, is, I believe, the heart of psychoanalysis. I take Bion's advice as reported by Marion Milner (1977/1996) that while we may get by with one theory, the many models generated by theory should be used and enjoyed. This does not solve the thorny problems of borrowing views that may contradict, but it does allow for the thought that psychoanalysis itself is contention: It disrupts the smooth surface of its own consciousness, finds meaning in the things farthest from one's mind, and makes terribly complex the humans' need for the human condition. Whether this destroys our illusions or gives us new ones is a question best left open. This debate belongs to education as well. Perhaps like psychoanalysis it, too, is caught in its own childhood.

Readers will see my preference for the genre of writing a little comment known as "the note." We first learn its form in early education and it may take years to divest ourselves from linking notes with compliance and then feeling required to study them in order to take an avalanche of school tests. We may remember asking teachers whether we have to take notes, if we can use our notes when taking tests, and if we can copy the notes of the Other. If it can seem like the note is a crutch for memory, we may also recall our school notes as reverie, holding our secret thoughts, becoming the love note, or as recording a fleeting thought that must then be passed to friends sitting across the room. We may come to recall our own history of taking and receiving notes. Beyond being an avid note taker and finding my study littered with small bits of paper containing my thoughts and free associations, beyond my habit of taking notes without knowing in advance what will become of them, I have been influenced by their use in clinical writing where many of the papers, including some from Freud, carry the note in its title. The note, it seems to me, may gesture to its own incompleteness and to the modesty of contribution. It may be returned to again to be altered or to mark one problem in the endless stream of theory. Notes can also suggest tentativeness, playing with ideas, and a prehistory. Like the artist's sketch, a note may later be returned to and used as a study for a larger work. Indeed, while compulsory education and perhaps university classrooms may be responsible for ruining this mode of writing for those subjects who felt forced to take notes during lectures or were subject to the terrible lesson on how to take notes and then how to study them, my hope is that this book may remind readers of what is lovely about writing them.

While writing this book, I have benefited from deep friendships, thoughtful discussions with colleagues and students in the university, and with my clinical affiliation as a candidate in the Toronto Institute for Contemporary Psychoanalysis. I have been influenced by lively exchanges with Professor Carol Zemel on problems in aesthetics and the history of art. My apprenticeship in therapeutic practice has been supported and enriched by discussions with Dr. Oren Gozlen, Dr. Gabrielle Israelievitch, and Dr. Art Caspary. Dr. Michelle Flax heard most of this text and many others; I remain grateful for her skilled, compassionate listening and novel education. In the life and in the writing life, I thank again Professor Alice Pitt. Her generosity, grace, love, keen advice, and analytic insight are deeply valued. I also thank Joe Kincheloe and Shirley Steinberg for their encouragement and friendship and for their efforts in seeing this book through and Chris Meyers from Peter Lang Publishing. I thank Dr. Sharon Sliwinski for her insightful work on the cover of the book, her friendship, and for introducing me—by way of the gift "Shake Hands Please"—to the artist, Yukari Yoshimoto. I am grateful to the artist Yukari Yoshimoto, who gave me permission to reproduce her work titled "Shake Hands Please" for the book cover. I hope that the spirit of this text meets the spirit of her art. I thank Christine Higgott and Peter Ford of Off-Center Gallery for facilitating my access to Yoshimoto. Many e-mails were translated between English and Japanese, and one of the most interesting for me was trying to explain through translators, what this book is about and why Yosimoto's "Shake Hands Please" contained what for me is lovely and anxious about becoming a self with other selves.

Earlier versions of a few chapters have been published elsewhere; the majority, however, were written with this text in mind. I am grateful for permission to reprint, in altered form, the following: An earlier version of Chapter Three was published in 2005 in *Race, Identity and Representation in Education*, second edition, edited by Cameron McCarthy, Warren Crichlow, Greg Dimitriadis, and Nadine Dolby and reproduced by permission of Routledge/Taylor and Francis Group, LLC. A shorter version of Chapter Four appears in 2006 in *Love's Return: Psychoanalytic Essays on Childhood*, edited by Paulo Salvio and Gail Bolt and reproduced by permission of Routledge/Taylor and Francis Group, LLC. An earlier version of Chapter Five appeared in 2004 in *Disciplining the Child via the Discourse of the Professions*, edited by Roxanna Transit and reproduced courtesy of Charles C. Thomas Publisher, Ltd. A shorter version of Chapter Six appeared in the journal *Changing English*, Volume 11, 2004 and is available at http://www.tandf.co.uk.

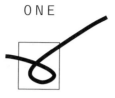

# ONE

# Psychoanalytic Studies of Learning and Not Learning

*In the best cases, analysis is an invitation to become the narrator, the novelist, of one's own story.*

Kristeva, The Sense and Non-Sense of Revolt

The invitation to narrate one's story of learning may lead to illegible experiences and so, to imagine Kristeva's (2000) best case, to writing many, many novels with a dedication to narration. As well, Kristeva involves the worst case: "What are the stories that Freud asked his patients to tell? Stories full of gaps, silences, awkwardness—in a way, novels deprived of an audience" (65). The best and worst cases are studies in the language of passion. Our concern is with their conjugation, with understanding obstacles to learning as intrinsic to obstacles to narrating learning.[1] Here is where the line between that which resists telling this novel story of learning and that which urges one to become a narrator is blurred, obscuring the boundary between the object of learning and the subject who learns. What kind of testimony to learning reaches into the conditions, values, and effects of its own production, including there what escapes and resists its grasp? What is involved in this novelness of narration? And how might we understand learning and not learning as affected by these experiences?

Try then to accept this strange invitation and represent the presence of learning without also recounting a story of being affected by the Other, without feeling something of one's own otherness, and without bumping up against the absence that representation signifies. There, too, traces of not learning are animated, whether we attribute this negativity to others who cannot or will not learn, or notice our own resistance. If this negativity can be recognized as part of the self, we may begin to ponder the difficult work of understanding that a narration is touched by the Other and by a failure within representation to grasp its object completely. Our thought experiment leads us to the heart of this chapter: Studies in learning and not learning are at once a play of the affects and an encounter with our ideas of them. Our studies bring into relief as well a history of the learning's invitation.

The psychoanalytic invitation asks us to narrate learning and not learning and in so doing, provokes aesthetic conflicts, doubt over what there is to know, what the good of knowing is and, whether knowledge matters to the Other. Psychoanalysts have their share of aesthetic conflicts because their invitation to narrate is received by them through special delivery and counter-transference will be the return address. That is, the act of inquiry affects the method; the invitation affects both the narration and its reception. Imagined this way, the story of learning we are about to encounter, the incredible one told by psychoanalysis, draws its convictions, at times against its own will, from literary and artistic designs, from the methods of novelists, artists, poets, and even toy makers. Aesthetic conflicts then ensue as to where psychoanalysis and its learning theory belong, a problem of boundaries so utterly familiar that we are apt to miss what anxiety putting things into their proper place defends against: an encounter with the groundlessness and insecurity of subjects who think.

It turns out that the psychoanalytic enterprise will be affected by the experiences it, too, narrates, thereby complicating further how psychoanalysis is conveyed and received. The large problems psychoanalysis sets for it concern placing its own methods on notice through attending to the intersubjective representation of structuring events of subjective life and our capacity to construct psychological significance from their affective qualities. This is why psychoanalysis receives its own invitation. It, too, writes many novels and worries all the while whether audience and author have gone missing.

The testimony itself is strange, for it begins with the worst and best case, the doubts over whether there will be an audience, whether there will be stories at all, and whether the affective world can be symbolized therapeutically. These doubts permit and permeate the psychoanalytic project and our encounters with it. As such, they, too, narrate a story of learning and not learning. To understand these subjective conundrums, I explore qualities of learning and not learning as leaning upon aesthetics and its preoccupation with what is sublime. More generally this chapter holds in tension the vicissitudes of influence and being influenced as a structuring impulse affecting both psychoanalysis and education. While often at cross purposes, both fields have their share in the affective disorders of learning and not learning. A few questions will orient us: How do we think about influence, not just influencing others but the way in which we are affected by our practices? What can one know without it being seen and with the insecurity of interpreting psychical events? What use is this speculative knowledge for associating the delegates of learning with not learning?

English has no word that conjoins learning and not learning, or that signifies the negativity that learning also contains. Indeed, the progressive word "learning" can represent procedures and hopes for goals, but cannot precede its objects. It can refer to the material to be known and the learner's refinement, or the work entailed in making a signature on knowledge. It presupposes an encounter with something or someone but cannot refer to its accidents, anticipations, grasping actions, or affective stumbles. The word learning cannot index to its own duration, its noncoincidence with an object, and its strategies of representation. If these last limits are shared with not learning, what separates them is that, typically, not learning designates the destination of an individual's failure, her or his negation, resistance, ignorance, or refusal to learn. Opposition may be its noisy underside. Not learning may be associated with regression, but as a backward movement, one is stretched to pinpoint its origin. Missed by rigid division is what they both require: the arts and crafts of mediation; the place of the Other; the passions and disappointments of an encounter; the anticipation, objections, and anxiety that are set in motion; and, the defenses against loss of the object, loss of love, and loss of self-recognition. What actually differentiates these two positions in learning, what dissociates and confuses, is when one position forecloses the capacity to think of its other, to reflect upon one's representations, even if this requires wild speculation that exceeds conscious experience. All these relations will be grouped under the transference, itself an obstacle to and impulse toward communicating the ways learning and not learning conjugate. Suppose, then, we imagine learning not so much as the victory over not learning but as playing with and even requiring its own negativity.

In my work as educator, I am often told that psychoanalysis and education are completely different fields, usually with objections such as: Teachers are not analysts and analysts are not educators; teachers cannot and should not analyze their students; no one has time for psychoanalysis. While application may not be the best arbiter for understanding our responsibilities to others, the transference—the transposition of affects—between these fields gives us plenty of hints as to how we may listen to their uneasy conversations. These objections which posit an absolute boundary convey an anxiety over the fact that both fields of practice and theory must be preoccupied with and affected by learning and not learning. A difference between these fields is, however, instructive. Whereas in the practices of education, we would be hard pressed to describe our work as learning and as not learning education, or as clarifying the procedures of not learning, psychoanalysts and their analysands have this as their problem: Undergoing analysis, from whatever side, is a learning of psychoanalysis and a curiosity toward bringing into relief a history of not learning. And this history of not learning as narrated in the analytic setting conjugates the past with the present analytic relationship. Not learning is analyzed through its affective compositions conveyed under the auspices of the transference. It is also an obscure resource because the transference resists its own representations and sets interpretation to work. This double problem of representing learning through remembering not learning further complicates Kristeva's invitation to become a novelist; it is rare, indeed, to write without writing.[2]

How others learn psychoanalysis and how psychoanalysis affects itself, or how the Other's affect mobilizes a psychoanalytic response to transform psychoanalysis itself, turn out to be intimately related. This is the education of psychoanalysis. Indeed, Freud's founding problems of presenting psychoanalysis to the general public, to his colleagues, and to his analysands transformed psychoanalytic theory from an assertion of its ideas of psychical life and then chagrin over their rejection to a curiosity toward exploring what we may see today as aesthetic conflicts in learning and not learning. Representing conflicts in learning is akin to writing a novel because the concern is with constructing a psychology of emotional reality; there we really do personify knowledge and make of its objects noisy creatures. From the theatrics of language we create metaphors of likeness from emotional reality, composite words that refer us to wishes and re-grets, and to phantasies of being. Through the freedom of imagination and in dreams, we can conceptualize what is not seen yet still exerts the force of absence. Through the unconscious we are affected by what conscious-ness cannot imagine. These events and the ways in which they conjugate perception with desire capture experiences of our being affected before knowing in advance meaning's migrations. Affect passes through all of this to associate meaning to places least expected: to phantasies of learning and not learning. Representing learning creates a fictitious space, not because learning is unreal but because learning leans on affect and desire which, in turn, mesmerizes representation. On this view, to conceptualize learning and not learning through the transference means attending to how the affective work of psychoanalysis acts upon and transforms its own edifice. While following the lines of a psychological narrative, this particular story of learning takes shape as a narrative on learning depth psychology.

## Madness and Aesthetics

To encounter the qualities, dynamics, adaptations, and force of the sub-jective world of learning, I draw upon aesthetic terms, many of which are literary. My style for thinking with aesthetics is interdisciplinary: a patchwork of psychoanalytic discussions on art, psychoanalytic writing's dependence upon literary truths as the means of persuasion, influence, and working through; and literary theory's occupation within the crisis of representation as sublime knowledge. Ricoeur's (1970) study of Freud proposes that theory and thought must suffer a complex of crisis—of lan-guage, of interpretation, and of reflection (56). His observations of what animates meaning will be useful over the course of my psychoanalytic studies because when these crises are felt, intersubjectivity becomes un-certain. After all, what brings language, interpretation, and reflection its purpose is that these intrigues of meaning both address the Other and invite our own Otherness.

There is no justification for my interests in aesthetic designs of learn-ing and not learning. There are, however, autobiographical details. Once, a long time ago, I was a high school English teacher. Working with liter-ary and aesthetic designs influenced how I came to think about education, my own and those of others. But also, I admit a particular estrangement from the world and my thinking about it that is best engaged through the solitudes of literary design and the intimacy of psychoanalysis. My own learning in psychoanalysis as analysand and as a candidate in the clinic of psychoanalytic education brings closer the problem of aesthetic conflicts. If these bare details can be accepted as flashpoints, they may only illuminate my passionate attachments and anxieties made in both education and psychoanalysis and my dependency upon literary representation to express something of how I feel. Objections will surely follow and oddly they will be reminiscent of objections to psychoanalysis. But they will also make apparent the aesthetic conflicts needed for any representation and reflection on it to matter. I mean then to discuss learning and not learning psychoanalytically; there will be curiosity toward displacement, defenses, and affect and so with the negativity of meaning. This aesthetic involves paying attention to guarded statements, utterances that mislead, misrecognize, and abject and taking note of the little procedures of resistance to interpretation that service desire. These are also the chances taken by novels and artistic expression.

In the analytic setting, the analysand's recounting of a novel or a news event may be a way to animate conflict and represent to the Other one's inner world of object relations. I have noticed in the psychoanalytic archive that its theory and clinical descriptions also draw poignancy from the work of the arts to represent psychical reality from the viewpoint of its affective travails. Psychoanalysis needs to affect representation, to create and take residence in the emotional impact conveyed and received, and thus borrows from the most affected representations—fiction and mythology—to notice the excess of desire, the volatility of affect, the play of meaning, and the accidents of life. Working through is an aesthetic undertaking even as aesthetics allows psychoanalysis to participate in the peregrinations of representation and its hesitation to stray. There are reveries and painful silences. Psychoanalysis allows aesthetics its madness, what Felman (1985/2003) calls, "the literary thing . . . the original, originative drive that makes us read" (5).

To grasp these strange affectations, I also borrow from the field of aesthetics to consider the vicissitudes of learning because the former tolerates the crisis of representation and links representation's failure, or its aporia, to being affected. Care is given to the vicissitudes of curiosity and what stops it short. Curiosity is an old word to describe the mind's movements, reveries, trespasses, transgressions, and forgets the boundary between imagination and madness. André Green (1986) will guide us here:

So what has become of madness? Rather than characterize it as a disorder of reason, one should on the contrary stress the affective, passionate element which modifies the subject's relation to reality, electing a part or whole object, becoming more or less exclusively attached to it, reorganizing his perceptions of the world around it, and giving it a unique or irreplaceable aura by which the ego is captivated and alienated. (223)

Without irony Green's depiction of madness is so general that it can gather under its sign our love affairs and our hatred with theory and fields of thought and practice such as philosophy, education, and psychoanalysis. But why pass passion through madness as opposed to, say, its sublimation? Because affect as sensation and as statement of need—and because of the intensity of the drive that seeks a representative—the thought of the object will be marked and animated through mechanisms of idealization and splitting and through aggression, hate, love, and worries over destruction and repair. Because between the ego's captivation and alienation, presence and absence may mortify, pleasure and pain become indistinct, and suffering erupts. In aesthetics, these contrary feelings are grouped under the experience of the sublime, where thought encounters its limits and becomes groundlessness, thereby alienating its perception. When thought becomes sublime we are unable to turn away from our fascination of being, at least momentarily, without our own nature to comprehend ourselves (Lyotard 1994). Because of our private madness, Green is interested in our relationship to reality as such and with the idea that our perception of reality involves passionate relations with objects. What distinguishes the psychoanalytic from philosophical preoccupations with representation is the former's attention to this passionate alienation: "It is," writes Green, "the psyche that suffers, that suffers the passion of a missing object" (235). Sublimation cannot prevent unhappiness even if its productions leave us happy.[3]

The philosophy of aesthetics considers loss from the other side. It notices a passion for absence through its preoccupation with representation's failure to capture the object and through placing the imagination in this gap. Guyer's (2005) history of debates on beauty in aesthetics summarizes a troubling dimension of knowledge dependent upon the arts: What does one make of "the cognitive significance of fiction" (x)? How does an encounter with fiction affect the churning of reason and our capacity and interest in apprehending the world? Given the freedom of representation that fiction permits, given this mad freedom, what becomes of our understanding of the external world? Will perception be ruined as meaning is deepened? Here, too, we wonder over the means for mesmerizing attention, perception, and recognition. What is the work of fiction as it gains its momentum from reconceptualizing the affectations of experience that it also creates? These questions we ask of cognition join freedom to the sublime: to a preoccupation with what cannot be seen, with an absence felt, and a remainder that may be thought of as an ache of representation. "To *see* something disappear again," Ann Smock (1982) writes in her introduction to her translation of Blanchot's essays on literature, "this is an experience which cannot actually start . . . [It is] an ordeal . . . [and] an incapacity to stop seeing what is not there to be seen" (9). Blanchot (1982) names this affectation without justification as "irreducible existence" (217), and then, more than once, he will see the effects of having to need and desire the lost object as "torn intimacy" (226).

These interminable problems of alienation, fascination, desire, and existence present themselves to the work of the human professions, thereby animating their own aesthetic conflicts. Within the human professions, there are gigantic objections to modeling its knowledge and techniques after the procedures and aporia of fiction, after the crisis of representation, language, and reflection. To be sure, their intersubjective conditions invoke anxiety over boundaries. We are likely to ask what becomes of our desire for objectivity and neutrality and why do we have these desires at all? What happens to the goodness of knowing the world if perception is affected through the animations of psychical life on its way to being further mediated and even displaced by language, interpretation, reflection, and the desires of the Other? These objections will disorient and mislead because they carry complex anxiety, an anticipation of danger without knowing in advance what specifically will be lost or destroyed when fiction is found. The worry is that with so much uncertainty and contention over the meaning of practice and theory and over the qualities of understanding our objects, the certitude of reality and even our love of it will disappear. Let us pay attention to these aesthetic conflicts with this double effort: arranging the objections through analyzing the anxieties over the loss of reality and love and treating all of these as entry points that already concern the work of conjugating learning and not learning.

The rehearsal of objections highlights what is sublime in learning since objections force attention to the dynamic conflicts between form and matter that learning leans upon and that not learning may try to give away. Learning can then be imagined as convening those elusive qualities of an uncanny encounter that compose the sublime: its variations on beauty, awe, and worthiness; relations of truth and knowledge; the disruption of what disappears with the desire for self-presence; and its work of the creation and destruction of meanings. The limits of our thinking, the relation between thinking and suffering, and the failures to synthesize the inadequacy of the concept to the thing of experience—all of these little implosions constitute the aesthetic conflicts that inaugurate and frustrate the travail of learning (Lyotard 1988). In regard to learners, an aesthetic orientation magnifies their affectations and may invite novel expression and symbolization.

## Presenting Problems

Near the end of his long career, Freud continued to question how to present his unusual ideas to the general public, his psychoanalytic colleagues, and to those in his clinical practice. It was an electric and an unruly audience he held in mind and one can only wonder how such a disparate group influenced the ideas themselves. These individuals were already subject to their own address, the unconscious—an overpopulated geography trading signification in special currency: resistance to rationality, loyalty to pleasure, and cancellation of time. And as if the unconscious is now sounding like its own private country, Freud further pried open its boundaries by speculating on its functions, wishes, affects, fragmenting strategies and resistance to translation. The unconscious will rule by its own unruly laws of primary processes: condensation, displacement, substitution, undoing, and reversals into opposites, all delightful deconstructions of symbolization. This incontinent law is itself an aesthetic undertaking, for there the world is transformed, conviction is made, affect is given free reign, and new realities are created. It is also a world where nothing ever goes away, where repression, as both the force and the content, would preserve and bury untenable ideas and affects, and where one of its representatives, the dream, would only drop hints that meaning is elsewhere. This logic of otherness plays well with secondary processes of consciousness, not in the sense that everyone gets along, but rather in what each would make of the Other through creative conflict. Both primary and secondary processes are required for something like thinking to occur but the primary will also mark thoughts, and this doubling played havoc with Freud's problem of presentation. There would be no unaffected bystanders. In this regard, the psychoanalytic presentation would draw its appeal to and susceptibility for the arts of existence from aesthetic design.

While presenting psychoanalysis to the reading public differs from an encounter with these ideas in the analytic setting, it is the free association in the analytic setting that influences the directions of difficulties noticed. The workings of psychoanalytic work—whether from the vantage of the analyst or the analysand—depend on the intermingling and confusion of rationality and irrationality and so begin not with understanding but with uncertainty. The assumption is that learning occurs before understanding, and so the work would be to notice the conflicts needed to accept this uncertainty, and only then for the allowance of knowledge to be made within self/other relations. The willing suspension of disbelief as shared convictions is needed for and emerges from psychoanalytic action: that the unconscious exists, that one can take pleasure in the incredulities of living, and that analysis matters. In the analytic setting, the transference—a signature of impressive history hardly remembered but terribly memorable—would tie uncertainty to knowing. This means that one's desire to settle understanding animates scenes of not understanding as well as infantile wishes to be understood without having to speak. In the play of the analytic relation, unconscious wishes are carried to the Other through the conviction of the affects. Moreover, through these telegraphed, projected feelings, through these unconscious communications, psychoanalysis conflicts with its wish to educate. It will be useless to rationally explain the symptom and then expect it to disappear. It will be useless to situate a final cause and expect the resistance to magically relax. Reason will fail, but it will never be so far away that its urgency will disappear. Psychoanalytic meaning will be carried by this enigma, adding poignancy to Freud's problem of presentation. How does one present ideas that undo the defense of rational thought, which depend on this undoing, but that then, along with this destruction, invite new forms of the resistance and of working through (Freud 1926)?

The creation, conveyance, and acceptance of psychoanalysis would become the founding presenting problem of psychoanalysis. And this problem will migrate to, and transform, the ways psychoanalysis thinks of pedagogy, learning, and creative life. It is a difficulty that will place psychoanalysis in conflict with what education can mean because the educational methods cannot know their own reception. Freud's (1940b) short unfinished paper whose title conveys a problem of education, "Some Elementary Lessons in Psycho-Analysis," begins with the psychological problem of presentation and with the suggestion that what is most elementary is the most difficult to accept. How can one introduce unusual ideas that seem to go against consciousness without also calling forth the resistance? There are two psychological strategies he will use and then discard, both of which are familiar to contemporary pedagogy and to child rearing practices. One strategy is "genetic." It addresses the accidental structure and the constitutional aspects of temperamental experience, presenting what is so familiar that once grasped, listeners will have already reached their own conclusions. Today we would see this as beginning from the knowledge of learners and only gradually, following from their experiences, introducing new ideas. It is one way learning occurs, leaning upon the familiar and slowly stretching the early understandings until they can be altered by independent views. Freud notes a problem with this approach. It is so gradual that by the time a new idea is accepted it is felt as if it is not so new and the learner may ask, "Is that all there is?" This approach also covers over earlier problems. How do the constitutional or the genetic come to be experienced as experience? Does the genetic approach actually begin inside the learner's beginning or does it animate that which allows the learner to begin, namely the pleasure principle?

Freud's second approach is dogmatic, or today, what we would think of as ideological, even authoritarian, in its scope and outlook. This approach borrows from didacticism and its obsession with the explication of events. An idea is asserted and explained, all with the rational expectation of its acceptance. It does not solve the paradox of how the rational can address irrationality or break through the defense of dogma. The dogmatic approach as well carries subsidiary problems, for dogmatic ideas do not brook well with those who do not hold them. They will want to argue with both the dogmatic tone and the idea, perhaps fighting rationality with rationality. And dogmatic ideas can feel prosecutory. So there will be some who will want to prove them wrong. Even if the dogmatic approach seems allied with the reality principle and so affixed to the contours of reason, dogma distorts reality into propaganda. Does reality then feel rigid and literal? And how can one create conviction from an approach that trades acceptance with compliance? Both directions, Freud warns, will suffer from psychological resistance. So readers meet the first elementary lesson: Psychoanalysis is not easy to accept, even if the approach is correct. The second lesson leaves superego learning to the side and brings into relief what has been called aesthetic conflict: a third way to consider not how to present an idea but what appearance and knowledge present to understanding. Here the issue becomes judging the value and the worthiness of feelings as ideas. Within this uncertainty, theory and practice will be at odds. And this needed gamble will animate thinking. Indeed, without these odds, there will be nothing more to think.

Freud's strategic opening exposition, whose approach might startle and create conviction, is entangled in his topic, which is the psychical. And the psychical, governed by the impressions of primary and secondary processes, registers and creates itself from their difference. The psychical projects into and introjects from the world of others and from the otherness of its own world. Understanding, therefore, will suffer from the unmeant, the misheard, the failure of representation, and from the object relations that carry this history. Wild theories will be made. Wishes and fears will confuse the communication, as will the suppositions of anticipatory judgments. Freud persists with his pedagogical question: whether there is a relation between this idea of the psychical and how it can be conveyed. He knows this intimate concept, the psychical, unhinges the personal from the rational, leaving us with our naked subjectivity and with persistent questions. Why is the psychical so incredible? Why, when the human is represented as a psychological being, as being affected by both the external and internal world and as having to make from this meaning, would anxiety signal so much danger? If ideas must be defended against, if ideas seem to make one flee from knowledge and from not knowing, and if the ego can signal danger but cannot flee from the danger it also creates, what becomes of influencing and being influenced? And, how to understand what comes to count as danger?

Freud's project aimed at therapeutic actions, beginning with the view that talk matters a great deal, that interpretation, or making words from things, has therapeutic action. Putting things into words was the only work, yet the procedure of free association ruled out the logic of intentionality. Free Association transported discourse into the realm of the unapparent, the erased, the unnoticed, and the things one did not mean to say. It was the accidental quality of the speaking subject, when misrecognition escaped the clutches of self-correction that required a special mode of listening. So Freud's question on the presentation of ideas spanned not just his own ideas and speculations. It also aims to listen, with stereophonic reception, to the presentation of the Other, now hearing the silence, gaps, and the resistance as the experience in listening, as the material to interpret. The analyst reads between the lines and puts into words what else has been said, staying involved with the unconscious communication.

Through listening to the Other, Freud elaborated a key conflict in the psychoanalytic approach. In sketching out some elementary lessons in psychoanalysis, the audience will be asked to learn from psychoanalysis without understanding it; they are asked to suspend their disbelief and keep in mind, without acting it out, their tendency to privilege consciousness and to equate inner life with consciousness of it. Essentially, Freud is inviting his audience into passionate discourse, to play with psychical actions as meaningful events that cannot know their own structures of representation. Speaking subjects must loosen their hold on what they think reality expects and on what they anticipate as reality. To relax, to let the mind's thoughts drift, to feel forgotten ideas suddenly pop into one's head, to mix metaphors, to say the opposite of what one thought one was saying, all these wild thoughts are heard as the language of passion. Freud's view was that the irrelevant and the repressed are not the exception to human experience, but oddly, a way into understanding its complexity. When inquiry makes its way into what is forgotten, missed, too present, lost, or thrown away, the dogmatic and genetic become useless. Thus the presenting problem is greater than one of proper strategy for once the psychical is admitted as a pressure, as a function, as a dynamic, and as affecting itself, nothing escapes its force, including what we take to be the proper and the improper. Indeed, the psychical spans ideas, perceptions, affect, consciousness, the unconscious, and the drives. Reality, too, will lose its transparency because perception will be a question of passion.

Many of these difficult ideas structure another of Freud's (1937) late papers, "Analysis, Terminable and Interminable."[4] Here, analyst and analysand are the subjects of psychoanalysis. Here, too, is the preoccupation with presentation, now accepting the stress of a resistance from the side of the analyst: "But we must not take the clarity of our own insight as a measure of the conviction which we produce in the patient" (229). Analytic insight cannot be dependent upon genetic or dogmatic strategies but must be a working through of these early forms of learning. Freud acknowledges more limits, specifically the one pertaining to the breadth of psychoanalysis. Analytic work will be only partial because old structures will survive its deconstructive efforts, because interpretations are never exhausted, and because psychoanalytic knowledge is not completed through its techniques. Analytic insight will be marked by its own frailty because conflict is the poesy of psychical life. What Freud called "cathectic loyalty" (241), or the sticky libido, will refuse to give up old objects. And this refers not just to the analysand but to the analyst as well. Old attachments can be stronger than new appeals, another reason for depicting genetic or dogmatic strategies as resistance to learning. How then is psychoanalytic conviction made if cathectic loyalty resists psychoanalysis? To be loyal to a theory that asks us to be disloyal is, perhaps one of its most radical requests. And this problem may have brought Freud to see the dogmatic and the genetic as a symptom of conflict when he wrote: "Analysis . . . is always right in theory but not always right in practice" (229). Analysis, too, draws upon the conventions of psychical life where one feels ambivalent, both psychically right in theory and unconvinced in bodily practice.

"Analysis Terminable and Interminable" revisits major psychoanalytic themes from the vantage of problems they present to the clinic. And the key tension is that psychoanalysis as a therapeutic action must come to terms with its own resistances to understanding its limits to cure. Readers meet archaic heritage, original bisexuality, the life and death drives, the transference, therapeutic action, negative therapeutic reaction, castration, penis envy, masculinity and femininity, and the flight to health or illness. These are all qualities of the psychical and the means for symbolizing them. But they live within the great aporia of technique and of theory and as such, affect both analyst and analysand with their difference. What becomes interminable, then, is the new conflict: the resistance to resistance.

This is not the first time that Freud is concerned with the psychical experience of psychoanalytic practitioners, but this paper seems especially insistent, deeply critical, of the work itself which now comprises the analysts' interminable analysis. Analysts attend to how this work affects their own mind and the analytic relation. Analysts must hold convictions, specifically made from their own analysis, yet this loyalty may create and rest upon hostility to others who disagree. Cathectic loyalty inhibits critical scrutiny into the analysts' beliefs. Perhaps this conviction is a way of being theoretically right and practically wrong. If these are two forms of the misuse of power—refusing the difference of the analysand and dogmatism in one's own view—a third breakdown is without an agent. "It would not be surprising if the effect of a constant preoccupation with all the repressed material which struggles for freedom in the human mind were to stir up in the analyst as well all the instinctual demands which he is otherwise able to keep under suppression. These, too, are 'dangers of analysis' . . ." (249). The analysand affects the analyst and this counter-transference slips the analyst's interpretations. The analyst's love, hate, and curiosity will be animated, as will envy, aggression, and early conflicts. The analyst's interpretation too is subject to analysis.

There is, then, a constitutive tension at the heart of the analytic enterprise germinating from the analyst's individuality as both effect and affected and flowering in the method of psychoanalysis. On the one hand, analysis may make the analyst ill, animating conflicts, distorting convictions, and using techniques as a defense against not knowing. On the other, analysts, too, experience their madness through analytic work and symbolizing this madness is also what the work entails. By now, however, consciousness has lost its hold and two unconscious subjects meet. What saves the analytic setting from fixating upon its own madness, then, is not the certainty of irrationality, but its capacity to be narrated and thus doubted.

Freud (1937) took the position that no one is perfect, that there is no subject presumed to know: "It cannot be disputed that analysts in their own personalities have not invariably come up to the standard of psychical normality to which they wish to educate their patience" (247). If this view seems to draw psychoanalytic work back to the ideal state of mental health, it may also be read as abolishing the standard of psychic normality. We are asked to accept the idea that the wishes one has for others are not those one may have achieved oneself. And we are also invited to examine these wishes for education by asking what else they may represent. Freud's recognition of how psychical normality as both an ideal and a fiction is transformed into standards that only provide a facade of certainty led him to see the urge to educate as a defense against one of the only resources upon which analysis is founded: the uncertain intersubjectivity made from two people in a room. Whether one takes a genetic or dogmatic approach to presenting this humanity, neither will be able to suppress nor cure individuality. Learning and not learning, it turns out, will be the expression of intersubjectivity, not a representative of the knowledge learned. And on this view, discourse and its object are altered by their aesthetic qualities.

"Analysis Terminable and Interminable" may be read as depressing advice on the problem of how analysis comes to an end and also when one's psychical education is complete. Yet this problem of when analysis is over is so entangled with the promise of outcomes and efficiency that the best Freud can do is to point these out. Indeed, he is left with having to admit the practical limit that analysis is over when two people no longer meet in the analytic setting. The shadow problem, which education must share, is that the idealization of outcomes protects its own wish for learning to be a prophylactic action against ignorance and not learning. The wish is that outcomes are not just things that happen but should carry an insurance policy guaranteeing that one is forever protected from any future conflict. Yet how can the future of conflict be abolished if the unconscious abolishes reality but cannot be abolished by reality? Moreover, how can one even know a conflict that does not yet exist? These views left Freud questioning what therapeutic action can mean. The issue, he concludes, is not how psychoanalysis does what it does but rather, with what it is, with its uses of the obstacles that stand in its way, indeed, and most radically, with its failure to cure. We have reached the negativity within the heart of learning. Through its failure as cure, learning is interminable and terminable. But so, too, is not learning.

Ostensibly, these last great essays speak to the limits of psychoanalysis and as many have argued, to the conflictive history of psychoanalytic ideas.[5] They hint at why the study of limits must also be an inquiry into the fragility of changing one's mind, presenting this struggle as it plays out in theory and practice. It is the confrontation with limits that permits the sublime to affect the structure's imaginary. After all, the symbolization of limits is also a story of subjectivity and its representation. From the dedication to what alienates narrative one learns this narrative courage: to make analysis interminable. All of these dilemmas belong as well to the field of education where we trade in ideas in the hope of making a difference to lives lived there. But we also mistake our convictions for student learning, project our helplessness in the form of demands to learn, borrow genetic and dogmatic strategies of presentation, dream of classrooms that work or fall apart, and experience, indeed, act out, the dangers of education. This is the teacher's illness, the teacher's transference of the fault lines of learning into the practices and theories of education. On this view there is no such thing as perfect learning and no learning that can prevent a future of not learning. And as with psychoanalysis, when the question of education emerges, when it can be posed, presented, and encountered without genetic or dogmatic defenses, and when learning and not learning can be read between the lines of theory and practice, then, it seems, the experiences that are education may be presented aesthetically, as interminably affected by what is sublime in the procedures of its own narration. We may become open to the work of the aesthetic, what Hannah Segal (1952/2004) terms "creating our world anew" (47).

## Literary Styles

"In the field of symptomatic acts, too," writes Freud (1901) in his book of mistakes, "psycho-analytic observation must concede priority to imaginative writers" (213). Hysteria, dreams, mistakes, sexuality, and jokes each make us all imaginative writers. In all these events, something happens to language. There is, in the words of de Certeau (1988), a "displacement toward the poetic or novelistic genre. Psychoanalytic conversion is a conversion to literature" (19). It will be a rewriting altered by its affects and so will compose a style of learning created along the lines of the poetic. Interpretation will hear what is not said and return this difference to the work of learning.

The hybrid procedures, structures, functions, and transpositions of psychical life repeat in the values of literary design. And while novels cannot feel the psychical life they represent, readers certainly can. Novels symbolize the affected world lending just enough distance for reflections to accompany and be alienated by their own crisis of representations. This theory of distance—the ego's capacity to self-observe—is how Freud thought of the relation between symptom and interpretation. As an action of its own accord, the literary invites the novel problem of presenting our difference from ourselves, by representing what else we mean and what has been missed. Neither genetic nor dogmatic, the literary can be thought of as a third term, whose surprise of association startles the reader's interpretation.

Though invoking an excess of meaning, the literary also does something to time. Aesthetic time runs slowly by exalting the moment and the detail and by inviting the past to mingle with present feelings. Moment to moment, history by history, magnified time can feel like no time at all. Losing track of time may be as close as one can get to feeling the timeless qualities of the unconscious. All this forgotten time however poses a paradox because the history of psychoanalysis, as it plays out in the history spoken in the psychoanalytic setting, is also a history of remembering our unfolding present. The time lag represented is the significance one feels today with the provision that the present cannot know itself as such, cannot anticipate its own time.

Freud's (1937) "Analysis Terminable and Interminable" keeps watch over this burdened time, seeing the analytic dialogue as only affecting conflicts presently in action, as opposed to conflicts that may appear in some distant future. Anticipating conflicts and trying to prevent them is, after all, a neurotic activity fueled by the steam of anxiety. Present conflicts are different since they converge in the transference and the counter-transference and so can be addressed. Freud calls out a poem to set his watch, quoting Goethe's *Faust*: "*Su muss denn doch die Hexe dran!* [We must call the Witch to our help, after all!]" (225). And he stretches Goethe's appeal to meet his own method, now imagining psychoanalysis as " . . . the Witch Meta-psychology. Without metapsychological speculation and theorizing—I had almost said 'phantasying'—we shall not get another step forward" (225).

Without a phantasy of knowledge, without that motivating fiction, and without an admission of something on the tip of one's tongue, with what one almost said, there is hardly a way to enter into mental worlds. So it is with this "witch meta-psychology." It proceeds, just as psychical life proceeds, through speculation, theorizing, accidents, and phantasying. And present conflicts will be called and addressed. The invitation is for the symptom to repeat through variations, its attempt to placate meaning by missing it. The context of the analytic setting, however, causes the symptom's confusion to create something anew, what Freud saw as "an artificial illness" (1915a). Conveyed through the transference, the displaced symptom will present itself as defamiliarization. Much earlier in the psychoanalytic archive, Freud (1905) saw aspects of these early explorations as sexual research. Children, Freud supposed, gave themselves over to the same aimless quality as the transference, the same desire to know against all odds. For the little sex researcher, theory was exciting because it needed neither external proof of its own existence nor any experience to secure its grounds. Indeed, theory's only purpose was its capacity for exciting symbolization. And this intimacy between thinking and sexuality, the sexualizing of thought, may help us understand why literary styles so excite, why Freud needed Goethe, why we need our private madness.

Early on in his writing, in his studies of the hysterics, Freud (1893–1895) noticed that his case studies read like novels and worried that these clinical discussions would then be dismissed as fiction, as a product of his imagination. In the midst of his discussion of Fraulein Elisabeth von R., one of the hysterics who ushered Freud into his talking cure, Freud interrupts his presentation to reflect upon the difference of his scientific background from his new career as analyst:

> I have not always been a psychotherapist. Like other neuropathologists, I was trained to employ local diagnoses and electro-prognosis, and it still strikes me as strange that the case histories I write should read like short stories and that, as one might say, they lack the serious stamp of science. I must console myself with the reflection that the nature of the subject is evidently responsible for this, rather than a preference of my own. (160)

The subject calls forth the method, something unusual for science to admit. It is almost as if the literary made Freud notice that illness is also a story, replete with its own logic, style, substance, and values. The story made Freud into a narrator, a novelist. Further, Freud came to see illness as making and preventing meaning. Freud (1893–1895) continues with his thought that even if these case studies are of a different order of narrative, even if they contain the Otherness of narrative called fiction, whereas the psychiatric cases of his day did not, the advantage is that only through the literary can there be made "an intimate connection between the story of the patient's sufferings and the symptoms of his illness" (161). This insight brings Freud to his boldness: He made from it the courage to represent this inner world as designing literary events, with the requirement that to understand what is being represented, one will have to read between the lines.

And, indeed, Freud's clinical case studies do read like novels, like affected discourse. There are plot lines, narrative flairs, rising and falling actions, and denouement. Through these features the author regards the subject's complexity, the literary qualities of the story as conveyed, and the method of understanding made from listening. The analysand's metaphors, slips of the tongue, negations, and strange grammatical constructions of self and Other are heard as wandering thoughts meant to communicate what is not known but nonetheless felt. Knowledge is not in charge but rather its unintended qualities become charged by the affects. In these clinical studies, one finds an interest in bringing together accidents and structures for the meanings they now carry. There, too, is tragedy and also the model for tragedy: the Oedipus narrative. Here is a stirring world of object relations and blindness to them. And this led Freud to consider illness as presenting a story of the development of suffering, where symptoms live between the lines of the narrative and the history of the complaint (de Certeau 1993). If the interpretation touches the gaps between the lines, it is because Freud, too, is affected in that other place. It is this object world of representation, the internalization of others as the transfiguration of emotional experience that would open psychoanalytic thought to a novel understanding of its own education. Education, then, would come to mean something more accidental, an altercation of a system through affect. Education would become not what we make happen, but what happens to us in our dependency with others and the sense we may make from that. Contemporary views of psychoanalysis and social thought will help us sort out how the preoccupation with presenting psychoanalysis becomes a problem of aesthetics and emotional responsibility. That will prepare the thinking for what these new links may mean for the question of commenting on the aesthetic conflicts of learning and not learning.

## Aesthetic Conflicts

De Certeau (1993) defines the Freudian Novel as referring to the patient's discourse, to a literary work, to the psychoanalytic archive, and as deriving from Freud's style of interpreting and writing. In bringing into relief the literary qualities of psychoanalytic discourse, what becomes novel is that this discourse allows for and welcomes its own incoherence for what it does not know, namely its own means of representation. By centering the literary as the model of the case study, psychoanalysis must confront the qualities of its own fiction and reconfigure what fiction signifies. De Certeau invites us to consider fiction as capable of surviving unmeant qualities of language, that the literary work has the capacity to say more than it means. But it also contains resistance to fiction. The reader's resistance provokes judgments over its unstable qualities and the writer may give herself or himself over to the urge to make a story coherent by tying up loose ends too neatly, or short-circuiting ambiguity through a dependency on stereotyped language. These forms of resistance are signs of distress, suggesting a confrontation with sublime affect.

"Psychoanalysis," writes de Certeau (1993), "takes up the definition given to fiction as being a knowledge jeopardized and wounded by its otherness (the affect, etc.) . . . In the analytic field, this discourse is effective because it is 'touched' or wounded by the affect" (27). De Certeau names the affect as "the return of the passions" (25), a madness that conveys more than meaning holds. Passion displaces conscious intention for something original. Fiction, then, will be affected by its own passion and convey passion, inviting mesmerizing involvement, inciting readers to return to their own lives with comparability and with difference. This passion will also include destructive forces, tearing meaning to pieces, fracturing satisfaction, posing doubt, bringing us to the place Blanchot (1982) noticed as "torn intimacy" (226). The affect erupts when one is least prepared for its emergence, thus heralding emphatic susceptibility. The discourse may purport to be objective and rational at the manifest content, only to be betrayed by a latent insistence. Leo Bersani's (1986) discussion of psychoanalysis and aesthetics also takes pleasure in this return of passion, finding depth by placing the literary as intimate with the designs of sexuality. Interpretation, too, will be marked with this otherness made from both the resistance to being touched and from the desire to be affected.

If the founding problem of psychoanalysis was one of presentation, our contemporary concerns revolve around the question of reception, encounter, and literary disruption. Bersani (1986) gathers these uncertainties under the name of aesthetic, itself a strategy of representation that gladly gives away mastery for its failure to represent. According to Bersani,

> Literature mocks and defeats the communicative projects of language; it both invites interpretation and makes language somewhat unsuitable for interpretation. It forces us to be aware of the density of words not as a function of their semantic richness, but rather as a sign of their inadequacy to the mobile sense which they cannot enclose. (67)

This other scene, which Freud named the drive, seeks release in representations and represents the affects. Unsuitable for representations but nonetheless pressuring and pestering meaning, the drive cannot be known, except for its affectations, aggression, and sexuality. Literature stages this conflict: a science of incomplete humanity in that it can suspend its own purpose while drawing attention to the problem of symbolizing life as such. Thus for Bersani, to read in the Freudian archive is to question, as Freud did, the basis of knowing, not to replace unknowing with a more authentic truth, but rather to encounter the ways representation fails to supplant the affect it requires for its formulation. As psychological allegory, the elementary lessons of the literary cannot and will not compete with self-improvement, heightened consciousness, or states of perfection. These activities belong to the events of the reality ego and its defensive, illusionary structure. The literary, however, belongs to that which is beyond pleasure, to the after life of events and to the return of the repressed. It, too, slows down time, permitting an uncertain freedom, urging what Freud called "free association"—an occurrence where the drive plays with and may destroy the representations it seeks.

Whereas in the early Freud archive works of art and literature were analyzed from either the view of the psycho-biography of the artist or author and as a means to illustrate the sublimation of the drive, contemporary debates on psychoanalysis and aesthetics propose an aesthetic of psychoanalysis that unsettles the psychoanalytic work. Kofman (1988) stresses the tentative and deconstructive work of analysis; she follows psychoanalytic distortions and displacements, turning to the affectations that sublimation cannot resolve. Kristeva's (2000) long-term project, a literary psychoanalysis, invites novelists and poets into the intimacy of the clinic because of their capacity for revolt through presenting subjective worlds as subversion. She finds in Freud's theory of signification aesthetic properties of revolt, where there is an overturning of conscious meanings in order to propose a new theory of language. In different ways, for Kofman and Kristeva, the psychoanalytic learning is interminable, not because we cannot know everything but because what we know is more than what can be said, and learning this takes one into what is sublime in subjectivity.

In the contemporary analytic setting, and drawing on the clinical work of Melanie Klein and Wilfred Bion, Donald Meltzer (2004) will call contact with an aesthetic object, an aesthetic conflict, needed for thinking to matter. Indeed, what else can the problem of presentation be but a problem of beauty, worthiness, goodness, and value made from worries of destruction, ugliness, and diminishment? These are internal doubts over the beauty of one's own inside but always because there is someone beautiful outside. Aesthetic conflicts are preoccupations with what cannot be seen but are nonetheless felt through their absence. They also invoke occasions for ethical encounters with others.

For this preoccupation with internal beauty to make sense, one must suppose that the first aesthetic object is the mother, whose beauty is mesmerizing to the infant. And if this supposition can be held in mind, aesthetic conflict, or the doubts that will be raised in relation to the exquisite meaning of the Other's love, also supposes that inner objects want to know their own beauty. It is not a logic for consumer society; indeed, consumer society may deaden these doubts and the search for beauty that follows. The aesthetic conflict is personal and archaic when one wonders if external and internal beauty correspond. The aesthetic conflict is animated by the desire for this ineffable knowledge—a poetic truth—where the self wants to know if its insides are as beautiful as the outside. But this means there will be alienation and fascination, an alienation from what cannot be seen and a fascination with what one cannot stop looking for. Melanie Klein will link this fascination and alienation with anxiety over the object needed for a new beginning of responsibility, what she saw as the urge for reparation on behalf of the internal and external Other. For creativity to be possible, Klein (1957) supposes, there must be both conflict and a need to make meaning from it, and she will link this need to the workings of gratitude. Klein and later Meltzer add life to Freud's binary of pleasure and unpleasure as motivating and captivating psychical reality and as setting timeless defences. They view our beginnings, our natality, in relation to the Other as the origin of object relations which then go on to found and inaugurate the affects of love, hate, envy, and gratitude, all needed to create the capacity to tolerate the passionate uncertainties of relationships with others. Aesthetic conflict contains this uncertain relationship to the Other, this slippage of boundary and order, and this passion. It is also a good enough description for conjugating learning and not learning.

It is in this regard that we return to Freud's great contribution, his calling upon artists, poets, and novelists, children's toys, jokes, the playthings of antiquity, and the aesthetics of the dream world, not to assist him in the confirmation of preordained views, but to become addressed by that other research, the research of psychical life and use its methods as a form of play, free association, freedom in mind. In his reminiscences on life in Vienna and as a member of Freud's circle of analysts, Richard Sterba (1982) recalls a Wednesday night meeting that took place on March 30, 1930. Freud was speaking about his current book, *Civilization and Its Discontents*, lamenting that he had left out of his discussion the possibility and chances of happiness. At this meeting, Freud continued to defend the psychoanalytic method and criticize the prevailing view that it did damage to people by its stress on unhappiness and now, by its newest mythology, the death drive. Not even the analysts wanted this theory. Sterba then quotes from his notes Freud's reply, but not before telling his readers that Freud never wanted his colleagues to take any notes during Wednesday night meetings. So here is the note which quotes Freud that Sterba was not supposed to take:

> It has been said that I am trying to force the death instinct upon analysts. However, I am only like an old farmer who plants fruit trees, or like someone who has to go out of the house and leaves a toy behind so that the children will have something to play with while he is absent. I wrote the book with purely analytic intentions, based on my former existence as an analytic writer, in brooding contemplation, concerned to promote the concept of the feeling of guilt to its very end. The feeling of guilt is created by the renunciation of aggression. Now it's up to you to play with this idea. But I consider this the most important progress in analysis. (116)

An invitation to write, to play, to be affected, to be permissive in our note taking: All these gestures of freedom compose the play of novel education.

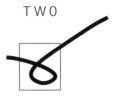

# TWO

# Five Excursions into Free Association, or Just Take the A Train

*Research no longer merely seeks successful compre-*
*hension. It returns to things it cannot understand. It*
*measures by fortifying its needs and methods.*

de Certeau, The Writing of History

## First Excursion

"What am I supposed to do?" the analysand asks. "Just say whatever comes to mind," the analyst replies. So begins the strangely frustrating psychoanalytic request Freud (1912a) called "the fundamental rule": free association. Rarely can a rule be so indiscriminating, although it is precisely through indiscretion that this rule miniaturizes the story of psychoanalysis: What makes psychoanalysis psychoanalytic is the unmooring of meaning from the speaker's intention and the interpretation of that gap as expressing unconscious meaning. Perhaps for this reason the rule is very difficult to accept, unless, of course, it can dawn on speakers that they are free to freely associate with their conflicts. Let us note there is nothing here to solve. Instead, this conflicted speech allows for all that will follow, not just in the analytic setting, although it is there where free association may matter most. But something like free association can take residence in the pedagogical imagination, where there, too, the fragility of language gives notice to the difficulties of freely associating and the utter importance of doing just that. What links these two fields together is the question of writing. The idea of free association began not with speech but with the poet's writing preparation, the taking of uncensored notes that recorded reveries.

The astounding paradox at the center of free association is frustrating. The more one tries to let whatever is on one's mind come out into words, the fewer words there seem to be, even as the obstacles tumble out in a negation: "I have nothing to say." Free association evokes the very trouble at the heart of the analytic encounter: How does one work through the ways the self cannot associate freely? How does one encounter a self made from intellectual inhibition, censorship, projection, self-deception, confusion, and rigid life narratives entrapping self/other relations? More simply, what can the act of narrative mean for learning to live and how does one come to care about narrative through something so careless as free association?

This rule of free association invites fundamental differences. First, it distinguishes psychoanalysis from other therapeutic practices and other theories of the mind through beginning with the emphatic unconscious: its lawless irruptions, its susceptibility to experiences not consciously noticed, and its inclination for welcoming the repressed. Second, in free association language resembles a photographic negative. This is the difference within language: There is negation, disavowal, slips of the tongue, forgetting details, and undoing what has already happened. Then, meaning unhinges itself for desire. It is as if in free association desire suddenly slips into the back door of language, or leaves the door open to the uninvited guest who arrives without reason or purpose. How easily this language can dissolve into too many meanings, crowd out the speaker, or go up in smoke. Even descriptions of free association as a practice and theory suggest the difficulty of putting this experience to words. This, too, is another version of psychoanalytic conflict between theory and practice.

Third, when utterances are carried away from their object through displacement, so too is listening affected, along with the strictures of interpretation. Something is there between the lines. The underside of language can be heard as if the aim of words is to set them free from their thing objects. Then, the literal becomes literary. There can be parallel realities, conflictive chronologies, crowded cities of narratives, all occupying the same space. This archive is dedicated to the transference. We are approaching a fourth difference: Free association creates, between the analyst and the analysand, new editions of attunement and resistance. Fifth, in this strange libidinal economy the meanings and doings of free association are also deeply resisted. We do not give up our points so easily, nor can we simply let go of the meanings we inherit or wish for. Yet the aimlessness and at times emptiness of meaning that is also free association can feel as if the speaker, too, is lost in words.

What begins as a technique of therapy, or, as Kristeva (1995) calls it, "a speech therapy," (105) soon becomes a theory of language. We are entering the talking cure but also any form of practice, including our own pedagogical ones, that requires a faith in narrative, the faith that words create forms of life. And this theory gestures to the difficulties of practice, indeed to the ways in which practice must resist its own theory in order to even encounter itself. In clinical writing on free association, beginning with Freud's descriptions, the resistance is emphasized, followed by the difficulties of respecting this fundamental rule, then comes the obstacle, both social and psychical, to its maintenance, and finally, the problem of listening to all this with what Freud (1912a) called "evenly suspended attention" (111).[1] Free association, then, is both a particular narrative and the resistance to making narrative particular. It simultaneously narrates the difficulties of and obstacles to a narration that structures, transforms, and contains experience. Words fail in so many ways, even as they may urge us along to notice just that. Curiously, it is language that disrupts the Kantian unity, the "I think that accompanies all of my representations."[2] There is the negation, the "I would have never thought of that," the "I" that cannot be accompanied, that has no representatives.

Consider, then, the "I think that accompanies all of my education." Does the field of education have a fundamental rule, an orientation to its practices that makes education qualify as education? How does a technique of education become a theory of learning? We educators do have a sense of the ways education resists learning and how our techniques contribute to this peculiar conflict. We are indeed familiar with student frustrations when, after receiving an assignment, they ask: "What am I supposed to do?" And we can ask here as well, "What am I supposed to do with this free association?" Many educators may notice the flummox made, particularly if the point of their assignment is to invite autonomy not yet made, to create the conditions involved for the writer to decide what it is to choose to do something at all. This choice cannot be taught. As with free association, our writing assignments are only a condition for learning and not the learning itself. If we respond to this student, "Just say whatever is on your mind," we, too, invite the stirring of free association and the resistance, for we may also understand that the very structure of education invokes dependency, compliance, and apathy, and renders association so one sided and unfree. Education, too, must play this guessing game until anticipations are no longer the goals, until it can be affected by the conditions of learning it wishes for others. If, as de Certeau (1988, 39) suggests, we create a research that no longer seeks its own comprehension and so has the courage to return to what is not understood, this very *Unheimlich* return, as both psychoanalysis and education know, animates the old anxious question it is meant to transform: Just what should I return to? Just what am I supposed to do?

## Second Excursion

Many of Freud's most cogent descriptions of the method of free association are found in his papers on technique written in the early history of psychoanalysis.[3] One of Freud's (1913a) most poignant descriptions begin with advice as to what the analyst may say to the analysand. In the beginning there is an unusual conversation:

> What you tell me must differ in one respect from an ordinary conversation. Ordinarily you rightly try to keep a connecting thread running through your remarks and you exclude any intrusive ideas that may occur to you . . . but in this case you must proceed differently. You will notice that as you relate things various thoughts will occur to you which you would like to put aside on the grounds of certain criticism and objections. . . . You must never give in to these criticisms . . . indeed, you must say it precisely *because* you feel an aversion to doing so. . . . (135–136)

Here we have an invitation to conflict, even if avoidance seems easier. These various thoughts, Freud implies, must be put into words, otherwise the criticisms, objections, and prohibitions make discourse autistic. In a more positive sense, Freud (1913a) concludes his advice to the imagined analysand with a moving metaphor: "Act as though, for instance, you were a traveler sitting next to the window of a railway carriage and describing to someone inside the carriage the changing views which you see outside" (135). Essentially, free association is a train of thought, a way of training thought to derail itself. Just take the association train.

Free association is a rule that stretches language to its furthest outpost of meanings. It means to relax language from the grip of censorship and criticism and unmoor it from the entanglement of endless clarifications, justifications, projections, intellectualization, and the rationalizations that conscious intentions call upon to keep meaning still. Free association is an encouragement to the waking subject to experience the dreamlike qualities of having language, to associate with one's discarded content, to encounter again the strange trancelike sensation experienced when trying to narrate a dream. This mesmerizing talk will call things never intended. It will be a walk-about, meandering into reverie. One may become lost in thoughts. Suddenly the speaker will find herself where least expected, maybe mired in unacceptable phantasies of love and hate, desire, and erotic wishes. Theoretically, that should not matter: Speaker and listener should be unencumbered by rules of relevance, sense, courtesy, agendas, objectives, goals and yes, even the Foucaultian confessional. A new quality of association can be made from this losing the censor. Moreover, in the intimacy of the analytic setting, there is no consequence for saying whatever comes to mind, except for the consequence of being subject to unexpected meaning. Here is research that returns to what it cannot understand. This meandering may permit a new and flexible sense of psychological knowledge, epistemology, and what we take as outside reality.

When Freud (1912a) first called free association the fundamental rule of psychoanalysis, he also described "the transference-resistance" (107): That which makes free association free is extremely difficult to maintain because of association. To involve oneself in free association means to give up, however briefly, one's sense of reality in the world, one's sense of actuality and its limits, and one's sense that language can be controlled, or be taken as the proving ground for Kantian unity. To participate in free association is to give oneself over to the Eros of language. And just as analysands are asked to hold in abeyance their self-judgments, they must also stop worrying about what the analyst who listens thinks about all of that. Both are to enter language and thinking, nothing more than that. But there is something more, for it is difficult to leave behind a certain history of education, a history of second guessing, of projection, of worrying without knowledge what precisely the Other will think. There is the school, the home, even the neighborhood. There is the fear of having one's mind read. These, too, are associations and so create the transference resistance.

Not only then is this fundamental rule extremely difficult to follow. It will also invoke its own mode of resistance. It is easier, Freud suggests, for the analysand to worry about how the Other will understand. It is easier to fall in love with the analyst; it is easier to throw one's hands up and blame the analysis, than it is to participate in one's own analysis. There will be, there must be deflection, Freud warns in his paper "The Dynamics of Transference" (1912a): "This struggle between the doctor and the patient, between intellect and instinctual life, and between understanding and seeking to act, is played out almost exclusively in the phenomenon of transference" (108). And yet, this deflection is psychoanalysis as well; without it we would be nothing.

## Third Excursion

In that strange address that is free association, there is always the Other. When Freud (1913b) spoke of free association, he also made a note on interpretation suggesting that the analyst's work is "to draw conclusions from the expressed ideas of the person" (208). These "conclusions" must not be in the service of moralists. Nor shall we tie them to party agendas, political platforms, or to parental and societal authority. This bossy social cannot save the analysand from embarrassment or hurt feelings. Moreover, one is hard placed to challenge authority when worrying what it will think. Rather, the interpretations, that is to say, the analyst's associations, are meant to provoke, animate, and perhaps help the analysand work through the resistance and the transference. If all goes well, the interpretation invites free association.

When Christopher Bollas (1999) asked provocatively about the goal of psychoanalysis, what distinguishes its methods from everything else and how it is that psychoanalysis becomes psychoanalysis, he returned to Freud's original request: Analytic sessions should be structured by the analysand's free association. And Bollas, too, recounted all that stands in the way of free association with the paradoxical suggestion that what stands in its way frees one to consider constraints: "Free association was never intended to provide ideal talk in which the observer noted from the train all the sights seen on the journey. . . . In theory one should be able to ride this train without hindrance. In practice it would generate and deploy the unconscious conflicts of the mind" (65). The A train may go out of service. In free association, theory and practice will be at odds and through this conflict—neither theory alone nor practice alone—insight would make its way slowly, hesitantly, shyly.

A new discourse will emerge and for Bollas, free association opens the crypt of Western epistemology from the inside out with the consequence of freely encountering the contradictions and conflicts previously buried through idealization or severed through splitting and disparagement. Then, Bollas suggests, when something happens to language, sociality, and thinking, as it may in free association, something as well happens to larger conceptualizations of epistemology: "To ask Western man to discover truth by abandoning the effort to find it and adopting instead the leisurely task of simply stating what crosses the mind moment to moment is to undermine the entire structure of Western epistemology" (1999, 63).

Truth, it will turn out, does not found reality. Nor is it made from the Kantian critique of pure reason or serviced through scientific control. Instead through the accidents that free association permits, truth will slowly emerge from the mine field of what Klein (1930) termed "unreal reality" (221), the phantasies that undergird our capacity for symbolization that may lead to making psychical life significant. [4] Paradoxically, truth undermines values of mastery and control and the accompanying desire to evacuate subjectivity from reason. Truth resides in the farthest thing from one's mind, in the crevice of negation, within the utterance, "I would have never thought of that." The train of thought derails from the aporia of language: the noncoincidence between thing and word, the belatedness of meaning, and the word one has just lost. It is not just that the subject is split, but this split subject splits itself further with language. In free association, development is uneven, noncontinuous, and subject to regression. There are vicissitudes, wild thoughts.

Epistemology in psychoanalytic dialogue, Bollas (2000) will say in his study of hysteria, becomes "an ongoing experimentation with the arts and crafts of ontology" (81). And in referencing ontology, we are back to our beginnings, both maternal and paternal. In free association, these different orders associate:

> The patient allowed simply to speak what came to mind seemed almost a maternal defiance of the demands to get to the truth; if so, then it only

borrowed from the psychic reality that no truth could ever be imposed, but rather had to be created. . . . The patient and analyst might conjure the medium of mother and small child—a world of overlapping reveries—but in this case the father would intervene with his discovery of important communications, lucid lessons, and the patient's hidden conflicts. (112)

To associate freely with these object relations, one must freely associate with phantasy. Sentiments from sociology such as "Oh, you are only stereotyping strong daddy and weak mommy" will be of no use. Nor need we read Bollas defensively, as proffering statements of overvaluation and derision. Rather, these reveries of feeling strong and weak, itself the ground for "lucid lessons," can be considered as difference itself, as containing an unknowable realm of truth, namely that one is born, that one has parents, and from these social facts, come a truth that the facts themselves cannot anticipate.

Free association comes as a surprise. François Roustang (2000) names this twisted language "un-speech [*déparole*]" (25). "In everyday life, speech is supposedly designed to communicate and transmit information, but also, obviously, to avoid transmitting information" (25). And so Roustang begins with a central paradox of language, that communication itself avoids communication, that communication severs associations. This deflection is sustained, many note, in our information society. We have so many ways of not saying what we are saying that it takes a particular kind of listening to hear desire in this void. We may see a potential revolt and think of free association as a protest against the order of our information society and perhaps our compliance to its consumption. Then we may answer differently Kristeva's (2000) question: "How does the patrilineal subject that each of us risks becoming confront a power vacuum, armed for discourse with only a remote control?" (29). Free association may be a refuge from the deadness of twenty-four-hour news that has nothing to say, from the stay-in-touch-demand of e-mail, and from the litter of discarded information on that superhighway known as the Internet. Free association, Roustang continues, is autonomous from intention, even as it leads back to the self in startling ways. "Un-speech is similar to delirium, in that it is speech that has been undone, a drifting speech that is no longer concerned with being directed at someone or inscribed in a social relationship in anticipation of an action or plan" (26). And here is where one difficulty emerges: How does one give up a plan? Un-speech, however, is only similar to delirium. Roustang suggests that what differentiates delirium from un-speech is that the latter is directed to the Other, whereas in delirium the audience or listener has gone missing.

If free association requires us to say anything, whatever comes to mind, and places this under the sign of "freedom," there is also the association and its address to the Other. Otherness is there all along, but so too is the Other. Bollas (2002) maintains that free association is "a new technique for thinking" (34). What invokes thinking, Bollas may imply, is the thought of the unfamiliar. Thinking works as an apparatus of association. It does something to thoughts, to language, to the thinker.[5] Prior to its act, the destination of thinking is not apparent; plans are of no help in this regard or even worse, they may actually work to help us miss the experience. Eventually, Bollas (2002) suggests, free association narrates a story of sorts, but "a story revealed not between the lines, but in the chain of ideas within the lines" (4). This is close to how Freud (1913a) describes the analyst's reading of the analysand's secret wishes "between the lines of his complaints and the story of his illness" (140). And it is not such a leap to de Certeau's (1993) contemporary description of Freud's novel writings: "It allows us to consider any narrative as a relationship between a structure and some events" (21) and so a link between "the symptoms of the illness and the history of the suffering" (20). The fabrication of discourse becomes caught not only in its incapacity to complete itself but through the incapacity to read its own story.

Free association reveals the trouble with language that we tend to place in a parenthesis to even speak at all. There is difference within, a necessary mismatch or conflict between the word and the urge, between the affect and the idea, between consciousness and the unconscious, between the self and the Other. Here and there language cannot serve to punctuate experience; it is experience. And as an experience, it can be missed, lost, and refound. But because it will always gesture toward what is absent, the desire for representation colors words with the affect of longing. We are free to associate with our affects.

As for the analyst's interpretation of the analysand's utterances, Bollas (2002) locates here another paradox: "Often the psychoanalyst will find that when he or she is making a comment the patient appears to have drifted off. Analysts discover that their interpretation is not used for its apparent accuracy, but as a kind of evocative form: Because the analyst is talking, curiously the patient is free not to listen! But in not listening, the patient seems intrapsychically directed toward another interpretation" (42). The interpretation may be heard as a "good night" greeting, as inviting sleep, and as the drifting meanings made in lucid dreaming. Where else does one go when one is not listening?

Freud hoped free association was the means for curing neurosis. Eventually, he thought, patients come to what is on their mind, allow language its unruly qualities, find significance in the most insignificant places, and become more curious toward psychical reality. Freud's Hungarian colleague, Sándor Ferenczi, took the idea from the other side. He thought that we are cured when we can freely associate. Ferenczi felt this special demand as what one learns from analysis as opposed to what one brings to an analysis. We are entering the psychoanalytic realm of the "talking cure," from its backdoor history. How this talk works will be the subject of deep controversy, then and now. We can say that free association is a very strange use of language and perhaps agree with Karen Horney's (1991) assessment that there is no other word for it. "What we actually mean by free association," writes Horney, "is the purposelessness of mental productions. There is no immediate purpose other than this: letting things emerge" (37).

## Fourth Excursion

Let us take a short excursion into the psychoanalytic archive and consider the *mise-en-scène* behind Freud's theoretical papers and the transference Freud tried to tame. These events associate friendship with the discovery of method, and with the creation of technical advice in the wake of painful mistakes and wild misadventures. Early in the voluminous correspondence between Sigmund Freud and Sándor Ferenczi, spanning from 1908–1933 in three volumes, an excited and maybe even manic Ferenczi writes to Freud about the latter's key discovery of free association.[6] Ferenczi could barely contain himself, so involved was he in learning the new method of psychoanalysis and so interested in his own analysis and its progress. It may be important to know that Freud was forty-three years old when he met the twenty-six-year-old Ferenczi, that Ferenczi idealized Freud and loved him deeply, but that over the course of their long association, kept the disappointed wish that Freud could be more than his friend. Ferenczi, too, would discover a method for the analytic setting, calling it "mutual analysis."[7] There, both the analyst and the analysand would trade their narratives and positions as a way to defeat the authority of the clinic, as a way of drawing closer, and to gratify each other. And Ferenczi would seal this analytic relation with a kiss. Ferenczi experimented with these methods; Freud would try to dissuade him by a letter and then turn to the question of the analyst's neutrality more formally in a paper on technique.

For an all too brief time, at least from Ferenczi's view, Freud was his analyst. Their long correspondence documents, informally, what one scholar has called their "psychoanalytic misadventures." Ferenczi's transference to Freud was painful. He wanted so much. And Freud knew this demand. Indeed, in the early letters, Freud tries to warn Ferenczi of "the danger of personal estrangement brought about by the analysis" (Brabant et al. 1994, Letter #393, 482). It is best, Freud seems to be saying, if one is analyzed by a stranger. Friends may be too subject to rescue fantasies, personal investments in the cure, or to protecting feelings and so not interpreting the conflicts. There is a question of how much truth a friendship can bear but also to the place of analysis itself. Analysis between friends, Freud suggests, will ruin the friendship. These warnings will find their way into Freud's (1912b) recommendations that analysts take the stance of abstinence and neutrality to allow the analytic setting to be the playground of transference. Ferenczi, however, preferred not to make a distinction between his personal and professional life. He desired mutual analysis, believed in kissing his analysands, and felt in these practices a rare and beautiful intimacy. It was as if Ferenczi wished to embody the spirit of free association. By the way, Ferenczi is often called "the tender analyst."[8]

Let us return to a time when these painful conflicts have not yet taken their place between friends, when a twenty-six-year-old Ferenczi had just returned to his home in Budapest from his stimulating visit to Freud's Vienna. On February 5, 1910, Ferenczi writes a long letter with a desire to stretch the truth into the delirium of Un-speech:

> Once society has gone beyond the infantile, then hitherto completely unimagined possibilities for social and political life are opened up. Just think what it would mean if one *could tell everyone the truth*, one's father, teacher, neighbor, and even the king. All fabricated, imposed authority would go to the devil—what is *rightful* would remain natural. The eradication of lies from private and public life would necessarily *have to*

bring about better conditions; if reason and not dogmas (to which I add the word "morality") prevail, a more purposeful, less costly, and in every respect more economical reconciliation of individual interests and the common good would ensue . . .

Here in Budapest I found everything the way it was, only I myself seemed to have changed, talking things out has eradicated the last traces of neuroses, and I sense—in place of the earlier inclination toward inactivity—a kind of urge to do something. (Brabant et al. 1994, Letter #109, 131–132)

This "urge to do something" consisted in beginning the work of founding the Budapest Psychoanalytic Society in 1913. And yet, in hindsight, the urge did not last as Ferenczi hoped; he experienced long depressions, painful writing blocks, and terrible indecisiveness in love relations. All of this was exacerbated by Freud's bad advice to Ferenczi on a matter of love. For the rest of his passionate correspondence with Freud, his hope that "the last trances of neuroses" would have been eradicated does not bear out. Indeed, the correspondence is a veritable testimony to Ferenczi's greater and deeper disappointment that he and Freud could neither achieve a mutual free association nor create equality in the passionate matter of the transference love. If something resists the capacity to exceed the place Ferenczi could only name as "beyond the infantile" where everyone can just tell the truth and get things off their mind, there is also that utterly necessary tension of the infantile as carrying its own truth, as still associating with an inclination toward inactivity, as still wanting a radical passivity and an urge to do something. Both the failure and the tender potential of free association rested in this divide.

## Fifth Excursion

In Ferenczi's excited letters to Freud readers may learn that if something can happen to language, if the writer's language can keep pace with the affectations that make writing letters so necessary, it is only because something more than language animates the urge to express. One of the roots of free association emerges from a literary method found in advice manuals written to burgeoning writers. Freud (1920) recounts this relation in his short paper "A Note on the Prehistory of the Technique of Analysis." Free association, or something like it, such as "automatic writing," was a method employed by mystics, poets, and writers. The surrealists were quite taken with this method. André Breton and Marcel Duchamp, for instance, tried to visualize the unconscious as a machine, representing its production of estranged meaning as akin to the hyperrepresentations Freud (1900) called "the dream thoughts." Rousseau's *Confessions* hitched the autobiographic impulse and so the autobiography to it (Todorov 2001). The literary modernists and their invention of stream of consciousness made scandalous art of it. And finally, yes, the philosophers have their say. Blanchot (1982) begins his study of automatic writing from its promise, to write with inspiration, a writing that writes itself. That promise gains its force from desire. But what its economy conceals, Blanchot concludes, is the aporia of language: "the insecurity of the inaccessible, the infinite experience of that which cannot even be sought, a probing of what never is evident, the exacting demands of a search which is no search at all and of a presence which is never granted" (178). Automatic writing then becomes a symptom of anxiety and its method of defense.

Here, then, are the mania and the depression for automatic writing can feel like the Ouija Board of discourse. There is the infantile desire for discourse to be telepathic, to give us what we wish for, and to automate without having to associate. It lures us into the answer we already knew was waiting. So come. Place your hands on the magic pointer, move right into language, and let it speak. Let language be magical and mean without effort.

Freud (1920) found this mesmerizing history of automatic writing in Havelock Ellis's short essay that argues since it is concerned with the mythologies of antiquity, psychoanalysis is an art not a science.[9] Freud, too, traced the history of free association back to Schiller's correspondence of 1788: "The great poet and thinker recommends anyone who desires to be productive to adopt the method of free association" (264). We note its literary birth and in this paper, Freud continues to quote the poets as well as the hacks. For our purposes of prehistory, Freud borrows from Ellis a passage of a short essay of advice to new writers that Ferenczi also read. "The art of becoming an original writer in three days," by one Ludwig Börne, written in 1823 tells us:

> Take a few sheets of paper and for three days on end write down, without fabrication or hypocrisy, everything that comes into your head. Write down what you think of yourself, of your wife, of the Turkish War, of

Goethe . . . of your superiors—and when three days have passed you will be quite out of your senses with astonishment at the new and un-heard-of thoughts you have had. This is the art of becoming an original writer in three days. (265)

To become an original, one must tell the truth, say whatever is on one's mind, write through censorship, through conventional morality, through cultural politeness, and through worries about what someone else will think of it. Indeed, go out of your senses, jump on that A train, and say everything. Some of this advice is given to contemporary students in creative writing classes and it seems quite easy to follow with modern technology. With the computer, for instance, we certainly work at breakneck speed, perhaps even become mesmerized by watching language speed across the screen. Yet in our own educational archive, this automatic technique is not equivalent to what we call cognitive mapping, brainstorming, or webbing, for with these latter methods, we are not to complain about authority, write down what we think of the teacher, or record bad thoughts.

The lost art that Börne describes so manically, and that Freud and Ferenczi may have joked about, that lost prehistory is not regained from filling the page, from having one's brain stormed. Automatic writing is not free association, really. It is just an interesting metaphor. It may be just the preliminary labor because the analysis and interpretation of this automatic talk, this un-speech, this free association leads to the very conflicts the discourse covers over. Here we meet once again the idea of Horney (1942) who writes to its limit: "Of course, free association is never free . . . it does not work magic. It would be wrong to expect that as soon as rational control is released all that we are afraid of or despise in ourselves will be revealed. We may be fairly sure that no more will appear this way than we are able to stand" (106).

Here, too, is where free association meets the resistance, perhaps where we have to stop listening but also where we may need to associate with silence. In free association we try to meet and witness, most accidentally, most sublimely, and without discrimination, the otherness within. Yet we need the Other to do this, the Other who, unlike a sheet of paper, can return our free associations back to us with their difference. We have arrived to the association, a history of the Other's history. That is to say, we are closest to the difference that is the unconscious when we notice its displacement, when we are not listening, when we say the opposite of what we mean, when we turn language inside out, when our grammar collapses under the weight of our desire, and when we have no regard for staying on the topic. We are closest to our unconscious when it can be witnessed by another, when the Other puts us on notice, gives us back our conclusions so that we can redo them again. Bollas (2002) writes, "The curious laboratory of psychoanalysis allows us to see how people think unconsciously" (52). We are no longer looking out of the window of a train to describe all of what can be observed. Instead, we are trying to look inside this train of thought and to see from this vantage its derailments. If we could make something of a curious laboratory in education, how then would we answer that question, "What am I supposed to do?" Would we, like Ferenczi, only tell the truth? Would we, like Freud, try to suspend our attention? Would we take the route of Bollas and Horney and simply suggest the curious laboratory of education creates only what it can stand? Or maybe, the question can return to what it does not understand, to how it is that the truth straddles both the urge to research and the difficulty of freely associating with that.

# THREE

# A Note to "Identification with the Aggressor"

Marcia Cavell's (1993) discussion on psychoanalysis and philosophy provides a provocative description that relates learning to live to its psychical consequences: "Freud found the source of human neurosis in our long dependency on others and our capacity for symbolization" (1). Neurosis is the name Freud lent to the strange composite of conflicts made from fear of the loss of the object and from infantile desires, wishes and defenses against these.[1] Meaning itself is compromised, resisting, and repeatedly missing its own significance. Only with new symbolization, with the understanding that there is another, can a turning against the self be worked through. Cavell's point is that having to be an infant—beginning in dependency and helplessness—matters quite specifically throughout the lifetime of an individual, but not because there are developmental milestones to achieve and leave behind. Rather, children's own theories about development that symbolize self/other relations—what will be called throughout this chapter "phantasy"[2]—organize both their emotional understanding of conflicts with social milestones *and* the figuring of their inner worlds. Moreover, emotional understanding of these experiences is never achieved once; they receive newer symbolization with the adult's return to the scene of childhood, heightening its meanings, adding reminisces, accruing losses, and bending the contour of time. Readers should keep in mind both symbolization and dependency as working along the lines of this "logic of the emotion" (Isaacs 1952, 89).

One of the most paradoxical emotional ties that confers poignancy to questions of dependency and belonging is an ego defense called "identification with the aggressor." For now, it is enough to state that this ego defense is one against anxiety of loss, that it is largely unconscious, and its symbolization is the means to carry conflicts within emotional states into meaning and to relations with the world of others. To follow this trajectory from inarticulate literalness and anxiety made from dependency and helplessness to the creative world of metaphor, narrative, and significance is to encounter the question of the Other's place in the formation of inside and outside worlds. It is also to ask, what is internalization that it should be so constitutive of these worlds?

Over the course of this chapter I suggest a need to understand the ego defense of identification with the aggressor from its most prosaic and typical forms. For while it emerges from dependent relations—the prototype is children's identification with their parents—as an ego defense its organization turns on anxiety over the loss of love. Its presenting paradox is that the ego will take inside its perceptions of outside threats but in doing so transform both itself and the threat through mechanisms of splitting the relationship into good and bad. It is impossible, on this view, to experience dependency and helplessness without trying to symbolize them. Yet attempts to symbolize loss of love occur as psychical drama: Anxiety, inhibition, and defense become confused with the work of thinking, reparation, atonement, and creativity. Identifications organize psychical life and these elusive desires for being and having come as a call to the Other. The aggression made from these desires is not easily understood. If we are used to considering aggression only in its catastrophic points, we are apt to miss the idea that a mundane psychology of aggression goes hand in hand with conflicts of dependency and symbolization and brings into relief the importance of thinking of the emotional side of representing self/other relations. And if we are apt to represent our relations with others as only equated with consciousness of them, we miss the problem of why aggression becomes such a compelling solution for destroying the world of dependency. I draw upon ego psychology and object relations theory to consider the complexity of this ego defense. While different in their emphasis, their combination holds promise for a theory of sociality that need not choose between understanding the individual's inner world or attending only to larger social processes. The issue is that the individual's emotional world is made from the world of others. And yet the lure of extremity—the need to find the worst case—as the most important explanation and the accompanying devaluation of the individual's everyday experience may also give us a clue to the working of this ego defense. It may also provide insight into the question of why an attention to individual development complicates understanding problems of social breakdown and our urge to repair it. Later in this chapter, readers will meet so common and small of an instance of this ego defense that it may seem almost irrelevant to discussions of social breakdown. However, the most irrelevant detail returns us to the significance of what we discard.

We may have many ways to narrate why aggression makes us nervous and why dependency is a vulnerable relation, but why should symbolization affect us in these ways as well? One reason is that having to narrate a self wavers between wish and defense, between the childhood of the adult and the child's conflicts of love and hate with the parents. Here, symbolization leans upon dependency coloring in the outlines of significance with emotional verve. Another reason has to do with the very qualities of putting things into words and entering into a metaphorical and interpretative world. Finding words, feeling understood and recognized, and thinking deeply with others are all experiences that allow symbolic confidence, a confidence with the sign and with others. Yet this work is slow. So a third reason is captured by Alice Balint (1954) who stressed the frustrations of having to learn when she noticed that the time of education occurs too soon, before the educator or parent can count on understanding, the understanding either of the Other or of the self. Learning and its symbolization, on this view, is composed of a radical and original uncertainty and a promise. Not knowing but still needing to respond can make one nervous. Balint may help us remember that mistakes and misunderstandings are not the outside of education but rather are constitutive of its very possibility. These unintended qualities of learning, more often than not, are disavowed through obsessions with corrections, themselves a defense against the uncertainties of learning. The belatedness that belongs to learning is difficult to express and tolerate, particularly during times when what is to be learned concerns both histories of woeful disregard and the pleasures of social difference. Balint and Cavell compose difficult dilemmas for any education that attempts to address the significance and pain of social conflict, misunderstanding, and the breakdown of meaning. They add as well subjective events skipped over in discourses of social justice such as how selves represent to others their singularity and need to belong and be recognized.

From the clinical fact of dependency and symbolization further claims on the pressures of symbolization emerge: What distinguishes the human from other forms of life is its need to self-represent, self-theorize, and interpret through symbols self/other relations (Laplanche 1989; Pontalis 2003).[3] Were it not for dependency, there would be no drive to symbolization. In psychoanalytic terms, however, symbolization is never simply representing more accurately the qualities of objects in the world. Nor is it a problem of decoding what is already there. Instead, symbolization is an emotional experience, itself needed in order to be affected by meaning. Symbolization serves to link feelings to their ideas and as such is a resource for relatedness. It bridges a lifetime of losing and refinding objects and its vulnerability and promise lean upon two precarious resources that are often at odds even as both require construction and interpretation: internal or psychical reality and external or historical reality. The external world is animated by one's feeling states even as it seems to demand particular feelings from us. But also, affect creates and sets in motion the internal world. This paradox of relationality plays well in psychoanalytic theories and is useful for understanding some of the constitutive difficulty that inaugurates thinking and that thinking assuages.

Symbolization, too, may entangle the subject with objects it never consciously called upon. It engages and disclaims the subject's psychological events of introjection, or taking in aspects of the world into the self, and projection, or sending out and putting into the Other either aspects of the self that are good, or parts felt to be bad. Because these phantasized events or object relations create a subject, their magnetizing qualities mean that projection and introjection are also places of identification. The bits and pieces of the self sent out into the world which seems to come from elsewhere invoke what Melanie Klein (1946) called "projective identification." Klein animated identification through her emphasis on seeing this experience as a means for the self to control the object which is actually a projected disparaged part of the self but also "the impulses to control an object from within it stir up the fear of being controlled and persecuted inside it" (11).

How dynamics of introjection and projection relate to symbolization is stated well by the British child analyst Susan Isaacs (1952):

> They refer to such facts as that ideas, impressions and influences are taken into the self and become part of it; or that aspects of elements of the self are often disowned and attributed to some person or groups of persons, or some part of the external world. . . . Now these mental mechanisms are intimately related to certain persuasive phantasies. The phantasies of incorporation (devouring, absorbing, etc.) loved and hated objects, persons, into ourselves are amongst the earliest and most deeply unconscious phantasies, fundamentally oral in character since they are psychic representatives of the oral impulses. (98–99)

Isaacs places introjection and projection under the sign of phantasy and in so doing, accommodates the conflicts of love and hate. These propelling phantasies, perhaps thought of as a representation of representation, persuade and compel because they emerge from internal aggression and defenses against it. Yet they also communicate and organize terrible and lovely self/other relations.

The aggressive qualities of projection and introjection do not equate with only the destruction of the Other. D. W. Winnicott (1945/1992) views positively these beginnings by understanding the infant's ruthlessness and anti-concern—the biting, screaming, and kicking, for example—not as a response to the world or a hatred of it but a way to call the world of others or reality into being. Winnicott's dialogical sense of aggression relieves this concept from the weight of moralistic discourses and from the view that dependency is a one-way street. In doing so, he allows us to notice not just babies' raw potential to make a place for themselves in the world with others but to create and find a needed relationship made from the Other's capacity to tolerate, without being destroyed, their aggression. Here, the question of the baby's intention originally belongs to its drives. And to think with Winnicott on these matters is to consider conscious intention as a secondary process, attributed only retroactively to actions. Sonia Abadi (2001) describes the paradox Winnicott presents: "For Winnicott it is not recognition of one's destructiveness that leads to the possibility of reparation, but instead constructive and creative experiences that enable recognition of one's own destructiveness . . . it is the attitude of the environment toward the child's primary aggressive impulses that marks both the fate of the aggression and the capacity for love and reparation in each individual" (81–82). There are then dimensions of dependency: our dependency on internal processes, our dependency on others, and how these others respond to our dependency. This complexity must be symbolized in ways that allow the self capacity to think. We again return to the question of education, now as a container for self/other relations and so as a third space where, as opposed to retaliation, interest and curiosity toward others and with others can be made.[4]

Psychoanalytic debates on symbolization, aggression, and dependency can be understood as a counter-discourse to such anti-interpretive school-based policies as "zero tolerance," compliance to school authority, and obedience to cultural and normalizing conventions, whether those are of a gender-related, sexual, or racial nature. Psychoanalysis itself is a symbolization, stressing, too, the difficulty of ever knowing for certain the dynamics it rests upon or even if its resting points invent the very subject of its theories. Radical uncertainty, however, is required for the claim that psychical life matters, that interpretations may stir new thoughts, and that creativity is possible. Still, epistemological and ontological uncertainty brought to difficult topics can also grate on nerves because if both the theory and the subject are so unstable in and susceptible to their own unknowns, how is it possible to even recognize reality? While cultural, sociological, anthropological, historical, and postcolonial knowledge of self/other relations, for example, have much to say on problems of social breakdown, on the historical reality of inequality and social strife, and continue to be central to conceptualizing the imperatives of anti-racist pedagogy, the processes of learning, thinking, and feeling made within history, however, and the work of tying knowledge to significance are just beginning to be explored (Pitt and Britzman 2003). One of the most perplexing problems for any pedagogy that engages the work of social repair concerns the status of the external world in our inner world, not from the vantage of attitudinal change or new epistemologist standpoint theories but from the ways the inner world can even be imagined (Britzman 2003a).

Along with many contemporary discussions that address and construct the cultural field of representing race and identity through psychoanalytic theory, I join these debates with some trepidation of being misunderstood. The misunderstanding begins with an objection that social structures and historical oppression will either be ignored or worse, that the latter will be seen as the grounds of pathology. Anne Cheng's (2001) study of racial

melancholia begins with an insightful deconstruction of the orienting bi-
naries of sociological, epistemological, and theoretical objections to psychoanalytic work: there are worries that the victim will be blamed or seen
as only damaged, that focusing on individual psychology wipes away social
responsibility and the history of woeful disregard, and that psychological
orientations universalize and therefore ignore differences between cultures.
Cheng summarizes these objections aptly as "a debate about the assignment of social meaning to psychical processes" (15). Christopher Lane's
(1998) understanding of a psychoanalysis of race considers the other side of
the assignment, that is, how psychical meanings symbolize social processes.
Lane proffers more difficulties to an over-reliance on appeals to consciousness and knowledge, using psychoanalysis "to ruin the myth that psychic
enigmas are best explained as racial conflicts, and to critique the assumption that conflicts over the cultural meaning of race can be resolved *without* our tackling or understanding the unconscious" (20). Young-Bruehl
(1996) demonstrates a sense of how the unconscious works in her index
on the history of social science's grasp of prejudice. She argues that the appeal of prejudice is precisely in its illogical character, that it takes neurotic,
psychotic, narcissistic, and obsessional forms, all of which lean upon unconscious desires. Prejudice is propped up and animated by phantasies of
omnipotence and rigid wishes for a "black and white" or unsymbolic reality. Social prejudices may be indicative of rigid ego defenses and desires for
a mastery that shut out uncertainties that are carried in symbolization. To
understand prejudice as a resistance to symbolization—to consider, then,
how hatred of self and others links resistance to interiority and so to rejection of the psychological significance of dependence—requires a working
analysis of affect and its vicissitudes, seeing affect not as pathology, but as a
constitutive feature of knowledge, sociality, and subjectivity.

## Agencies

Freud (1933) described the internal world through its agencies and their
functions. His structural model of psychical life split the subject into
three: the id, the ego, and the superego (or the it, the me, and the above-
me). Respectively, they articulate the conflicting spheres of pleasure, reality, and morality. The contents of these spheres vary widely; the ranges of
their intelligibility depend upon culture, accidents, and the history (both
imagined and actual) of one's upbringing. Melanie Klein (1937) represents

the internal world as made from object relations, which refer to constructions of the self's representatives of its relationships with its first others[5]
joined to the premature self's symbolization of the anxieties these early
beginnings entail. Phantasy is the representation, then, not of actual others, but one's feelings about feelings. It is an anxious commentary on the
fragility of symbolization and the need for a semblance of meaning before there is something like understanding. On this view, pleasure, reality,
and morality emerge from the baby's expelling and taking in parts of its
world of others, yet its decision as to what is good and what is bad passes
through and is distorted by the anxiety of helplessness and dependency.
In object relations theory, for example, the superego forms early from a
combination of what is desirable about parents but also encompasses their
prohibitions and their parental strangeness. Whether one works from
Freudian or Kleinian theories, internalization is a complex of phantasies:
The unconscious action of taking in the object relation transforms both
the object and the ego.[6]

Regardless of whether one conceptualizes the self as seeking pleasure
or as seeking relations, its most unknown motivation is the unconscious.
Here is "the logic of emotions" in all its glory. The unconscious knows no
time, no negation, and tolerates contradiction. The unconscious may be
described metaphysically as the development of development. To understand the work of symbolization from this vantage and its importance for
becoming a subject with agency is to speculate on the ways in which the
human comes to give up wishful and omnipotent thinking, mourns losses,
tolerates new representations, respects the difference between internal and
external reality, and grasps, indeed, makes pleasure from, the actuality of
others as separate from the self (Hinshelwood 1991).[7] These psychological processes loosen symbolization from identifications, indeed, allow for
difference between affect and external events themselves. Symbolization
gradually eases ego boundaries just enough so that the ego risks learning
and change with a measure of confidence that it and the world can survive
the evitable mistakes, illusions, and misunderstandings that symbolization
with others also carries.

A psychoanalytic narrative of the ego's learning, then, begins within
infantile dependency and theorizes the ego's anxious experience of and defenses against the helplessness dependency entails. Here the world matters personally, although not in ways that are predicable. The residues of
culture in its most intimate and dematerialized, or introjected, form leave

us with questions as to how culture then becomes psychologically significant, where it loses its import, how it is affected by the psychical reality
of individuals and the structures of dependency created from this needed
relation. From this susceptibility to self and the Other, Freud (1926; 1933)
came to view the bodily ego as the seat of anxiety but also, because anxiety is the earliest form of thinking, it creates the potential for the ego to
observe itself and the world, judge reality, and think by joining wish, perception, and conception with reality. Associating affect or thing with idea
or symbolization is not just the ego's work but its passionate possibility.
Here is where the ego may be seen as affected by the outside world it also
affects. From this relation the ego defends itself against any perception of
danger, the key one being the equation of the fear of loss of the object with
loss of love. Its defenses, however, refract anxiety and so distort the danger, as if through a fun house mirror, all for the purpose of working over
anxiety. Imagine, then, such internal actions, or mental gymnastics meant
to protect the ego from inevitable loss: identification, turning around
upon the self, projecting onto the Other one's own intentions and worries,
changing ideas into their opposite, undoing what has already happened,
isolating idea from affect, denial, splitting into good and bad, repression,
idealization, altruism, and identification with the aggressor. These mechanisms affect the very functions of the ego—its cohesiveness, its flexibility,
and its curiosity toward the world. They also are the ego's unconscious
commentary and communication.

## Identification

Many analysts and academics begin with the promise and peril of identification, a special psychical process that allows the ego to attach to others
and to take inside the outside world. In educational contexts, teachers
hold a keen desire to create ways for their students to make identifications with others, knowledge, and events in the past. There is a hope
that emotional ties to social justice can be made from the study of social
devastation (Britzman 2000). There is also a fear that the identifications
themselves may impede an awareness of difference and an acknowledg-
ment of what is incommensurable (Simon 2000) and cannot be identified with. Psychically, identification organizes ego boundaries. Yet because aspects of the ego are unconscious, the decision to formulate one's
emotional ties—where and why they begin, how they lose their interest,

freely associate, protect, or turn against the self, for instance—does not rest with consciousness. Recall that identification is both an ego defense and its first means of becoming. It is also the way the ego splits itself, constituting its own superego. Freud (1933) described the superego as a history of libidinal identifications and abandoned objects "and as a structural relation . . . not merely a personification of some such abstractions as that of conscience" (64).

As with many concepts in psychoanalysis, the meanings, functions, and structures of identification and the processes called identification will take readers into the psychoanalytic archive: One will then meet foundational concepts such as introjection, projection, mourning, splitting, and object relations. Identification is not a cognitive, willful process or a result of rhetorical persuasiveness. It is not voluntary as in a conscious choice made from the world of possibilities. Rather, identifications compose one's internal world and the solutions one needs there. They are a psychical representation made from internal impulses and their fragmenting qualities make this ego defense complex. Identifications are partial and incomplete. A whole object is not taken in: They are contradictory in that two opposing qualities of an object can be incorporated or fused for incorporation and they are ambivalent, bestowed with both love and aggression. Freud pressed the view that consciousness for the human is the exception and also suggested it served as a defense against overwhelming stimuli. This may be one reason why he was so skeptical about consciousness raising through rational appeal. Yet, there remains his insistence that consciousness, or the ego's capacity to think over instinctual conflict and test its relation to what will constitute its feelings toward reality, allows the ego its ethical responsibility. Melanie Klein (1937) named this work "the urge to make reparation"—a desire to keep the Other in mind, to repair what phantasy breaks, and to understand the Other's vulnerability.

One of Freud's (1940a) last published papers, "An Outline of Psychoanalysis" contains a chapter simply titled "The Internal World." In its primal helplessness, the ego cannot distinguish itself from the other, and though its boundaries are a developmental achievement, they are never so absolute or settled because ego development is ongoing through the continuous mechanism of identification and by this means the ego splits itself to make a super-ego: "A portion of the external world has, at least partially, been abandoned as an object and has instead, by identification, been taken into the ego and thus become an integral part of the internal world. This new psychical agency continues to carry on the functions which have been performed by the people [the abandoned objects] in the external world" (205). In the very process of taking in what is no longer there, in the very awareness of loss and of love, and in its passionate and longing perception in the world, from all these positions, psychical agencies come into being. But also, the taking in is a libidinal process, meaning that love of the object and worries over its loss represent the logic of emotions and constitute our emotional ties to the external world.

So, since all losses cannot be noticed, what portion of the world is taken? Here is where identification becomes more complicated since it is tied to a desire that is in excess of socialization and logical processes of thought. We may identify with qualities of others as like the self but also may identify with a wish to have a self like the Other. We may wish others to be different from whom they are in the world and this wish to transform what is absent is taken in. While being and having are two of identity's events, our hope for relations blurs such distinctions. These blurry dynamics find representation in the inner world and in doing so, transform that world and the object relations taken in. Even if the external object is destructive, identification is a means to maintain a lost emotional tie. And identification is also a residue of an emotional tie, however unlikely.

## Identification with the Aggressor

The concept of "identification with the aggressor" has worked its way into social science research and into social and political thought. Readers meet echoes of this term in the writings of Fanon (1952/1986, 51) when he speaks of ego withdrawal and developmental impairment in the colonial Manichaean world.[8] A hint of this concept finds its way into W. E. B. Du Bois's (1903/1989) idea of "double consciousness"—of watching oneself through the eyes of the Other.[9] Another variation motivates Ogbu's (1974) notion of the burden of acting white, where identification wobbles through worries over race betrayal and self betrayal. The emphasis is on how the ego splits the world into good and bad, with the further effect of experiencing divided loyalties and ambivalence. In the literature on school bullying, the concept of identification with the aggressor is tied to the acting out of aggression as opposed to its internalization. In consciousness-raising discussions, identification with the aggressor takes a detour through the vague concept of "internalized oppression." Then it is likened to both the victim and the victimizer's internalization of homophobia or racism, although it can also be used to refer to the psychological after-effects of social inequality now introjected and transformed to animate an inferiority complex and self-hatred. In anti-racist pedagogy, identification with the aggressor may be used to explain the persistence of white working-class racism and why social solidarity fails. But it can also be the reason and justification, in educational programming, for the use of role models to instill, for those with low self-esteem, new identifications. All these orientations, while suggesting the perils and potential of identification, however, gloss over the psychical dynamics of defense and its effects on the ego's representational capacities. Bracketing the external world for a moment to try and take in the logic of emotions at play in this defense asks a great deal of educators who must also consider individuals in relation to larger groups and to the tugs of their own pedagogical desires, identifications, and nightmares (Gardner 1994).

We are apt to forget that the psychoanalytic concept of identification with the aggressor describes an ego defense. In the psychoanalytic archive, identification with the aggressor has a peculiarly contradictory history, reaching both into the problem of unconscious phantasy and projection and helping with the slow dissolution of the Oedipus complex[10] and as a critique of authority in psychoanalysis. "The aggressor" may be an actual person in life or a phantasy of an aspect of a beloved object. The identification is with the emotional logic of the relationship. For the child, it may be any figure who represents authority or is felt to be an authority. Again, we meet up with the symbolization of dependency and a defense against this helplessness, now in the form of identification with the aggressor. That is, the ego introjects the powerful Other and at least in phantasy, can then meet the Other now as more powerful because in the logic of emotions the powerful other is destroyed through its incorporation. There are, to be sure, actual aggressors, people who hurt, humiliate, and crush the life out of others. But the early groundwork for the conflict between dependency and helplessness as needing to be symbolized does not emerge from this cruel extreme. Rather, this ego defense is concerned with the emotional logic of dependency grounded in the social fact that early life requires care to survive and the authority of the Other in order to learn. The problem this human condition raises for educators concerns how we may encounter the spurious nature of identifications as also defying literal correspondence, causality, or even, any explanatory power. Indeed, we can glimpse the radical instability of the ego's mechanisms by taking them through phantasy and the fragmenting dynamic unconscious.

Anna Freud (1936/1995) codified the ego's mechanisms of defense, identifying twelve of them. The problem is not that we have them, for after all, the bodily ego has three partners to placate and experiences danger from each: the external world, and the contrary demands of the id and the superego. These three sources of anxiety—anxiety over others, over pleasure and guilt, and over morality—require different strategies of reality testing. When testing reality in the world the ego judges the veracity or truth of things: that the objects in our mind can be found again in the world. Our internal world requires the understanding of the adequacy of feelings to internal and external events. The problem is that mechanisms of defense may distort the nature of the danger and the ego's response to it, whether we are considering *realangst* or the ego's attempt to protect itself from persecuting feelings that emanate from its internal world. The ego is affected by its defenses and the very defense employed may incur more ego anxiety. Anna Freud advises her readers not to get caught up in deciding the origin of the ego's defense in terms of whether they emerge because of external reality or internal reality: "Even when we admit that the ego has not an entirely free hand in devising the defense mechanism which it employs, our study of these mechanisms impresses us with the magnitude of its achievement" (175).

One of the last ego defenses Anna Freud (1936/1995) noted was "identification with the aggressor." Even in its most prosaic form, this mechanism is a complex relation. "The aggressor" for the child is usually a loved adult who tells the child what to do and in some way, limits the child's pleasures. The child feels passive and persecuted. Father and mother may be felt as the aggressor, ruining the child's omnipotent wishes to be the parent or to have the parent. This defense transforms passivity into activity. Here is Anna Freud's description:

> Even when the external criticism has been introjected, the threat of punishment and the offense committed have not yet been connected up. . . . The moment the criticism is internalized, the offense is externalized. This means that the mechanism of identification with the aggressor is supplemented by another defensive measure, namely the projection of guilt. (118–119)

At its most brittle, identification with the aggressor is tied to indignation toward others, to pointing out their wrong doing and to expelling one's own guilt. Moral anxiety is transported through condemnation of the Other's morality. There are strong feelings of paranoia and incapacity to understand one's own contribution to the creation of anxiety. The ego and superego are essentially in conflict and perception charged with the ego's projections will be as angry as the internal world of object relations. So splitting into good and bad, feelings of moral superiority or inferiority, and moral anxiety become more exaggerated, as would be feelings of idealization and disparagement.

Sándor Ferenczi coined the term "identification with the aggressor." While Anna Freud generalized Ferenczi's concept as an inevitable outcome of a child's development toward autonomy from the parent's love, Ferenczi was able to hold in tension internal and external reality, the problem of guilt, and the dilemma of authority in the relation between students and teachers and analysts and analysands. It is in this latter sense that the concept turns to critique the psychoanalytic world. First, however, Ferenczi considered a more traumatic beginning to this defensive function, namely sexual abuse. He pointed out a child's confusion of libidinality made from the adult's misreading of the child's tenderness as seductive behavior. Ferenczi argued that the child's identification with the aggressor emerges from the seeds of a traumatic relation with an adult and thus sets the stage for the child's terrible compliance. His paper "The Confusion of Tongues between the Adults and the Child" (1933/1988) explored children's needs to love their parents, even if the parent's actions upon the child are devastating. The child would rather identify with the aggressor than give up on the parent. "It is difficult," writes Ferenczi,

> to imagine the behaviour and the emotions of children after such violence. One would expect the first impulse to be that of reaction, hatred, disgust, and energetic refusal. . . . *The same anxiety, however, if it reaches a certain maximum compels them to subordinate themselves like automata to the will of the aggressor, to divine each one of his desires and to gratify these; completely oblivious of themselves they identify themselves with the aggressor.* . . . The most important change, produced in the mind of the child by the anxiety-fear-ridden identification with the adult partner, is *introjection of the guilt feelings of the adult* which makes hitherto harmless play appear as a punishable offence. (201–202, emphasis original)

Ferenczi's conceptualization of identification with the aggressor highlights specific qualities of introjection made from scenes of abuse. Even if it means the destruction of the ego, for the ego losing love is so catastrophic that it would rather take in the threatening, bad object. Then a network of associations, tinged with guilt, anger, and despair are turned inward. Here, the identification is with the adult's guilt and the punishment it implies. The child abandons self-defense for identification with the parent.

There is also, however, a less traumatic form, having to do with the child's desire for autonomy and the need to identify with what is more powerful in order to even imagine a future autonomy. This relation may however agonize the adult who cannot yet give up the desire to control. In describing this aspect Ferenczi closes in on a dilemma of education, how its social relations put into place what he calls "an oppressive love" (204):

> Parents and adults, in the same way as we analysts, ought to learn to be constantly aware that behind the submissiveness or even the adoration, just as behind the transference of love, of our children, patients and pupils, there lies hidden an ardent desire to get rid of this oppressive love. If we can help the child, the patient or the pupil to give up the reaction of identification, and to ward off the over-burdening transference, then we may be said to have reached the goal of raising the personality to the highest level. (203–204)

Ferenczi launches a critique of psychoanalysis to remind those in authority of their charges' vulnerability to and desire for the Other's love. What is easiest to forget, he implies, is that there is a thin line between needing help from the Other and feeling one must be submissive in order to receive it. Paradoxically, Ferenczi suggests (and Winnicott will develop in his theories), there is an aggression required for the ego to become itself. In this way, identification with the aggressor also holds a key to the developing ego's wish for autonomy.

To understand something of its more prosaic qualities from the vantage of the ego who uses this defense, Anna Freud (1936/1995) recounts an example from August Aichhorn's work with children.[11] It has to do with a child making faces at an adult, which is interpreted as the way the child, when feeling threatened, transforms the received threat into making threats:

On such occasions he made faces which caused the whole class to burst out laughing. The master's view was that either the boy was consciously making fun of him or else the twitching of his face must be due to some kind of tic. His report was at once corroborated, for the boy began to make faces during the consultation, but, when master, pupil, and psychologist were together, the situation was explained. Observing the two attentively, Aichhorn saw the boy's grimaces were simply a caricature of the angry expression of the teacher and that, when he had to face a scolding by the latter, he tried to master his anxiety by involuntarily imitating him. The boy identified himself with the teacher's anger and copied his expression as he spoke, though the imitation was not recognized. Through his grimaces he was assimilating himself to or identifying himself with the dreaded external object. (110)

So many dilemmas are noteworthy here, but for the purposes of my discussion, three will be raised. They add up to the fact that in the confines of identification with the aggressor, there is no real Other to discover, that the "dreaded object" is not yet the Other, only the heavy trace of its affect. Before exploring this paradox—that the identification is with anxiety and in the process of identification, passivity is changed to activity—let us trace the various threads. First, identification with the aggressor is with a quality of the aggressor's aggression. In Anna Freud's example, the student identified with the authority's anger. He did not want to become the teacher, only master his anxiety made from the dependency on his teacher. Second, the acting out of the identification worked to deflect the boy's worries. The boy made his class laugh and sent the teacher on a wild goose chase of gathering the bits of a crumbling class. The teacher is now chasing the grimace. Third, even if the object is dreaded and here, the object is a part object made from the worry over the teacher's retaliatory anger, a relationship will be attempted, now in the form of the boy's relationship to his own feelings. The grimace symbolizes the transformation of passivity into activity. The ego will make a strange alliance with the dreaded external object in such a way that the relationship will repeat the breakdown. There is not yet another because there is not yet symbolization.

Earlier in this chapter I suggested that identification and projection go hand in hand. I now want to think about another side of this relationship, what Melanie Klein (1946) noted as "projective identification." This is where phantasy takes an unconscious social turn, for in the case of making a face at an authority, there is also an anticipation of what the authority will do next and, indeed, the action of making a face will affect what the Other in fact does. Others read the grimace and may respond with the force of their own anxiety, attuned, so to say, to the child's notice of a crisis within authority and so with what else the child's anxiety calls forth. The defense that is the grimace, and in a sense, the little private scenarios of aggrieved affect, calls forth the Other's aggression. It is almost as if the face said, "The dreaded object will retaliate, just as I expect it to!" Thus in projective identification, we can see that while the anxiety may emanate from within, there is also the Other it seeks and affects. If we turn to Winnicott's sense of aggression as a way to call others, the fact of this contest and the extent of damage made must depend upon *how* the Other responds, not in the technical sense of imposing procedural rules but in the emotional sense of not retaliating and so creating the space for affective bonds to be made. This is another aspect of dependency, where the Other's thoughtfulness is a resource for the self.

Now making faces is a rather common occurrence between children and adults in families and in schools. If one confines its meaning only to oppositional defiance, one is likely to miss the communication that is also difficult to receive. The grimace condenses a self-representation, a social representation, and a commentary on the very impossibility of holding both. This funny face blocks insight into the difficulty that makes a grimace the response that it is. At its worse, we are reduced to making funny faces to each other, a carnival trading in insults meant to ruin our dependency upon one another. Here is where retaliation overtakes mutuality. Stereotypes and manic name calling, for example, work in these destructive ways defending as they do against interpretation, symbolization, and the creation of meaningful psychological relationships. When dependency and helplessness are communicated to others there is still the work of others symbolizing the significance of the communication. This is perhaps why Ferenczi thought of identification as a reaction, as organizing what he called "oppressive love," a shadow dependency where there are no chances for either the surprises of an actual self or the reply of an actual Other.

## Representation, Again

Psychoanalysis is a theory of the meanings and transformations of human suffering. Indeed, Freud attributes to human interiority a particular madness that is both creative and detritus. Something about living makes us nervous and this anxiety lends longing to the work of symbolization. Interaction with others and symbolizing that significance carry a kernel of this neurosis, not because so many things can go wrong when people get together—although this is also the case—but because our dependency upon the outside world animates phantasies that then structure both our inner world and our perceptions of and wishes for the outside world. We are absolutely affected by what we try to affect. However, if it may then seem obvious to state that psychoanalysis is a depth psychology, less obvious is what this "depth" is made from and how our natality creates from relations of dependency and symbolization something like a self. These observations also raise a further question of what understanding these beginnings can mean for conceptualizations of thoughtful education that take a psychological approach to understanding the phenomenology of aggression.

In an essay that examines the nature of creativity and compliance, Adam Phillips (1998) offers a difficult warning that comes precariously close to the paradox of education: "Psychoanalysis should not be promoting knowledge as a consolation prize for injustice" (50). I take this to mean that however elegant our explanations may be on the designs and structures of our inner world, however much we invest in the therapeutic action of understanding, indeed, of "finding neurosis," and working through it, knowledge of these processes cannot be a substitute for transforming injustice in the social world. On the other hand, identifying this limit cannot be the end of the story because thinking with others is the only means for the self to transform itself. It, too, is a mode of freedom, a means for mourning, a possibility beyond oppressive love, the grounds for symbolization, and an expression of singularity. The capacity to think well about injustice and justice belongs to beginnings and now to education, which, after all, is the ego's second chance.

One of the common objections to psychoanalytic views on understanding social destruction and the construction of the human begins with the objection that compared to doing something about the conditions of poverty, social abuse, and civil war, what difference does it make to be able to think within the sophisticated and complex process of psychical life and recognize its capacity for suffering and reparation? I believe educators must be able to participate here by asking whether this binary must be our choice. The passage from individual difference and subjectivity to social difference and various modes of subjection is not a maze one travels through to reach an outside. Development is uneven, recursive, regressive, and retroactive, dependent upon others and the symbolization of the dependency. The objection that splits—one either analyzes or is an activist—is not a choice because it forecloses so many resources we require. The problem, rather, is how we will think about self/other relations in ways that take into account the complexity and creativity of psychical life, but also hold in mind that psychical life is not the after-thought of social history (although it is its own after-history). As for education, it can be made from understanding its own acts as beyond and even in contradiction to consciousness. We are entering the space of thinking about thinking, an exploration, however uncertain, of how one feels in the world of others and what this intimate knowledge may mean.

In another study that wonders if freedom and equality are at all compatible with human sociality, Phillips (2002) considers again psychoanalytic knowledge, not in terms of its use value, or application, but as potential space for the work of symbolization: "Psychoanalysis as a treatment and an experience, like democracy as a political process, allows people to speak and to be heard. Indeed it encourages people to give voice to their concerns, to be as difficult as they can be, because it depends upon their so doing" (15). This mode of "doing" is the other side of our capacity to self-represent. Here then is a new dependency, now on difficult symbolization. And this act of speaking and listening, so central to the structures of education, permits new considerations on how the self makes, from things like dependency and symbolization, something beyond oppressive love.

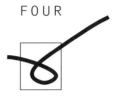

# FOUR

# Poor Little Oedipus: On the Pleasures and Disappointments of Sexual Enlightenment

*Psychoanalysis is about the unacceptable and about love, two things we may prefer to keep apart, and that Freud found to be inextricable.*

Adam Phillips, Terrors and Experts

Let us begin with the assumption that one of the most controversial, difficult, and even murky relations within the history of both education and psychoanalysis concerns matters of imagining and expressing love and hate. And let us assume that the difficulties of these matters elude certainty. Nor can their contours be anaesthetized with logical, unaffected thought because matters of love and hate are impressive, then magnetizing and affecting, even contagious. And let us also imagine that love and hate occupy, through personification and allegory, an internal world of object relations.[1] Indeed, inquiry into these things called love and hate requires gigantic narrative detours, novel imaginative leaps, fantastic speculations, and so the suspension of all credible things. Our epigram gives us more than a hint of the range of thinking needed. Psychoanalysts are no strangers to these views: theirs, too, follow curiosity toward love's migration to "unacceptable" conditions, situations, phantasies, objects, and breakdowns. All in the name of love one can find so many aggressions: crimes of passion and seduction, scenes of jealousy and envy, aggression and violence, and then an ordinary Oedipus complex that takes heart from the curiosity made from the child's sexual researches and games of let's play house. These vicissitudes of love are also our own, and clearing them from the rubble of social convention allows us to ask surprising questions about the nature of meaningful existence. In fact, if love has no alibi, it does permit our susceptibility to psychical reality and our capacity to be affected by its epistemological reverberations. In love, selves are crafted and deferred, objects are lost and refound, thoughts become poetic and absurd, and from these internal experiences knowledge is made.

Our beginning dilemma is this: The concept of love—the one that so easily finds its way to the unacceptable, the one that crumbles into a thousand tiny suspicions and so scatters broken hearts here and there, the one that seems to persist and take its own time despite pleas to let it lie dormant, to wait until one grows up, or to forget homosexual yearnings, and the one that startles the language of poets and novelists, yes, this cacophonous complex of love, for psychoanalysis and education—frays credibility and our logical foundations. Indeed, the story of love psychoanalysis tells is incredible, disillusioning cultural beliefs that love is the absence of aggression, that our parental love and love for our parents do not involve sexual feelings, and that infantile sexuality is either meaningless or nonexistent. Psychoanalysis begins otherwise, placing what Phillips (1996) noted as "the unacceptable" (xi) within an allowance of love's working, all to electrify the heart of psychical development and, too, its own methods for cure: the transference-love. Our inquiry will be a curious undertaking because our "educator" is not an actual person but made from an emotional experience of relating that becomes the basis for furthering the Eros of meaning. Freud (1916) hinted at this uncertain relation when he suggested love's influence: "Side by side with the exigencies of life, love is the great educator . . ." (312).

This chapter narrates an unusual psychoanalytic love story, having at its center peculiar relations in love, hate, and knowledge. From this admixture I explore the affective underpinnings of philosophical reasoning since any education must contain, however implicitly, ideas about the workings and breakdowns of good and bad knowledge and how we come to decide which knowledge will be loved and which knowledge will be hated. Let us set aside the narrow, instrumental view of education as application of knowledge onto the body of a student and as material set in stone. Think instead of what else we do with one another when we go about a particular relationship of trying to learn. Representing love will take us into discussions of philosophy and psychoanalysis and what each gives away for education. Yet whereas the field of philosophy pondered the problem of human existence through reason and judgment, psychoanalysis realized what is immanent for this question to even be asked: the playground of love and hate, there from the beginning. It would take the child analysts to see in this question of existence something startling in both the child's work of learning to live with others and in the adult's childhood of philosophy. To make this argument, I take some detours through past and present speculations on learning to live found in classical and contemporary psychoanalytic archives.[2] I need them to suggest that without a complex conception of love as a meaningful experience that contains what experience cannot master, there is no way of understanding our inner world and its passionate currents. And, by bringing into relief the problem of meaning from the inside out, I begin with a style of thinking that wanders over the work of psychological significance, when mind and body feel recognized and meaningful.

Psychoanalytic stories of love's learning assume many difficult names: the Oedipus complex, the drive, infantile sexuality, and the transference. Education, too, contemplates these conflicts when it can think about influence, authority, autonomy, curiosity, and affection. All of these relations entwine theory and love with the wish to create one's own life and still be recognized by the love of others. In due process, then, trying to know the reach of our inner world becomes entangled with phantasies of knowledge and resistance to this knowing. Add to our list the passionate question of ignorance, and we can begin to consider why learning from others is a passionate affair. This erotic epistemology, composed from putting all these urges into words for someone, is the condition, not the guarantee for psychological significance.

What then can knowledge mean for understanding desire, satisfaction, ignorance, unpleasure, and our relations with others? Qualities of this question preoccupied eighteenth-century philosophers of the Western European Enlightenment. They, too, would write about education to tie it to child rearing, to the work of emerging from dependency and immaturity, and to clarify the responsibilities of thinking and autonomy. And these philosophers saw salvation and hope in public discourse, considering that public talk on these matters is the equivalent to becoming influenced and influencing others (Schmidt 1996). In the beginning of the twentieth century the field of child psychoanalysis would try to borrow from philosophy this faith in rational understanding needed for judgment and reality testing. They called their private enlightenment sexual enlightenment. Eventually, child analysis left this wish behind when it began to listen to a child without recourse to a romance of innocence, an insistence upon children's sexual ignorance or asexuality, or didactic instruction. These were the unsatisfying choices a belief in sexual enlightenment made. How they came to be so unsatisfying is part of the story. The other part is how the vicissitudes of love become infused and thereby transformed again with themes of existence and psychological meaning. And we will see how listening anew moved some psychoanalysts to extenuate questions of love and hate in order to encounter an inner world.

Readers will meet the early theories of psychoanalysts, notably those of Freud and Melanie Klein through their disagreements over the work of love in thinking and in education. I consider some pedagogical and existential dilemmas in two of their early case studies: Freud's (1909) "Little Hans" and Klein's (1921) report on "Fritz." Though about fifteen years separate their publication, in the strange chronology of psychoanalytic knowledge, they are also contemporaneous. If each case represents both an initiation and a rupture in thinking psychoanalytically, their commonality resides in the fact that these case studies also prepared the ground for significant revisions to technique in child analysis and more urgently, to general psychoanalytic theory. My psychoanalytic approach analyzes how a philosophical idealization of enlightenment transformed into to a psychoanalytic dream of sexual enlightenment and then confronted a psychoanalytic problem, namely, that enlightenment cannot touch the question of existence. In highlighting questions of existence I explore an unreasonable reason at the heart of our sexual theories and in our internal attempts to conjugate knowledge with love. Looking inside will help us think differently about the problems of enlightenment and Kant's (1784/1999) worry over a self-incurred immaturity that he thought prevented the goal of rational judgment. Psychoanalysis sees this regression—from maturity to immaturity—as another name for the queer return of the infantile. Most surprising is that recursive infantile sexuality is a needed condition if there is to be any courage for thinking at all.

# Early Years

Melanie Klein was part of the second generation of psychoanalysts. As one of the founders of the field of child psychoanalysis and object relations theory,[3] Klein's understanding of psychoanalytic interpretation—what should be interpreted, how interpretation works, and what conflicts may be animated—developed with her work with very young children. Freud's clinic was with adults and his patient's psychoanalysis began with reconstructing a childhood that had already passed. Still, their shared commitment was only though a strange exchange and combination of words and play: the analysand's free association and the analyst's interpretation. And initially, at least for the adult, the words uttered were largely heard as historical and archeological. But whereas Freud's view of the child was primarily made from adult reconstructions—an adult trying to look back on experiences that were hardly remembered but terribly memorable—Klein's view of the child became terribly untimely. Through symptoms caught in play and drawing, children constructed in her analytic setting something unanticipated: a time before meaning could ease the mysteries of and anxieties toward trying to understand, when phantasy as the representative of an inner world of object relations worked overtime. This surreal timing may be thought of as a misstep of chronology that has tripped upon its own desire. Certainly, there was an overhearing of internal worlds that could then be thought about with a new language. What Klein suggests then, is a creative relationship of listening and speaking. There was no need to love the actual child or to teach the child to love. Her focus was on children's conception of love and hate as their own instructions. Within children's speech, Klein would overhear intimate and involuntary worlds of object relations as they played—sometimes aggressively, other times poignantly—with their theories of inner life and with their projective identifications with others. And what Klein listened intently for were affects of love and hate.

In its earliest years, however, psychoanalysis was also caught in this conundrum: Though having a faith in cure, in reason, in rational persuasion, and in the analyst's educative efforts, analysts kept meeting or having to pursue the estranging psychological meanings of hopelessness, inhibition, and anxiety. If one side spoke to cure, the other side had to learn to listen without idealization. In the developmental model, however, cure seemed the dominant direction, and analytic work mirrored this progressive march from repression, to memory, to consciousness. These efforts were corrective. At first it was thought that realistic knowledge would allow for some new catharses, thereby creating attachment to and curiosity toward the actual world of others. They thought that once the proper representatives were supplied, or found, or remembered, the neurosis and its symptoms would diminish. Freud's theory of the drives[4] pushed aside the wish for sexual enlightenment to pose the problem of representation. Yet as the field of child analysis was becoming itself, this faith in education was formative: Knowledge of sexuality would demolish the remnants of infantile theory and so, to that which works to inhibit thinking. Klein's work on thinking, however, suggests that without our infantile theories, what she called "phantasy," there would be no thinking at all. For phantasy was not just what the child imagined about the world. Rather, phantasy preexisted knowledge of the actual world and represented one's feelings. Phantasy is the carnival of children's feelings about their inner worlds and their object relations. Attempts to sexually enlighten children with objective information could not reach this depth.

One small admission in the early history of child psychoanalysis cast doubt upon the progression of knowledge as a mechanism for cure. Even as child analysts assumed, in the beginning, the goodness of knowledge to affect rational thought, there was a difficulty in understanding what made knowledge good or bad. This uncertainty emerged from their explorations of the underside of education since so many of their young analysands could not bear going to school. There was also, then, the idea that education itself made the child and the adult nervous, contributed to inhibition or the cessation of thinking and enjoyment, and created its own learning difficulties and problems with authority (Britzman 2003a). In education, little scenes of civilization and unhappiness were being played out. There does not seem to be, in contemporary education, a comparable sense of doubt toward its own motivations and goals. I think this may be the case for a number of reasons. Our educational efforts do not begin with a theory of the inner world or of the workings of emotional life. Second, given that mainstream education is so enamored of brain theory and theories of cognition, resistance to thinking of emotional life as the grounds for thinking itself—both from the perspective of the teacher and student—is even left unthought. And third, the chilling effects of the testing industry, of having to prove education works before its time, contribute to an instrumental, repressive orientation to knowledge. The procedures of content, comprehension, and skills domi-nate pedagogical interactions, and there is hardly time for curiosity into the mysteries of being.

By the time of Klein's disagreement over the nature of psychoanalytic education, the skeletal outlines of psychoanalysis were in place. Freud had already published his inaugural text, *The Interpretation of Dreams* (1900). Working from his own self-analysis, Freud speculated that psychical life was governed by the pleasure principle and its myriad wishes, that dreams unfettered by conscious censorship were the royal road to interpreting unconscious wishes, and that the dream-work itself (or the particular op-erations dreams employ to distort representation and maintain a sleeping state) reworked unconscious wishes. In dreams, representations appeared as wishes and so were distorted by displacements, reversals into opposites, substitutions, and condensation. In this strange scene of otherness, words turned into images or things. And dreams, so linked to the wish, were un-apparent knowledge: love, hate, and knowledge could be barely discerned. From this dream theory, symptoms of distress could be traced to a repres-sion of pleasure, to a libidinal fixation, and also to an actual trauma. This was the adult's progression.

The twentieth century ushered in psychoanalysis for children. And as with all new beginnings, the young field of child psychoanalysis looked to the future. It was tethered to an impossible promise to prevent the future of neuroses by lifting the veil of superstition and lies that obscured both the children's understanding of sexuality and the meanings of their pursuit of pleasure. As both a critique of societal hypocrisy toward sexuality and the damaging effects on development of repressing desire, child analysis heralded objective knowledge by telling children the truth. This is where the goal of sexual enlightenment as only an adventure with consciousness entered the picture: The child's supercilious theories of sexuality would be replaced by the adult's truthful knowledge.

Clinical work ruined the theoretical dream of a prophylactic analy-sis that emphasized education. Theory was not far behind. First, Freud found something beyond pleasure. By 1923 Freud (1923) would rethink the structure of psychical life not through pleasure and unpleasure but as a great conflict of pressures, investments, affects, and desires organized by the life and death drives. The life drive would become a metaphor for psychical binding and integration through qualities of Eros. The death drive would work in the service of unbinding through the accession of aggression and its only reason: the reduction of all tension. There would then be a negativity at the heart of psychical life. Following this conflict, and secondly, Freud began to understand that what he called "the cure of love" would be a terrific battle: people do not give up their symptoms easily; consciousness is too fickle, even inattentive, to affect itself; and there would even be a secondary gain from illness. From these limits the work of analysis focused upon the resistance to analysis. Constructions then were made for the sake of insight into more general existential problems, relating learning to live to having to create meaning from the fact of existence. And third, Klein, when she listened to children, stretched all of these new views to their furthest outpost. Klein took the problem of hate and love so seriously that the reasons for these emotions, why we have them at all, became strangely unmoored from a love of reality and from the original goal of child analysis: sexual enlightenment through didactic education.

## Enlightenment and Its Discontents

The early goals of child analysis were influenced by the philosophy of the Enlightenment. Indeed, to understand something of the reach of the question of sexual enlightenment and why it was so central to the early psychoanalytic archive, we must go further back in time, to the eighteenth century, and consider a problem Kant (1784/1999) raised when he wrote his 1784 newspaper editorial "An Answer to the Question: What Is Enlightenment?" His enlightenment was intimately shaped by his idea of education and why we have it at all. Kant stated his reasons directly in another of his essays, first published in English in 1899, and titled "On Education." There, Kant (1803/2003) begins with our beginnings: "Man is the only being who needs education. For by education we must understand nurture (the tending and feeding of the child), discipline [*Zucht*], and teaching, together with culture" (1). Kant's turn to natality and the fact of dependency as justifying adult responsibility to the child occurs at a time when many Continental philosophers were preoccupied by humanist concerns with the nature of human nature, with what it means to become a human, with how to conceptualize needs and desires, and with how judgment, autonomy, and action in the world come to influence development (Todorov 2002).

For Kant, enlightenment depends upon the acquisition of education and literacy. That is, in order to think for oneself, one has to have something to think about and education provides this material. Kant's (1784/1999) answer begins with his assertion of the importance of publicly performing one's reason: "But by the public use of one's own reason I mean that use which anyone may make of it *as a man of learning* addressing the entire *reading public*" (55, emphasis original). Yet this address can become confused because the learning man is not a man of learning. A hint of misrecognition occurs when Kant defines enlightenment as "*man's emergence from his self-incurred immaturity*" (54, emphasis original). Immaturity is another way to describe being unable to understand or think for oneself. Now all kinds of problems occur if autonomy is thought of as isolated—such as having to borrow language, overcoming the position of the Other in subjectivity, ignoring the split subject, forgetting alienation and dependency, and so on (Steuerman 2000)—but the unthought problem is with an aggressive faith in education as a representative of knowledge capable of transcending what Kant saw as "the second nature" that is adult immaturity (54). This faith cannot account for why there is something like "self-incurred immaturity" (54). Why does the human regress?

Almost two hundred years later, Kant's question became variegated when it found its way into an early debate in psychoanalysis. By the early twentieth century, knowledge and love became part of the discussion of psychoanalytic orientations to education and thereby made a new question: What is sexual enlightenment? Yet despite our leap in time, despite the nearly two hundred years between the Kantian and Freudian question, both began with the problem of a body: its archive of desire as not being in correspondence to its index of knowledge. Psychoanalysts eventually came to the idea that in order to even understand something like the desire for sexual enlightenment and what it may defend against, one must be willing to meet the limits of one's thinking about thinking. In psychoanalysis, this limit leads us to a speculation Freud called "the drives" and to the problem Kant mentioned, namely, a regression from maturity to immaturity.

The concept of "the drives" is a theoretical speculation I describe shortly. But two considerable problems previously unavailable to psychoanalysis emerge from Freud's theory of the drives as the urge that motivates psychical and social life. First, if sexual enlightenment was meant to enlighten sexuality, how is sexual enlightenment even possible if the sexual is related to the drive and the drive insists but cannot be directly represented? Freud's speculation on the drives permits a different understanding of the Kantian problem of a return to something primordial that resists enlightenment—what Kant noticed as "a self-incurred immaturity" (54) which must be overcome if there is to be something like a second chance for Reason. Second, there is the problem of regression: Why does the self return to its earlier state?

## Modes of Knowledge

One of the unusual qualities of psychoanalysis is that it considers its object of knowledge in terms of its functions and structures, and through the mechanisms required for its representation. How we come to know is not just the result of an investigative procedure. We know that psychoanalysis entangles knowledge with desire and posits that the first libidinal relationship with the mother is a "template upon which all later relationships are based" (Verhaeghe 1999, 37). This template is actually an impression in two senses of the word. The impression is a theory kindergarten, a constellation of infantile sexuality and its phantasies, conveyed and animated by projections and identifications. So my impression of the world beyond me emerges from my feelings toward a world inside me. My impression is projected outside of me, but because it comes from me, I am tied to these objects through identifications. However, these impressions, or phantasies, can seem as if they are coming from the world, directed at me. More improbably, something must be taken in, introjected, to leave behind an impression. In the second sense, the impression is of an introjective nature, constituting then a groove, or pleasurable indentation to which mesmerized knowledge migrates to and is magnetized by, but cannot fill, the hole, the lack, or the division. This template, then, affected by and created from our first mode of loving and being loved, must also mark a loss. Too soon a flurry of knowledge is being made, things that cannot be understood yet still demand to know and to be known. One consequence is that we will use knowledge as a defense, as an attempt to settle the longing and emptiness. Resistance to knowledge will be the counter-force.

Freud's (1905) "Three Essays on Sexuality" describes this drive quite simply as "the drive is to be regarded as a measure of the demand made upon the mind for work" (168). Ten years later Freud (1915b) will call the drive a psychical representative, emanating from within the body and performing itself through its four vicissitudes or transformations: "reversal into its opposite, turning round upon the subject's own self, repression, and sublimation" (126). In the case of reversal into its opposite, Freud theorized the transformation that will concern us the most has to do with love turning into hate and hate turning into love.

Even before this theoretical advance, Freud (1905) tried to characterize another kind of drive, the drive to know (*Wissentribe*), when he described children as "little sex researchers." Curiosity, or thirst for knowledge, carries and is charged by tinges of anxiety and desire. This is because there is a certain delay in knowing which impresses upon the construction of knowledge: Children encounter experiences they cannot understand and only later, with new knowledge placed over the old mysteries, does sexuality come to mean something different from what was first felt, thought, and encountered. For Freud, curiosity will be a shorthand for sexual curiosity. This curiosity is directed outward, resembling a sociological push to understand sexuality. The seriousness of inquiry is there, but it is distorted by an infantile phantasy of omnipotence, aggravated by an impossible wish to possess mother and father in order to give birth to the self. Curiosity will express itself through feelings of love and hate. And the research of the child, the particular knowledge of sexuality, will be affected. Contradictions will then accrue, marking the theory of the child's theory. Meltzer (1998) for example, in his discussion of Freud and Klein, finds ambivalence: "Since Freud's idea seems to be that this curiosity is fundamentally driven by anxiety and hatred, it is very puzzling that he should think of it as something that should drive the child in the direction of wanting to discover the truth" (67). This drive to know, then, has some constitutive flaws: One both wants and does not want the truth. This leads Lacan to further complicate an understanding of the drive to know through what he called "the passion for ignorance" or the myriad ways our search for knowledge performs negations and resistance (Felman 1987).

Klein (1928) will take this uncanny complex of desire, anxiety, and knowledge and give it an even more precocious chronology. Not only that, she will insist that the drive to know pertains to internal affairs, wanting first to know the inside not the outside. And she will give it an awkward name, calling it an epistemophilic instinct, a drive to know the inside of the mother's body. This drive is aggressive, sadistic, and intrusive, tied to wanting to take possession of the mother by knowing her insides. Love and hate will be confused, protecting the inquiry, destroying the object, destroying the inquiry, loving the object. With Freud, Klein kept the idea that the drive to knowledge is a defense against the anxiety of not knowing yet urgently needing to know. But unlike Freud, Klein will see this drive as if it were a desire for x-ray vision. That is, it is not the outside world that the child wants to know but the inside world. Here then is the model for aesthetic conflict. Why, however, should the inside of the mother's body matter so much to the child? Klein speculated that the first object for the infant is the mother's body, while the first existential problem for the child concerns conceptualizing a time before birth (Meltzer 1998). Moreover, Klein used the concept of the epistemophilic instinct as a way to characterize the flora and fauna of the inner world of object relations. Meltzer's (1998) description of Klein's contribution is lovely:

> It took somebody like Mrs. Klein, listening to little children talking about the inside of their mother's body with absolute conviction as if it were Budapest or Vienna, as an absolutely geographical place, to realize that there really is an inner world, and that it is not just allegorical or metaphorical, but has a concrete existence—in the life of the mind, not the brain. (98)

For Klein, internal reality would be like a crowded city in rush hour traffic, not the stillness of the archeological site of Freud's view of the psyche, but more active, more dynamic, more real. And the propulsion of affect would gain lightning-like force from this carnival world, creating, announcing, urging, and addressing object relations.

The drive to know is conviction and it is the outside world, then, which seems absurd. In this confusion, the adult's insistence for an accurate, unaffected knowledge is of no use because of the nature of the questions that a child must ask. Verhaeghe (1999) posits three questions that form the child's curiosity: "What is the difference between me and the other sex, where do children come from, and what is the relation between my mother and father?" (127). As I will suggest later, sexual enlightenment fails because these questions posit a first nature—the infantile—and the infantile entangles its own nature with theoretical worlds of love and hate. If these inquiries pull us back to this first nature, their power resides in what cannot be answered: the lifetime question of existence as such. It was Klein (1921) who first theorized a strange "resistance to enlightenment" as a return of the infantile sexuality. She then stretched the idea of *this resistance* to the problem of having to be educated (Britzman 2003a).

## "Little Hans"

For those not familiar with Freud's (1909) "Little Hans" case, of which the original title was "Analysis of a Phobia in a Five-Year-Old Boy," here is how Freud, seventeen years later, and in his structural theory of psychical life (where now there is a profound conflict between two drives—Eros and Thanatos) summarizes the presenting problem: "Little Hans refused to go out into the street because he was afraid of horses. This was the raw material of the case" (Freud 1926, 101). The horse, we learn, is not really a horse but a father whom he both feared and loved. So the conflict has a measure of ambivalence. And Freud (1926) distinguishes Hans's fear of having a horse bite him or fall down in front of him from a phobia with the simple statement, "What made it a neurosis was one thing alone; the replacement of his father by a horse" (103). We are back to the question of symbolization. From here, Freud elaborates a theory of knowledge that resists its own unity. With anxiety, meaning is unmoored from the sign and Hans creates "a horse father." This dreamlike transformation harkens back to Freud's theory of what happens to meaning in the dream-work: Meaning will be broken into bits and pieces and rearranged and reorganized through condensation, reversal into its opposite, substitution, and displacement. "As we see," writes Freud, "the conflict due to ambivalence is not dealt with in relation to one and the same person; it is circumvented, as it were, by one of the pair of conflicting impulses being directed to another person as a substitutive object" (1926, 103). Here, then, is the emotional logic that can assert without negation: "Yes, my father is a horse." But how does one make sense of this irrational reason?

Around 1926 Freud retracts his earlier metapsychological speculation that repression causes anxiety and turns it around to the idea that anxiety, specifically as signaling internal danger, allows the ego to create repression. Now, repression will be an *after-repression*, a secondary defense rather than as a reason for anxiety. But the defense will only be known if the repression has, in some sense, failed. The nature of the failure will be marked by a symptom, itself a placeholder for something missed (Freud 1926). Hans, for example, may repress his hatred for his father, but the hatred does not go away. Rather, it returns in the symptom of a phobia, fear of horses that fall down or bite him. The Little Hans case helps Freud understand this sequence when he traced the disjunction between an idea which is repressed and the affect which is not. Essentially, by splitting representation into the thing and the presentation, the idea may be shut out of consciousness but the affect is carried over to another object. Spitting, displacement, and substitution are processes we have seen as necessary to the dream-work. Knowledge, too, works along the lines of a psychical apparatus in that it cannot be complete, self identical, or hold its own boundaries without a tendency toward alienation and fixation. Knowledge, too, will be affected by the dream-work.

Divisions, reversals, and dissociations of affect and idea are working models for understanding the symbolic procedures set in motion by a traumatic perception of helplessness, passivity, and loss. The ego must face two kinds of losses: the loss of that first object and the threat of its unrepresentability. To return to Little Hans, the boy wanted his mother (the first object) and hated his father. Yet how can this phantasy be even spoken; how can his desire here be representable? What exactly did Hans want from the horse? I suspect that he wanted a private knowledge to contain the force of the loss of the first phantasy. Here, as stated earlier, knowledge will be a defense against this loss. An object has been lost; libidinal cathexes have been withdrawn, and a traumatic search for symbols is set in motion. In psychoanalysis, this remembering, repetition, and working through are also models for thinking and making theories: thinking over drive conflict, finding adequate symbols, and mourning the unrepresentable loss that the drive also animates. Hence what Freud (1914) called "working through" will now consist not of the recovery of memory but an encounter with one's own need to symbolize: tolerating the arbitrary nature of the signified and sign, encountering and even taking pleasure from the gap between psychical life and historical life; and learning to love psychical reality and to accept that hatred is part of this world as well. The problem is that in this search for the signifier, itself an index of loss, something primal, an existential agony, repeats. There is no way around this constitutive fault line. There is no way around this self-incurred immaturity. Indeed, it may become our first resource. Knowledge, too, will carry this burden, and Freud (1909) hinted at this conundrum when he called Little Hans "our Little Oedipus." Who would have thought that phobias had something to do with love and its losses?

Little Hans is precocious and worried, ostensibly afraid of horses that would bite him or fall down. There are other worries too, of which we might surmise distorted glimmers of the three questions of the child: that someone will see him making wiwi; that he will turn into a woman; and that his father's questions are somehow beside the point. These displaced occupations were also enactments of early attachments: Hans was afraid of crossing the street and so leaving his mother behind. His solution is rather ingenious, for here is where Hans attempts to represent the drive, and it is no mistake that he calls for his mother. That first impression, what Verhaeghe (2001) will see as the way the drive is linked to the Other, will also mean that the quest for existence will be at odds with the drive to know. Freud (1909) observed this tension in his introduction to the case with an example of Hans wondering, at age three and a half, if his mother has a "widdler" like his father's. His mother replies, "Of course. Didn't you know that?" and to which Hans answers, "No. I thought you were so big you'd have a widdler like a horse" (9–10). Freud commented on this absurd mismatched exchange: "Thirst for knowledge seems to be inseparable from sexual curiosity. Hans's curiosity was particularly directed toward his parents" (9). And Freud also asked readers to remember the horse.

Let us take a closer look at Hans's worries in relation to the development of psychoanalysis for it was not just that Hans wanted sexual knowledge. He was also trying to figure out a chronology prior to his existence, and he was trying to do that through seeing if his own body meant anything to his phantasies of femininity. Would he give birth as well when he grew up? Hans could not figure out his hatred for his father and then, whether love and hate carried any significance at all. And the more his father explained, the more frustrated Hans became. There was something about Hans that Freud could not address, namely, the significance to the child (and to psychoanalytic theory) of the child's phantasies of the mother, all children's femininity phases, and the unconscious registration of these impressions. Klein will begin with these impressions, attributing the femininity phase to girls and boys.

Freud's "thirst for knowledge" has two conflicting sources: One emerges from infantile sexuality which allows for curiosity or the drive to know and bestows its theories with omnipotence and grandiosity, suggestive of the oral phase. The other source encompasses anxiety and internal danger, a pushing away of the distress made from the loss of the original object. Anal defenses against this distress occur, and the distress reappears in a new guise, projected into a different object. As for knowledge, children try to make sense of their family and their place with their parents. Phantasy, however, will have other adventures. Meltzer's (1998) thoughts on "Little Hans" suggest that Freud was not yet at a cross road where love and hate would be more useful than a theory of instincts. For Meltzer, "Little Hans" also proposed something enigmatic about this thirst for knowledge: "that the thirst for knowledge is driven by anxiety, and that knowledge will inevitably be used for defensive processes" (52). That is, entangled in trying to know the truth is also a fear of truth, and this makes for a confusion between good and bad knowledge. It also charges a regression of history. The Kantian "self-incurred immaturity" is a defense that is never so far away.

## Fritz and Company

Klein's (1921) "The Development of a Child" endorsed sexual enlightenment as a goal of child analysis. In Part One of the paper, Klein has a sharp critical wish: "We can spare the child unnecessary repression by freeing—and first and foremost in ourselves—the whole wide sphere of sexuality from the dense veils of secrecy, falsehood and danger spun by a hypocritical civilization upon an affective and uninformed foundation" (1). Readers are pulled inside the dream of sexual enlightenment, itself a "necessary repression" of the infantile stage. Part Two of the paper, written a few years later, discards this faith in the power of rational knowledge to overcome the symptom. Klein now considers naive her early insistence on the usefulness of a prophylactic psychoanalysis. In leaving this faith, it is almost as if Klein is asking, "If education cannot prevent the neurosis, then what is it doing?" Klein's difficult contribution was to wonder if there is a place where education cannot go, but where, nonetheless, knowledge can become. But this knowledge is of a different order, expressing itself as the inexplicable reach to phantasy, thus opening our educational archive to its own otherness, thus rewriting Freud's story of thinking as reality testing, reminding us that there is no thinking without phantasy.

Klein began a psychoanalytic education with her son with the idea of enlightening him in what she called "sexual matters." By answering any of his questions with honesty, she thought she could help him avoid the future of neurotic tendencies and also "deprive sexuality at once of its mystery and of a great part of its danger" (1–2).

Things get rather absurd. At one point, the five-year-old Fritz believes he is a gourmet cook, can speak French fluently, and can fix any object that is broken. While Klein explains patiently that he does not yet know how to do any of these things—that he must learn—Fritz replies calmly:

"If I am shown how just once, I can do it quite well" (3). He holds tightly to this great refrain; it is his last word. Something about having to learn is being skipped over, and Klein places what is missed under the ominous heading "The child's resistance to enlightenment." It is possible, I think, to wonder who or what is being resisted, given the fact that other divisions of Klein's case study paper gather Fritz's struggle under the grand theme of existence. That is, Fritz wonders about the nature of reality and his judgments of it, the qualities of time, history, and memory, the definitions of his rights and powers, the future of his wishes and hopes, the meaning of birth and death, and whether there is God.

These are exquisite problems, and they take us to the dreamy realm of trying to symbolize our encounter with both reality and phantasy. And if Fritz is now sounding a bit like Kant, trying to know things-in-themselves while bumping up against the limits of trying to know, his questions force Klein to move as close as she ever would to confronting her own wishes for enlightenment. From this confrontation there will emerge the question of phantasy and a Kleinian view of an infantile life that will speculate upon not a self-incurred immaturity, but a constitutive immaturity that will set thinking to work. Here is where Klein begins to think about infantile omnipotence differently, as both a defense against being small and helpless and as a mode of obdurate thought that even if buried by having to grow up, preserves our wishes for learning and existence.

Klein had difficulty figuring out the nature of curiosity—where it comes from, what it represents, how it loosens itself from its object and so, what it means to urge *this* facility. These questions also animated something new about her own curiosity. Klein discovered, along with the child's resistance to enlightenment, her own resistance to what else the child asks. We are entering the psychoanalytic field of the transference: the exchange of unconscious wishes, the displacement of our first love onto figures of authority, and the transposition of symbolic equivalences of old and repressed conflicts onto the understanding of new situations. Significantly, Freud (1912a) writes of transference as a dynamic, as a relation, and as an obstacle, and he links its indelible signature to permitting an impossible investigation. In trying to know something new, our psychic archive is animated and perhaps agitated. The transference, Freud writes, emerges from "a compromise between the demands of [the resistance] and those of the work of investigation" (103). Something within the very work of investigation resists and animates its own demands. And in psychoanalysis, this resistance may symbolize a paradox: There is mystery to sexuality and knowledge cannot take this away. But there is also mystery to knowledge because we have sexuality. It is here that our elusive education, our elusive enlightenment, flutters and flounders.

It is useful to return to Verhaeghe's (1999) summary of the three questions that preoccupy the child: "What is the difference between me and the other sex, where do children come from, and what is the relation between my mother and father?" (127). Klein's study of Fritz gives a sense of how chaotic, desperate, unreasonable, and insistent these questions feel though the following report on the nature of the mother and child's conversation reproduced below was Klein's attempt at a "sexual enlightenment." The breakdown of meaning provoked by the mother's instruction begins to give us a sense of the gigantic mismatch in needs and desires sexual enlightenment animates. This passage also harkens back to the exchange between Hans and his mother:

> When I begin once more about the little egg, he interrupts me, "I know that." I continue, "Papa can make something with his wiwi that really looks rather like milk and it is called seed; he makes it like doing wiwi only not so much. Mama's wiwi is different to papa's" (he interrupts) "I know *that!*" I say, "Mama's wiwi is like a hole. If papa puts his wiwi into mama's wiwi and makes the seed there, then the seed runs in deeper into her body and when it meets with one of the little eggs that are inside mama, then that little egg begins to grow and becomes a child." Fritz listened with great interest and said, "I would so much like to see how a child is made inside like that." I explain that this is impossible until he is big because it can't be done 'til then but that then he will do it himself. "But then I would like to do it to mama." "That can't be, mama can't be your wife for she is the wife of your papa, and then papa would have no wife." "But we could both do it to her." I say, "No, that can't be. Every man has only one wife. When you are big, your mama will be old . . . Your mama will always love you but she can't be your wife." . . . At the end he said, "But I would just once like to see how the child gets in and out." (34)

No wonder Klein places this conversation under the heading "The child's resistance to enlightenment." Fritz, like Oedipus, demands all of the positions: he is baby and father, son and lover. He is egg and seed, big and old. And these positions regard his mother's appeal to a future as ridiculous. The child cannot give birth to himself and cannot witness his own birth. Yet there was something Fritz needed to know: What is going on inside of the mother? This was how Fritz wondered about his own origin. Yet it was mistakenly answered through the mother's desire. That is, Klein told the story of her love with her husband. And this leaves out little Fritz, who was not only not there during parental intercourse but whose parents could not have even thought of him at the time. How is Fritz to understand that he had no existence in his parent's sexual intercourse, that what had existed then was not Fritz but the parental erotic love which excludes him? The enlightenment Fritz resists, then, is that his parents have a life without him and that Fritz cannot yet use the knowledge his mother offers to make sense of either his origin or his desire to know. We have reached the crevices of the Oedipus complex, not so much the story of exclusion but the yearning for knowledge to complete the mystery of existence.

Klein, too, is unsatisfied with the nature of her explanation for she has not reached a phantasy nor even interpreted the anxiety that Freud spoke of as also being a part of the child's sexual curiosity. She is still early in her own education although she manages to link Fritz's persistent questions to an inner world where there is mental pain made from not understanding. Here is where Klein (1921) begins to grapple with the problem of think-ing emotional worlds when she comments on how Fritz struggles with his desires: "That a certain 'pain,' an unwillingness to accept (against which his desire for truth was struggling) was the determining factor in his fre-quent repetition of the question" (4).

Where there is existence, there is a certain pain, an ambivalence that is also an impression. Here is where love and hate begin their efforts. The child's questions, Klein came to suspect, were an unconscious plea both to possess history not yet formulated and to formulate something that can never be history, to have his own private enlightenment by answering the question of existence prior to his existence. Even more, Fritz already knew how babies are born. He wanted to know where he was before he was born, and this leads him back to that first relation with his mother's body. Once Klein could give up on explaining the world as it is or more actually, in a language she supposed her son would understand, she could allow herself to listen to the child's worries over existence made from wanting to known an inner world. The ethical turn is hinted when Klein leaves the drive to know and so, her own drive to tell and instead considers that range of love and hate in the inner world and how these feelings relate to the child's theories and meanings. Many years later, Klein (1946) will speak of psychical positions needed for thinking. She will see this inquiry as wavering between the paranoid-schizoid and depressive positions. The paranoid-schizoid position is a phantasy of knowledge, created from splitting the object into good and bad but then needing paranoid anxieties to defend against the object which has been hurt by splitting and so may take its revenge. In the paranoid-schizoid position, the concern is only with protecting the self. Then follows a sense of the object as a whole object which allows for the development of a knowledge of phantasy, what Klein would call "the depressive position." In the depressive position, pining, loss, and depressive anxiety may become integrated into the fact of existence because existence is with others. The infantile wish to give birth to itself, to possess the other, transforms into a concern for the Other, which now includes feelings of loss, remorse, and reparation. Rather than only be left with the Kantian subject, the "I-think-that-accompanies-all-of-my representations," we have what instead is an inner world capable of thinking one's thoughts, of doubting representations, and of accepting ambivalence. In the depressive position archaic defenses of splitting, idealization, and envy give way to feelings of love, reparation, and gratitude. Love and hate, on this view, are never so far apart, but neither are they so close that each would lose its respective uniqueness.

## Mind the Gap

Originally, Klein put great faith in the value of psychoanalytic education to cure ignorance, settle confusion, and perhaps, even, correct the mistakes of existence. *Bildung,* or moral training, is what Kant (1803/2003) hoped education could direct in order to create the conditions for reason. Reason then would insure a move from self-incurred immaturity to autonomy and individuality. Both of these views of education sustain a phantasy of knowledge: that knowledge can, in and of itself, transform the self and its superfluous infantile theories. They do not yet reach a knowledge of phantasy or the Kleinian depressive position. The self-incurred immaturity that so worried Kant is emblematic of two demands whose conflict is the prerequisite for thinking: infantile sexuality with its wish to have no knowledge (the Lacanian passion for ignorance) and the drive to know one's own origins, fueled by the paranoid-schizoid position.

Klein leaves us with a question as to whether enlightenment can even be useful to any working through of the phantasized events of the child with a theory. She also allows us to question the phantasies of that other theory: enlightenment. It was Klein who, in depicting a concrete inner world, relaxed the grip of enlightenment and turned to the tumult of love and hate. The movement is from a belief in the phantasy of knowledge to overcome immaturity to an analytic style whose only goal was knowledge of phantasy. What her young analysands did with this new knowledge, and here Klein supports a very different sense of autonomy, was theirs to do with as they wished.

In more contemporary terms, Verhaeghe's (2001) summary of Lacan's view of knowledge brings us to the heart of the matter:

> The fact that the unconscious is not a thinking being, but first and foremost an enjoying being who does not want to know anything about it. This cannot be captured within a traditional articulated knowledge. Beyond the illusion of mirroring, then, there is a "relation to being" that cannot be known. There is a discordance, a cleft between being and knowledge on *our* side, that is, at the side of the subject where the latter is indeed not-whole. (113)

Self-incurred immaturity may signal this not-whole, passing over an interpretation of enlightenment only to confront the uninterruptible dream of existence. This mystery is what the drive may animate but cannot solve because what else can the drive be but a preview story of love and hate? It is this discord that the work of integration attempts to contain and that the work of thought must tolerate to go on thinking. And the discordance between being and knowledge, the conflict philosophy may try to solve and that education may try to ignore, may be another way of thinking about love and hate. If education is to "mind the gap," it must consider the phantasies of its own workings, its own dream-work, but not mistake how it understands itself as settling the research of either the child or the adult.

# FIVE

# Melanie Klein, Little Richard, and the Psychoanalytic Question of Inhibition

## Prehistory

For those outside the psychoanalytic field, encountering the language of Melanie Klein and her work with children is a strange, if not shocking affair. If readers think of her interpretations of children's play as irrelevant, consider her case studies as her attempt to anchor causality through the Freudian fiction of psychical structure, or suppose her theories of psychical life install the very pathologies they claim to reveal, then one may as well not read Klein at all. And yet Kleinian theory presents contemporary readers with a dramatic theoretical conundrum. Klein begins her narrative of the subject not with a discussion of how external reality influences or affects it but instead with the poiesis of psychical reality, of an inner world of object relations. Hers is a narrative that entangles theory and its origins with a biological drive she called the "epistemophilic instinct"—the drive to know, to master, to control. By hitching the fate of the subject's knowledge to the fecundity of the unconscious drives, distinctions between epistemology and ontology no longer matter; left over is the shadowy internal world of phantasy as the first means and resource for encountering the world of others. This resource is prehistoric, populated with a bizarre puppet world of theories.

No wonder Klein takes learning away from education and instead supposes that learning occurs in confrontation with the drives. It is not that the outside world matters little. Rather, Klein imagines preconditions for its encounter, namely, the anxiety that calls forth the internal world of object relations. She thus can raise the crucial question of how both the internal and external worlds can be known at all. Thinking, interpretation, and narrative emerge from and are marked by this anxiety. The difficulty of learning is not so much clarified by Klein's general insistence upon the power of an asocial death drive. Yet this pressure afflicts subjects, prior to their capacity for language and understanding, with a persecutory anxiety so profound that it can feel as if the attack comes from the outside. What reduces the opacity of this schizoid world is Klein's claim that the confusion between bodily boundaries—what is inside and what is outside and so what belongs to the self and to the Other—begins the question of good and bad boundaries. Emerging from this terrible splitting are both psychical representatives of anxiety and the capacity to think about them. These creatures can be thought of as personifications of anxiety and defenses against it. Klein will call the precocious group that arrives before knowledge of the world, phantasy, and thinking about them will constitute knowledge. So the drive is the conveyer for both the subject's destruction of objects *and* her first resource for repairing their meaning. Klein will dedicate her theory and practice to elucidating these phantasies because her commitment is with how insight into this anxiety allows the self the creativity for interpreting the stakes of constructing reality. Good and bad, inside and outside, self and Other, reality and phantasy, these are the object relations of the capacious Kleinian subject.

If, then, we have something like psychological meaning before we have understanding, Kleinian speculation opens the ostensibly settled question of what biology can signify if the problem of making psychical significance is where we must begin. Klein raises meaning, or knowledge of reality and phantasy, as the first terrible problem and so she attributes something original and frustrating to the infant: a lively, desperate, paranoid, and an urgent struggle to symbolize, to understand, and to relate. Biology is no longer a clichéd destiny. Instead it is a symbol for that mythic battle, the movement of meaning with relating: how even the barest flutter of significance emerges from and is marked by the violent recursiveness of terrifying literalness; how interpretation undoes concrete representations to make room for symbolization; and how thinking can come close to atonement or thinking of the Other. Klein's principle may go something like this: *Where deprivation was, there frustration, symbolization, gratitude, and reparation shall become.* There can be made from this progression human tolerance for language, interpretation, and so for metaphoric freedom. This is what Klein means by poignant thinking. And she insists upon language and narrative as the means for working through the confining confusion of infantile reality. Klein, therefore, will not invite a novel to be written since she expects the difficulty belongs to the novel already written and now defended against. For Klein will maintain that perceptions of reality as only stringent and punishing are projections of an internal world of hostile object relations. The rigidness is preserved through a fear of interpretation and so of psychological meaning. These fears and their defenses against them are what Klein means by inhibition, and why she is concerned with difficulties in and obstacles to psychical freedom.

Working with some Kleinian conundrums, I develop the theme of psychoanalytic freedom as a way into the question of inhibition. Klein links freedom to the capacity to think about phantasy, to value interpretations as a means of knowing reality and of loosening its hold, and to take pleasure in the designs of psychological meaning. The other side of freedom is inhibition, and her theories on inhibition and narrative open contemporary debates on the status of the concept of psychological freedom during times when we seem to be more adept at describing social processes of normalization and subjection than we do in describing the problem of learning to live and what it can mean that we are susceptible to both conscious and unconscious forces. Indeed, critical theories of the subject emphasize the ways we are affected through external conditions and so present our susceptibility to discursive design as an effect of discourse. Interiority is thus viewed as an after-thought; psychological significance becomes a ruse of social structure. Klein's theories challenge this docility, even suggesting that if inhibition can be the royal road to normalization, it is also a lively, aggressive, and powerful dynamic and paradoxically, a nascent challenge to docility. I explore this paradox throughout and suggest that Klein's theories of learning and not learning can be thought of in three registers: as a response to historical and cultural circumstances that supposed women and children were incapable of thinking; as psychoanalytic arguments with Anna Freud over the question of what the child is capable of accepting in the psychoanalytic setting; and lastly as clinical provocations to the child and to theory itself.

While there is great difficulty in making a context outside of the psychoanalytic field for Klein's clinical practice, particularly because of her interest in speaking in a language of archaic anxiety, it is clear what Klein's practice and theories were responding to in the world of child analysis: the influence of education, or better, the belief that education, if properly conducted, can cure neurosis and inhibition and can prevent the future of neurosis. Adam Phillips (2002) ties the quest to determine childhood, education, and cure to the desire to systematize. He argues that the concept of childhood is one procedure of knowledge:

> In simple terms, the Freudian child suffers, so to speak, from an intensity of desire and an excess of vulnerability. It was not, as Aries was among the first to show, that this was news about childhood. The news was in the need, beginning in the eighteenth century, to make the child an object of systematic knowledge. (151)

The news is the need. The systematicity of knowledge must pass through the distortions and condensations of the unconscious, thereby marking knowledge with affect: obsession, fixation, anxiety, and paranoia, for instance. In Allan Bass's (1998) view, systematicity is not just a codification or procedure of knowledge but a structure of defense: "Whenever one finds systematicity, one can, from a psychoanalytic point of view, ask the question of what unbearable piece of reality is being defended against by means of the system" (426). This is the news that put education into question and where Kleinian theory of knowledge begins.

## That Other Education

Melanie Klein (1882–1960) was responding to the inhibitions within her own generation; perhaps in this return to Klein we are responding to something that resists in ours. There are those biographic details that open and may serve as an emblem of, but not the explication for, the early twentieth century. As a daughter of the Jewish Enlightenment, the *Haskala*, she began with great faith in the promise of education. She had hopes for herself to be a medical doctor but instead, by 1903, married a business man, Arthur Klein. Then over the next ten years came three children, along with what might have been a return of a deep depression. Around 1914, Klein entered psychoanalysis with Ferenczi in Budapest; there, with his encouragement, she practiced in that new field of child psychoanalysis as well. During that first part of the twentieth century, Klein moved from country to country, language to language, and through different psycho-analytical theories. The reasons are dramatic: depression, civil war, family obligations, constraints, analysis, and finally her work. Perhaps there was also a need for recognition or escape from what can only be too recogniz-able. By 1919 Klein became a member of the Budapest Psychoanalytic Society. By 1921 she had moved to Berlin, joined that Society, and in 1924 began another analysis with Karl Abraham. A year later with Abraham's premature death, the analysis abruptly ended. By 1926, Klein divorced and emigrated to London. These idiomatic events, now residues of his-tory, also congeal in her theory, or perhaps they set the stage for what her theory of object relations will become: places of sudden change, of desire, and of mourning and reparation.

In his discussion of Klein's legacy, J.-B. Pontalis (1981) thought her theories attempted to work toward a difficult question: "What holds the child back?" (95). Contemporary commentators of Klein's theory and life such as Grosskurth (1987), Likierman (2001), and Kristeva (2001a) con-sider the concept of inhibition as her core dilemma. It is a question, Pon-talis suggests, that exceeds *savior faire*, resting in neither knowledge of the object nor with the subject-presumed-to-know:

> If in her first text, Melanie Klein's attention was held above all by the child's inhibitions, it was because they assumed an exemplary value for her: the child had more to say for himself than what he actually said. This was why she refused to see this or that 'characteristic' of the child as a deficiency that . . . one should relate to his nature. . . . She there-fore chose not to define the conditions which should be fulfilled by child analysis, but to submit psychoanalytical theory and methods to the dis-concerting text of the child's speech. (95–96)

Here then is a practice with children that counters application and adjustment, which refuses to define itself prior the unfolding of its own events. Her approach is other to education and child rearing because the problem she posed is psychic freedom, with what holds one back from thinking about one's thoughts, with how inhibition is the self's means of normalization and theory's defense against affecting itself. Yes, Klein will say: Inhibition is the self's defense, a means for the ego to reduce anxiety, but also, to reduce the world and itself. And yes, there is a certain tragedy. The strategy for warding off anxiety only accrues more, so the cost to the self is as severe as the reality it diminishes. Where there is anxiety there may be theory, but it is a theory that is precarious, dangerous, schizoid and paranoid.

Let us try to place Klein's theory of inhibition alongside much that inaugurates our age of testimony: the emancipation of women, the right to divorce, the Jewish problem, diaspora, exile, genocide, human rights— all forces that come under the heading of what Kristeva (2001a) called, in her study of Klein, "The Psychoanalytic Century." It is the century preoccupied with affect, subjectivity, and narrative, a century of sublation, of preservation, and overcoming. But it is also the century of the return of the repressed, of repetition, of suffering, of thinking, and so, of the unconscious. If the Psychoanalytic Century is one of witnessing and testimony, it is also qualified by trauma and through its disavowal. In our own age, where depth psychology is dismissed as an imposition on the subject, and so where interior life is reduced to an after-thought, to a discourse effect, or denigrated by critical theory as illusion (Adorno 1959/2001) and where the depressive society dulls our capacity for revolt, passion, and Eros (Kristeva 2002; Roudinesco 2001), Klein's theories of authority, knowledge, and psychical life are there to remind us of the consequences of eschewing the elaboration of psychological knowledge for adults and children.

Yet it is difficult for the self to accept and elaborate psychical reality and this idea, too, is part of her theory. Klein places resistance not in processes of learning but in designs of phantasy. There is the refusal to know, a defense against knowing that one knows. In resistance, one can glimpse the terrible volatile nature of unconscious anxiety: when phantasy cancels reality, when there can be a world of no difference. Pointing this out takes language to its limits. She understands the fragility of psychological significance, how easily it can get lost, become wrongheaded, collapse into itself. To see the world as more than an imposition or as a reflection of one's own internal reality, to encounter reality not as a sealed fate but as a problem of interpretation requires a return to that other world, phantasy. This return will require the capacity to enter nonsense, to speak the language of a puppet world of theory. Kristeva (2001a) gathers this discourse of madness under the sign of Klein's stunning achievements: Klein accepted that there was something foolhardy, ridiculous beyond compare, in psychical life and articulating this could only be done through performing the absurdity of language and desire. The Beckett-like paradox and achievement are that Klein took psychical life so seriously that she could see at its heart something deeply foolish, incomplete, and then human.

Some of the terms she would lend to this foolhardiness, this urge for theory to wrap the world tightly, this urge against all rational odds, sound like tin to the sensitive ear. By the middle of her career Klein would no longer assert her theory of the epistemophilic instinct, or the sadistic grounds of the desire to know. It would become her first commentary on the problem of where knowledge comes from. And so this drive, what could be awkwardly spoken of as "the highest flowering of sadism" (Petot 1990, 186) was an attempt to describe both the internal devastations of control and the omnipotence, when not knowing equates with danger, when danger means helplessness, when helplessness means annihilation. And yet, without this terrifying danger there would be no reason to press knowledge into shape. Klein will place her theory of inhibition in this conundrum and counter-intuitively view inhibition's withdrawal as necessary and as paranoid, as devastating on its own accord but also, even as it influences, as capable of being influenced. Inhibition will hold one back. Against all odds, Klein will call it forth.

Certainly inhibition is a form of intellectual withholding. But withholding what? Adam Phillips's (2002) essay, ironically titled "Against Inhibition," takes us in one direction with a story of education: a teacher encouraged a student, who eventually became a famous poet, to explore through narrative his rather violent phantasy of crushing babies' heads. The idea was that putting feelings into words dissipated the violence of feelings but also that words were of a different order than actions, even if the words described despicable actions. This writing was "against inhibition"—a way to explore the difference between reality and phantasy, the difference between omniscience in thought and woeful disregard in life. The narrative may be an ingenious way of getting around the problem of imagining forbidden things and the desire to communicate them. Perhaps this young author felt as if his head was being crushed, or he felt like a baby and then had to destroy that feeling.

Klein's sense of inhibition began with the problem of only imaging forbidden things. In her narrative, inhibition is an attack, a murder of curiosity, because inhibition is a heightened state of being plagued by too many answers. "Where there was a text," writes Phillips (2002), "there will be a set text. Inhibition—the whole sadomasochistically staged drama of it—is like a ruse of the ego in its relentless project of negating the unconscious" (73). One can inhibit the self so there is no otherness. Inhibition is thus emblematic of profound negativity, a wish to destroy one's creativity, a hatred of not knowing, what Kristeva (2001a) considers as a particular effect of subjectivity, that there can be "a phobia of being" (84). Here is the force of the death drive in its intimate sense, the loss of curiosity, the fear of reality, the denial of phantasy, the hatred of psychical life. Something in the drive to know destroys itself, and so Klein leaves us with a theoretical discord: If we have knowledge before we have something like understanding, what unbearable reality must knowledge defend itself against? Her response is the fear of what is already there: the death drive.

Jacqueline Rose's (1993) return to Klein begins with one of the key dilemmas a theory of death poses to social thought: If death has psychical meaning, then the child, and everyone else, is always embroiled in spinning, projecting, and fleeing meanings marked by an inescapable negativity. "What seems to be outrageous," writes Rose (1993) in her discussion on the status of negativity in the work of Klein and hence on the problem of subjectivity and politics,

> —paradoxically harder to manage than death as a pure force, as something which assaults the subject from outside—is this internalization of death into the structure. If death is a pure point of biological origin, then at least it can be scientifically known. But if it enters into the process of psychic meanings, inseparable from the mechanisms through which subjects create and recreate their vision of the world, then from where can we gain the detachment with which to get it under control? (160)

Because of the drive, knowledge will always be a painful problem, calling things never intended, substituting for a primal loss, throwing out other things it may also wish to preserve. And objectivity will have to accept this conflict as well in order to reach its own difference from dissociation and stasis. It will mean not only the acceptance of subjective meaning but also the courage needed to comment upon its negativity.

Without an awareness of the workings of phantasy—itself a problem for objectivity—there can be no reality, only compliance to an unforgiving, sadomasochist authority. This is the painful experience of inhibition, where the encounter with authority repeats something archaic: helplessness, hatred, paranoia, anxiety, and against all odds, the potential for revolt. John Phillips (1998) argues that Kleinian knowledge begins from this extreme:

> The Kleinian notion of knowledge must be considered in terms of her account of its *possibility*. . . . A deeply objective knowledge in the Kleinian sense demands a knowledge of phantasy itself, as well as an understanding of the inhibiting power of authority. Without this, the "reality principle" is just another tyrannous master, because the phantasy of omniscience remains undiminished. For Klein, objective knowledge is a step towards understanding of phantasy. (163)

Klein's approach to the problem of knowledge is paradoxical. Objective knowledge comes as close as possible to understanding the paranoid/schizoid state of subjectivity and what makes it so susceptible to omnipotence, rigid conceptualizations, and intellectual inhibition. Yet objective knowledge must also be marked by these very qualities even as such knowledge is an attempt to think about thinking. Knowledge of phantasy allows for theories of reality. This is what Klein understands as objectivity: knowledge at one degree removed from enacting the charge of phantasy yet still affected and so able to comment upon it from the inside. The analyst's utterance does not direct meaning but only calls attention to its own activity, to what it can mean to think about thinking and too, to accept depressive anxiety. Thus there will also be something foolhardy about interpretation itself, an antiauthoritarian gesture laced with sadness.

## A Second Chance

In the analytic setting, feelings of domination, compliance, and normalization are indexes of unresolved conflict, and ironically there they are given free reign. While Klein thought a child's play with small toys was akin to the adult's free association, there was nothing benign. "Play exists," Kristeva (2001a) suggests when speaking about Klein's work, "to the extent that it moves forward, burns, breaks, wipes, dirties, cleans, destroys, constructs, and so forth" (49). This destructive or dematerializing drama sets the stage for Klein's utterance: Interpretations are meant to pull the kicking and screaming psychical states into the playground of language.

If psychoanalysis places faith into language—as the means for complaint, free association, negation, interpretation, and therapeutic action—Klein's interpretations point to the vulnerability at the heart of even having language at all. Subjectivity is deeply at odds with reality since subjectivity is noncoincidental with consciousness of itself. So language must provoke this divide to speak of itself. Kristeva (2001a) stresses the evocative work: "By respecting the fantasy and interpreting it, the analyst does not establish the reality to be known or the law to be followed, but gives the ego a chance to constantly create a reality that, while increasingly objective, is the only one that is thinkable for me, livable for me, and desirable for me" (238). Here is the ego's second chance. While respect for phantasy will be where Klein will place the interpretation and freedom, it will also be where meaning will break down.

Contemporary readers may well find Klein's prose difficult to interpret because at one level Klein's writing performs a stunning literalness matched only by what she claimed in the name of the child. She tried to put into language "memories in feelings" (1975, 338), a linguistic repetition where words, too, provoke the very affectations they try to contain. Klein does what analysts must do, eroticize language, and enliven it so that the subject can experience language as relation rather than as an imposition of a heartless authority. "Analysts mobilize affect," writes Kristeva (1995), "by openly presenting themselves during interpretation as a magnet of libido" (99). Kristeva goes on to describe the analyst's words as performing two functions.

> [A]n analyst fosters desire (including of course the desire to speak) despite inhibition and depression. Second, the therapist must be a *speech therapist* who maps out an individual program for each child (since "theoretical givens" do not apply to everyone) and then helps these children understand the linguistic categories that will allow them to add symbolic productions to their subjectivity. (105–106)

Where inhibition was, there desire, language, symbolism and the Other shall become. But also, the analyst is a magnet for the analysand's hatred. In the beginning, the analyst encounters a terrible anxiety content that is bellicose, aggressive, sadistic, and paranoid, that announces the inner world as hostile and angry and that is projected onto the outer world. From this compost of meanings emerges the world of object relations:

concreteness, symbolization, sociality, and individual history. Phantasy will be the means for Klein (1930) to speculate on this puppet world that she will call without irony an "unreal reality" (221). Because we are discussing the experience of knowledge in psychical reality there can be no appeal to the outside as a means of explanation or motivation. It is a style the analyst Kohon (1999) describes as "a literature of excess based on interpretations" (156). It is a literature that mobilizes affect, the second chance for both the subject and for theory.

What is repeated in play is the articulation of a prehistory and the repetition illustrates the linguistic conundrums Kleinian theory proposes. The language of psychoanalysis may use everyday words, but their usage sends meaning to the furthest outposts of nonsense. Words are even meant to question the scene of meaning. Language magnifies its use: dreamy, insistent, echolike. Kristeva (1995) has described language as "a complex psychological event . . . [where] psychic representatives are displaced from affects as well as from the drama of desires, fears, and depressive fits that have a meaning for children, even though they are unable to join the world of everyday language's coded signification" (108–109). An interpretation of anxiety, for instance, takes its residence in the performance of the phantasy that is the anxiety. As for the relational difficulty, Klein's theories are theories of phantasy—she has to imagine a time before language and education, a time that diminishes all time, that does not yet exhibit chance. If this strange temporality is the anterior time of anxiety, it is also, for Kristeva (2001a) a time of resistance and so closure. There is the wish not to know:

> The child's unconscious forces us to confront *another form of knowledge*, an enigmatic knowledge that characterizes the *fantasy* and that remains resistant to "enlightenment," a knowledge that does not wish to be *familiar* with the real world through learning and adaptation to reality. Such *knowledge* staves off *awareness*. (40, emphasis original)

Klein claims she could witness the child's unconscious and hear what else the child says. She eschews appeals to authority, to promises of betterment, to the goodness of the child, to the best intentions of a helping relation, to morals, indeed, to all that secures the grounds of normalization. All that is left is to enter anxiety. And Klein places at risk her own intelligibility with a contact that symbolizes, repeats, and calls to attention the paranoia, aggression, depravation, and frustration that are the phantasy. If at first Klein repeats a terrible discourse, she must also make this discourse into difference, a commentary on the nature and risks of knowing. So Klein tries on a doubled discourse, speaking simultaneously to theory and the child's theory. This borderline discourse is what Jacqueline Rose (1993) also sees as foolhardy:

> Let's note that the genesis of the persecutory object in Kleinian thinking casts a shadow over interpretation, since, according to the logic of negation, interpretation comes as a stranger from the outside. And let's note too that if Klein makes of the analyst a fool and a fantast, it is from this place that the analyst has to try to speak, bridging the gap . . . between the baby ignorant of the external world and the scientist aware of nothing else. (169–170)

## Helpless Education

By the time Klein moved to London in 1926 arguments with Anna Freud over how to conduct the analysis of children were in full swing. There were significant debates over what children were capable of and whether they could be psychoanalytically involved. Her early biographical details suggest Klein was drawn to the problem of inhibition. By the middle of her life she may have been asking something crucial of her own field: What holds interpretation back? And so from where does psychoanalysis come? Her arguments with Anna Freud suggest a radical uncertainty about the status of the concept of influence in learning and in self/other relations. And nowhere did this argument become more fantastic than when it turned to the meaning of helplessness in both psychoanalytic work and in psychical life (Britzman 2003a).

Both analysts agreed that human helplessness and the utter dependency of the immature human were a structuring condition of psychical life and so carried over to relations with others. They accepted that helplessness found residency within the very beginnings of thinking itself. They diverged on the future of helplessness. Was this also influence? For Klein, helplessness enraged and frustrated the infant to such an extent that anxiety and aggression marked the time of development. Anna Freud did not attribute such formative aggression or sadism to the infant and felt instead that the ego, with the help of its defenses, its actual parents, and its capacity for love, made its own second chance. In her work with children, Anna Freud offered "a helping hand," and an ego ideal that she hoped could win over the child. She was prepared to open some possibilities through confidence building and foreclose others by rational persuasion and the position of authority. Education, particularly as *Aufklärung*—the bringing up of childhood and culture, or Kantian enlightenment—was the desirable goal. Klein was directly opposed to enlightening the child in the analytic setting.

If for Anna Freud there were three sources of anxiety—the object, the instinct, and the superego—for Klein anxiety was constitutional and had only one source: the death drive, and so a fear of annihilation. The difference here is rather stark. Anna Freud argued that educative measures should be joined with child analysis, for education could offer the child strategies of reality testing and, through the analyst's solicitation of the child's help, encourage the child to develop an interest in being needed, helping others, and sublimating aggression. To Klein, these needs in the psychoanalytic setting are irrelevant, indeed, they render psychoanalysis helpless. Moreover, Klein viewed education as an inhibiting force for two reasons. The internal world does not affect itself through rational appeal. But also many of her young analysands were sent to her because their education made them more miserable, compliant, and suspicious of the teacher's intentions. Thus Klein argued that the alliance of analysis with education only repeats inhibition.

Here is the dilemma: Klein developed psychoanalytic theory by turning history inside out. She assumed the infant enters the actual world with a precipitate psychological knowledge that predates having to learn it. She used this idea as the resource for interpretation of unconscious phantasies. This orientation opened new tensions for what cure can mean and how symbolism or putting things into language actually allow for thinking, relating, and affecting one's narrative world. She made in child analysis a new psychoanalytic object, leaving the child's conscious preoccupations and listening to the child's unconscious anxiety. And this meant a radical change in her understanding of the child, the nature of knowledge, and psychoanalytic cure. Klein would come to believe that phantasies inaugurate development. In the case of psychoanalytic encounter, Klein would leave her desire to mold the child's character and so abandon educational goals for the uncertainties of free association. And finally, as for knowledge, it would no longer be on the side of adaptation to reality. In this redrawing, epistemology emerges in the wake of anxiety and phantasy, and knowledge becomes knowledge of phantasy, or what would later be thought of as "thinking about thinking." Petot's (1990) study of Klein's radical shift makes the argument that when Klein left the idea of education, she could also see inhibition as one of its effects:

> The child's good social adaptation and success at school cannot be the goals for the child analyst; they are at most secondary . . . "normality" cannot be stated in terms of objective criteria, but in terms of liberty, fluidity, and the variety in the creation of fantasies . . . no references to external criteria can be acceptable in psychoanalysis . . . the objectives of the analysis of children can be defined only in psychoanalytic terms. (44)

If Klein raises the fantastic question from where does reality come, if she can put in parentheses, at least during the analytic hour, the world beyond her clinic, her answer would be just as incredible: The condition for constructing any knowledge of reality at all is phantasy.

## Toy Soldiers

A year after Klein's death, her case study of Richard was published under the title, *Narrative of a child analysis: The conduct of the psycho-analysis of children as seen in the treatment of a ten-year-old boy* (1961). This analysis came to a premature end, but the notes she refined years later detail a total of ninety-three sessions (more than four months in 1941) and almost all of Richard's drawings made through their analytic work. Klein notes in her introduction that Richard's symptoms of being terrified of other children, his worries that strangers would attack him or follow him and overhear his thoughts, his worry of being poisoned by his nanny, and his refusal to go to school began during the outbreak of World War II in 1939. There was for Richard a profound emotional inhibition but also an intellectual precociousness. His symptoms of claustrophobia, of not being able to go to school, of worrying that he would be attacked by other children, all communicated the danger his inhibition attempted to solve. Richard had theories of the world; the problem was that he could not understand what his theories, what having to mean, meant for his relations to others. He did have keen, albeit solitary, interests. Richard was an avid follower of the British navel maneuvers and the war theater. He knew many of the

European national anthems and occasionally would burst into these songs at a particularly crucial moment in his play. Richard also collected with pleasure a miniature fleet of toy navel ships that he brought to most of the sessions; leaving them at home was a communication as well.

"Mrs. K." provided the paper, pens, and crayons Richard would use to draw. Seventy-four drawings are included in this text; their maturity and articulateness vary with Richard's emotional states. When he was mad at Mrs. K., she would appear in these drawings. In one she is a triangle body with giant breasts, glaring eyes. It is the only picture he will be embarrassed over, and it is one of the few times that Klein will try to appease his worry. She will also have second thoughts and rethink her own desires in that appeasement. In another picture Richard draws a line across the middle of the paper and happily announces that whatever happens on the top of the picture matters; whatever happens at the bottom half of the picture does not. This splitting organizes his drawings: Empires are divided and battles are fought. Toy soldiers destroy or they are destroyed. There are strange starfish animals, each prong representing a family member. Sometimes the starfish are arranged in military formation. There are intricate maps and there are scribbles. The analysis begins with Richard fighting the interpretations; as the work progresses and near the end Richard begins analyzing his own thoughts.

Meltzer's (1998) lectures on Klein's case study summarize and comment on each of Klein's sessions with Richard. The clinical work of 1941 is written up almost seventeen years later when Klein's major theoretical breakthroughs on schizoid mechanisms, on envy, gratitude, reparation, and the depressive position may affect how this case is read today. Meltzer identifies where Klein departs from Freud. Instead of the ego, readers see a self, and the inner world begins its geography immediately: There are good and bad objects and confusion between them. This is a crowded world. At the time of the analysis, Klein was interested in overcoming inhibition; today the discussion would lean toward an attention to Richard's attempts to repair an inner world of object relations. Richard's analysis, however, prepared the way for Klein's own theoretical development. Their work freed Klein to place in the heart of our humanity, a psychical reality. The consequence of this shift, from overcoming to encountering psychical reality, Meltzer points out, "requires an immense shift in one's view of the world to think that the outside world is essentially meaningless and unknowable, that one perceives the forms but must attribute meaning. Philosophically, this is the great problem in coming to grips with Kleinian thought and its implications" (1998, 230). It is not that the world does not exist, but that for it to come into being in any meaningful way, interpretations must be risked. Inhibition, then, is when one loses a symbolic grip, when the attribute that is meaning is symbolically equated with the thing in itself.

Here, then, is where Klein finds Richard's confusion, seeing the way he strangulates meaning even as he mourns its loss. Over the course of these ninety-three sessions, Richard is preoccupied with enemies, sometimes wondering, for example, if Mrs. K. and Mr. K. (who had passed away although Richard had difficulty believing it) are German spies or even if his housekeeper is out to poison him. All these worries and their strange narratives come with a special language that Klein learns from Richard: There are Mrs. K. cruisers, big jobs, bird mummies, giants, blue-mummies, the Hitler-penis, the brute Mrs. K., lonely Rumania, 'Roseman'-genital and lunatic-genital, and then many silly coincidences (such as a ship named the *Vampire* and Mrs. K.'s interpretation of Richard's greediness), mishearings that take on a life of their own, denials of symbols, and Richard's strange corrections of Mrs. K.'s interpretations. The transference and its interpretation begin immediately.

The analysis occurred in a Welsh village where Richard and Klein stayed during the London *Blitzkrieg*. Klein rents a playroom and this means that after each session, she must pack up her materials and ready the room for other renters. Richard is quite preoccupied with what happens in the room without him and also with what else Klein does with her time when they are not together. Although Klein gives readers a brief history of Richard's upbringing, the majority of the study's nearly five hundred pages are composed of Klein's notes of the sessions, taken immediately after each hour ended. These notes are verbatim ethnographic details, a curious combination of Klein's observations of Richard over the session, their reported speech, summaries of her interpretations, and descriptions of the detours through which she and his interpretations are sent. Occasionally Klein adds a further note years later to comment on her technique with children, tensions in practice, errors in her judgment, and problems in analyst/child relations. Readers also glimpse, through Klein's eyes, the flora and fauna of daily analysis, the detritus of interpretation, and the quotidian qualities of the analyst/analysand's relations. There are moments of great poignancy but also practical jokes that Richard plays on Klein, such as when he gives her a jar of face cream that when opened becomes a jack-in-the-box.

Richard is a precocious ten-year-old child, able to read adult desires and, by his own admission, manipulate them. Yet by the eighth session, Richard speaks of his analysis as "the work," and Klein wonders if she had used this term or if it was his own description. Work it is and from the beginning Klein interprets deeply whatever she perceives as Richard's unconscious anxiety. Not only do children have a wide range of phantasies, but these emotions for Klein refer to an internally complex world of object relations. Perhaps anticipating her reader's resistance to her method of interpreting deeply, of asking about sexual fears, Oedipal phantasies, and hostile wishes, by the twenty-first session, Klein considers the benefits of her approach:

> It is in fact striking that very painful interpretations—and I am particularly thinking of the interpretations referring to death and to dead internalized objects, which is a psychotic anxiety—could have the effect of reviving hope and making the patient feel more alive. My explanation for this would be that bringing a very deep anxiety nearer to consciousness, in itself produces relief. But I also believe that the very fact that the analysis gets into contact with deep-lying unconscious anxieties gives the patient a feeling of being understood and therefore revives hope. (Klein 1961, 100)

With the revival of hope, Klein learns, comes resistance to the analysis. Each session stages a tiny play: the transference calls forth another cycle of the conflict and defense against it. Scenes change rapidly to accommodate zany plots, bizarre object creatures, foolhardy theories, flashes of insight and then again, the creature resistance. Against these odds there emerge feelings of being understood for both Richard and Mrs. K. and feelings that can create between them a special understanding which can welcome their doubts.

Their twenty-fourth session occurs on a Saturday when Richard brings with him his doubts and what they may mean. Richard doubts Mrs. K.'s interpretation of his hostile wishes toward her and his mother: "Do I really think this of all of you? I don't know if I do. How can you really know what I think?" (111). He may have been asking how thoughts come to matter at all. Klein continues:

*Mrs. K.* replied that from his play, drawings, and what he was saying and doing, she gathered some of his unconscious thoughts; but he expressed his doubts whether she was right and could be trusted. These doubts, Mrs. K. interpreted, had come up together with his general distrust of her and Mummy, which had been more marked in the last few days. . . . Recently he had unconsciously expressed his death wishes towards Mummy and Mrs. K., and found it very painful and frightening when Mrs. K. interpreted this. But he felt relieved and happier afterwards . . . (111–112)

Meltzer's (1998) interpretation of this scene returns to Klein's theory: "You cannot attack the inside of the mother containing your rivals and enemies without harming the mother herself" (159). Richard desired to protect his objects, and much later, after the analysis, Klein will see Richard as entering the depressive position, a concern for the Other. He wants the truth. If one has bad thoughts, can the mother still be all right? This question ushers in a new desire: reparation, the urge to restore the goodness of the internal object and the self's relation to the external one.

What were these unconscious thoughts? For Richard, they could be about the war, the terrible one he was living through and the internal one that fascinated him, the one that housed what Klein spoke of as his "internal Hitler." And when she spoke in that way, using words like "Hitler-daddy" or "Hitler-penis," Richard would become anxious and begin walking around the room, looking in cupboards, Mrs. K.'s purse, or any closed object. Near the end of that session, Richard begins to squeeze a little ball between his feet and then marches around the room doing the goose-step:

*Mrs. K.* interpreted that the little ball represented the world; Mummy and Mrs. K., squeezed by German boots—the goose step. In doing this Richard expressed his feeling that he not only contained the good Mummy but also the Hitler-father, and was destroying Mummy as the bad father did. Richard strongly objected, saying that he was not like Hitler, but he seemed to understand that the goose-stepping and the squeezing feet represented this. (114)

Still, the interpretation affected Richard. As he was getting ready to leave the room, he turns off the electric fire and says: "Poor old radiator will have a rest. He carefully put the crayons according to sizes into the box . . . and helped Mrs. K. to put the toys away in her bag" (114). After a rather poignant description of Richard bidding the room goodbye, reminding Mrs. K. to bring his drawings back to the next session and his lingering there as the room was being prepared for the next group, Klein interpreted:

> *Mrs. K.* interpreted his fear that she might die at the weekend—the poor old silent room. That is why he had to make sure about her bringing the drawings; this also expressed his wish to help in the analysis, and thus to put Mrs. K. right and preserve her. This is why he wished for Mrs. K.—the poor old radiator—to have a rest, not to be exhausted by her patients, particularly by him. (114)

And of course Richard is preoccupied with death, wondering if his thoughts can destroy the world and then, wondering in another session who will psychoanalyze him if Mrs. K. dies? Richard is worried about Mrs. K.'s travels to London. Will she return to him?

These questions come before a long break. When the analysis resumes, Klein believes Richard's resistance had reached a certain climax:

> While Richard at times wished to leave the room when anxiety welled up more fully and resistance reached a climax, he never actually left early. . . . What he did on a number of occasions was not to bring his fleet, which usually expressed his feeling that he had left a good part of his self and of his objects at home. The analysis of this splitting often had the effect that he brought the fleet again in the next session, and that he was able to make another step towards integration. (192)

Richard is beginning to think about his thinking, to understand that when he represents the outside world he is looking from the vantage of his emotional wishes, that his theories of the world are not coterminous with reality. And others can notice his communication and so allow the fleet to return, itself a good object. Richard is also learning to have a very different kind of conversation about language, where the poor old radiator is not just a radiator but can represent his worry in their analytic work, that perhaps his badness has destroyed or taken the steam out of poor old Mrs. K. And here is where his confusion begins to recede. Richard is learning to mourn.

And so with the understanding that there is or can be a mismatch between affect and perception, questions become a second chance. In the middle of his analysis, Richard asks Mrs. K. what grown-ups are afraid of, whether "grown-ups are afraid of other grown-ups?" (231). But he was also interested now in psychoanalysis: "It seemed such a secret to him. He would like to get to the 'heart of it.' Mrs. K. interpreted that while he was actually interested to know all about psycho-analysis, he also wanted to find out all Mrs. K.'s secrets" (231). A few sessions later, Richard returns to the topic of psychoanalysis: "Was it a rule amongst psycho-analysts that they were never to get cross or impatient? Would it harm the work? . . . Mrs. K. interpreted that she stood for Mummy and he expected her to become very hostile about his desires to rob her of Daddy's good penis and devour it. But Richard also hoped that Mrs. K. was not actually like Mummy; because she was a psycho-analyst and was doing this work to find out his thoughts and help him with them, and she would not be cross and he could speak freely to her" (246).

As Richard begins to ask more and more questions about Mrs. K. and psychoanalysis, he slowly gets to the heart of the matter for himself. The fifty-second session occurs on a Sunday, a full seven-session week. Richard wonders if analysts go to church, and Mrs. K. asks him if he thought it was wrong not to go to church on Sunday. This exchange begins to move slowly into other matters that Richard might feel are wrong:

> *Mrs. K.* pointed out his strong doubts in psycho-analysis; he felt it to be very wrong. Because Mrs. K. discussed with him matters which he thought improper and which he had even been taught to consider as improper, he felt that she was tempting him and allowed him to experience sexual desires towards his mother and herself. These desires seemed all the more dangerous to him because they are connected with hate, jealously, and destruction of his parents, whom he also loved. . . .
>
> Because she stood for the good and helpful Mummy, it was also painful to him to suspect that she was also the improper and tempting Mummy. He was afraid that the powerful Daddy—God—would punish Mummy too; lightning which struck the Nazi aeroplane punished the treacherous and disloyal Mummy as well as Mrs. K. . . . (255)

We are very close to the foolish heart, the language of anxiety, the puppet world of theory. When we hear what we do not want to hear, it feels as if we are being both persecuted and tempted by these ideas. Ideas become symbolically equated with actions and then are defended against rather than thought about. This splitting into good and bad is the basis of moralism, itself a defense against understanding the anxiety of emotional life. Here is Mrs. K. She is willing to speak this nonsense and so convey these worries back to Richard so that he can symbolize them, learn what he wants. Klein is letting Richard know he is not a leaf in the wind; nor is he the lightning that downed the plane in his drawing. He need not become his phantasy.

At the end of four months of work, after seeing Richard for ninety-three sessions, Klein's closing note is dedicated to the hopefulness Richard has made:

> Another sign of the increasing predominance of the life instinct, and with it of the capacity for love, was that he no longer felt impelled to turn away from destroyed objects but could experience compassion for them. I have referred to the fact that Richard, who so strongly hated the enemies threatening Britain's existence at that time, became capable of feeling sympathy for the destroyed enemy. (466)

Our enemies should only have to be destroyed once so that there can be an afterward for the object relations of the self and the Other. The trajectory Klein describes for learning is as follows: anxiety, persecution, splitting, phantasy, identification, resistance, envy, repair, cooperation, reparation, gratitude. This difficult beginning, those early defenses, are needed for what will follow. This describes as well the ways her theory progresses.

## Reparation

Over the course of Klein's narrative there are two lines of discourse. Along the lines of technique, Klein interprets the unconscious anxiety of Richard's free association. She does this immediately and so calls forth Richard's anxiety. He presents his associations through bodily movements and actions in the playroom, his drawings and play with toys, and his running commentary as he plays or draws. Along the lines of therapeutic actions, the second discourse is more illustrative, meant to show Richard, through interpretations and responses, that his activities, doubts, questions, and refusals also are an index of his attitude toward his object relations, that he is always communicating something, and that even if this something is hostile, Mrs. K. will survive his phantasies because they are only that: commentaries on anxiety and defenses against it. Indeed, the mechanisms of defense are phantasies and oddly, the means to know them. This is a world where the child is capable of metaphorical meaning and so of destroying and constructing knowledge. Through narrative, thinking about thinking, one can elaborate psychological knowledge. But the analyst must be willing to serve as a magnet for both love and hate, the analyst must be ready to become the poor old radiator. And the child must come to the terrible understanding that while it is easy to break things, to repair the object takes a great deal more: the toleration of frustration, an urge to repair the object for its own sake, and a capacity for remorse and sadness, what Klein (1940) will call mourning.

These two lines of discourse, Klein's techniques and her discussions of their therapeutic actions are now debated. Meltzer's (1998) discussion considers a danger involved in Klein's technique of inviting and invoking terrible anxiety as a gamble that may exacerbate confusion between internal and external worlds. Object relations become terribly literal so that they really do destroy; they really do split into good and bad, and they really do annihilate one another and others. In this supercilious world, there can then be no coincidence, no unfortunate world events that do not then feel as if the child's feelings have caused them. The danger is that the transference will be confused with omnipotence, or that Klein's technique will be incapable of understanding itself as a construction, as a work of language.

Other commentaries on this case study point to the problem that Klein is not paying enough attention to Richard's external conditions—the war, his separation from his father and brother, his family's safety, his worries about the United Kingdom and Mrs. K., and so on. Adam Phillip's (2000) complex essay, "Bombs Away," urges analysts to remember that history indeed is taken personally by the child and that actual bombs are not just universal symbols for internal hostility. The tension is between Klein's theoretical preoccupations and Richard's actual history, between trauma as an internal and external catastrophe and how these catastrophes, wherever they are located, become symbolized. The narrative of Richard's analysis may hint at this conundrum, making history can also mean inquiring into the nature of the relation between external and internal danger. It is, however, always a problem of meaning. And this problem raises the question of what it is to take history personally. For Klein, history personalized when metabolized by a prehistory she calls phantasy. Indeed, to take history personally, one must grapple with what is significant about the personal. One may have these doubts, Klein believed, without accompanying them with the defense of inhibition.

Contemporary readers may also hold an incredulity toward the induction of symbolization, of what it can mean to call forth the hostilities of the internal world, our attitudes toward our object relations and so encounter psychical representatives in the form of, say, a Hitler-penis. This world is terribly literal, and Klein's interpretations suggest that if that x stands for y, if the toy ship can stand for the father's penis, then symbolizing this trajectory of the affect—understanding the way it migrates to and identifies with its own bad objects—can diminish its persecutory nature and the mesmerizing destruction of the paranoid-schizoid position. When language is encountered through its associative and metaphoric links, thoughts may become uninhibited, indeed the difference between thoughts and events, memory and perception, can be allowed. It is this allowance that Klein saw as the depressive position. Literalness, the wish for and fear that reality can be one thing only, is precisely where the defenses of both omnipotence and inhibition reside. It is also a condition for war and destruction, of needing to repeatedly destroy enemies. If Klein was foolhardy in trying to determine which comes first—psychological knowledge or knowledge of the world—Richard offered a glimpse of what it is to experience the force of both as a dilemma for knowledge.

Perhaps it hardly needs saying, but where else than in the analytic setting would a child and adult have such a conversation about life, learn why meaning is so fragile, so subject to splitting, so difficult to maintain, so sad to repair? Where else can such affects play out until they become so tired that they may be refreshed through the Other's language? Where else would a child be invited to explore terrifying doubts, to speak his mind, to change his mind? What one notices in the world, what counts as an event, how one notices the eventfulness of the event, all these processes suggest something about the qualities and conflicts of one's internal world of object relations. This is why there must be a parallel or shadow dialogue in the analytic setting, why interpretation is interpretation of what is not yet thought but nonetheless enacted, why language must be eroticized. While education may feel sure as to what moves the child forward, the direction of Klein's curiosity is otherwise, with what holds the child back, with what holds theory back, and with what the child thinks of that. Over the course of her long career, she will try various formulations, perhaps her most sustained attempt at trying to know, wrestling with her own epistemophilic instinct is found in the narrative of analysis with Richard.

Klein was well aware that she was making a narrative about children and on the nature of child psychoanalysis, not as a prescription, and not as Kristeva (2001a) argued, as "a system of knowledge," (104) but as a narration, an occasion for constructing thinking with children and with theory. In this regard, Klein wrote a novel education. She sent education away from the analytic setting, by keeping the world in a parenthesis. In creating a psychoanalytic world, Klein also had to refuse its trappings: she left the position of role model, moralist of the child's drama, and cheerleader of positive thinking. She found these positions as too subject to superego anxiety. Klein was able to step away from these pedagogical habits because she was most interested in the ways the child represented phantasy, the child's object relations. She was foolhardy enough to think it was important for theory to represent these dilemmas of form and what it means to give meaning creative chances. She may locate these attempts as inviting psychic freedom, an internal free association.

Through anxiety's representations one could glimpse the painful defense of inhibition and normalization, a hyperagency that she would see as superego anxiety, whose properties of harsh judgment depend upon splitting and idealization, and the confusion of good and bad. In this puppet world of object relations, hating a parent feels as if the affect did murder the parent and that the parent may now return to murder the child. This tiny drama may repeat more horribly in the devastations of war. Klein insisted that it was only through exploring the forbidden that knowledge of reality could ever be made because however wrong-headed, aggressive, hostile, and foolhardy, phantasy is the beginning of interpretation. This made all the difference in her work with children; they, too, were the interpreters affecting her theory. If child analysis begins with the supposition that children can receive and understand the psychoanalytic utterance, it concludes with the view that it is not just the idea that children can be understood. To leave knowledge there is still to stay in the realm of inhibition. The idea is that children, too, are very capable of self-understanding, of thinking about thinking, of understanding why we have to have understanding at all. The idea is that theory can contain these dilemmas of knowing and not knowing the world of self and Other, even if it cannot resolve the uncertainty that symbolization also carries.

# SIX

# Monsters in Literature

## The Archive

Thirty-odd years ago I began teaching in a public alternative high school. The summer before, I was to meet the students and learn their grade; I was expected to create and then teach an interesting new course. I called my first high school curriculum "Monsters in Literature." This creature inaugurated my student teaching in English studies. What these events could mean, however, eluded the time of their unfolding. Thinking through the significance of this absence is where this chapter begins. If meaning is given after the fact, the fact is made from understanding this uncertainty and the distortions it may continue to carry. This understanding can seem like the opposite of the events that did occur because it centers phantasies that animate the need to make memory significant, bringing into relief a particular history of uneven development that is difficult to remember. Here is where learning to teach enters the picture. Constructions of learning to teach become an exemplary problem for memory itself. Present conflicts call back and migrate to untimely scenes of childhood, whether these be the actual childhood or the childhood of teaching. And, in the events of teaching itself, beginnings are further distorted because the future that the teacher anticipates depends upon what has already happened.

For the teacher to appreciate, long after the fact of her beginning, something of the uniqueness and use of her own unconscious wishes made from the childhood of teaching, the construction of memories must no longer be thought of as representations of what actually happened. Rather, constructions are the work of sorting out the distortions of memory and analyzing what the early Freud (1899) called "screen memories" or vivid details of insignificant content, that serve as a place holder for the forgotten. This material, however, is rich because the churning memory is stirred by adults looking upon their own past as they wished it to be. The events that we take as "what happened" are already worked over through desire and the lens of a later time. Yet this act of memory is creative.

I use my present understanding of teaching to construct my early days of learning to teach as a means to raise thorny questions on the work of learning from the teacher's beginning, seeing the exercise not as scene of cognitive mastery, where an original object becomes refurbished and set down in the museum of pedagogy, but as an occasion for an analytic turn needed to understand the psychical difficulties I believe we teachers have in remembering our beginnings, our learning to teach. Symptoms of not remembering emerge, I think, when we become frustrated with our students who do not learn as we imagine, but also when we divide our work through the measure of good or bad days. To illustrate the difficulty of the teacher's memory, two fragments of autobiography are set into tension with a general problem in English education and its preoccupation with teaching students literature. It turns out that this imperative links two experiences not typically thought of as belonging together: our conceptualizations of the literary in both thinking about teaching and learning are also a commentary on the emotional states of the teacher and her uses of the literary.

Let us pause to consider the newly arrived teacher's developmental conflicts. So far, I have managed to elude the aesthetic conflicts that bring me back to make new sense of old events in my teaching career. These conflicts are two sides of the same dilemma: that which can be made from the literary text that involve the teacher's fragile grasp of the literary in pedagogical events. Before turning to these actual aesthetic conflicts, and for any working analysis to occur, it is useful to work within a psychoanalytic frame for understanding the qualities of emotional states that are in need of recognition. Both psychoanalysis and education are concerned with the problem of what makes for a fact, or an awareness of shared reality that can then become the grounds for further work and thinking. Thinking with the work of Bion and Meltzer, Robert Caper (1999) identified three qualities of emotional states that compose "a clinical fact": Bion's notion of a sense of isolation in intimate relations, or an awareness of the separateness of individuals when working together; Meltzer's view of an aesthetic conflict, where an interpretation animates both the sublime and so an unbearable conflict within its significance and use; and an awareness of one's role in creating emotional states. Noticing these qualities of difference are the preliminary grounds for a working analysis and so Caper defines a clinical fact as "what becomes clear in an analysis when these emotional states are observed to obtain" (3). Admittedly, there is much uncertainty and insecurity in constructing such "facts." More so, in both analysis and education, these intrasubjective and intersubjective conditions are neither automatic nor apparent. Much will occur to animate ignorance and forgetfulness. There will be resistance to implication, a desire to be unencumbered by the Other, and censorship or repression of the erotic ties these emotional states also depend upon.

As for the newly arrived teacher, there are not yet "pedagogical facts" waiting to be picked up along the road of experience because it takes a great deal of time to actually notice students in the room, to consider how they are affected by the teacher's emotional states, and to recognize how student differences can be erased by the teacher's projections. Caper's conditions for a working analysis are useful in trying to understand the teacher's work where the teacher is separate from the student and so may wonder about the seductions of immediate gratification; where the interpretations the teacher uses give rise to new aesthetic conflicts; and where teachers can think about both their contributions to the emotional world of the classroom and the classroom's contribution to their own emotional world. With these conditions in mind, we can return to the particular dilemma the literary poses to the newly arrived teacher's defense against aesthetic conflicts in the classroom.

One aesthetic conflict that belongs to English education concerns the status of the concept of the literary in curriculum and teaching. Literary knowledge, as Felman (1987) has argued, is knowledge that is not in control of itself and because this is so, it must perform its ignorance. Yet this performance defies the script of classroom control and to notice this disjuncture is a key to analyzing the experience of aesthetic conflict. A further tension involves the artist as creator. The creation of a work of art is in excess of the artist's intentions. So, too, is its reception. Kofman (1988) describes a particular paradox of creative work where "the author plays out the knowledge without possessing it, and because of that he makes a work of art" (41). But this means that the literary or the artistic calls into being both affective states of knowledge and ignorance and the work of thinking about them. Here is one dimension of the aesthetic conflict: There is knowledge that cannot be in charge of itself yet charges us to wonder about our thoughts. Another dimension is its timing: A quality of this conflict is deferred and there is experience before understanding. These dimensions of mistiming and misrecognition are a shared problem for both literary and pedagogical events: There is knowledge yet the question of its significance eludes the conscious awareness of teacher and student, even as they will perform some of what is being repressed. In the meantime, "screen memories" will be a placeholder for this missed encounter. As for pedagogy, Pitt (2003) suggests that the culmination of this needed confusion signifies "an unsolvable knot [that should] . . . remind us that our pedagogical efforts set into motion experiences the outcomes of which we cannot predict and often do not want" (114).

How does this "unsolvable knot" play havoc within the childhood of teaching? From a reconstruction of a bungling beginner's dilemmas of misunderstandings centered on the tensions the literary opens, I explore more general thoughts on psychoanalytic problems of learning to teach and the aesthetic conflicts that are a part of this work. My working analysis draws upon insights made from psychoanalytic research into the qualities of difficult knowledge in teaching and learning, where memories of teaching and learning blur the distinction between obstacles to learning and obstacles to narrating learning (Pitt and Britzman 2003) and where learning itself may feel traumatic and so lose significance (Britzman and Pitt 2004). I also draw upon some ideas from two psychoanalysts of a different generation, flavor, and scope: Sigmund Freud and D. W. Winnicott. From Freud, I consider a constitutive dilemma of memory that opened this chapter: Psychical forces compose memory, yet the narration of these events symbolizes the obstacles to thinking about them. Whereas Freud performs one way to analyze resistance to the autobiographical event, finding within resistance a literary truth, Winnicott magnifies the aggression that resistance can symbolize. He brings into relief beginnings, those early relations between self and Other by presenting a surprising distinction between object usage and object relating. This difference brings me to the problem of curriculum and opens awareness into why few developmental paradoxes are needed for a working analysis of the newly arrived teacher's aesthetic conflicts.

## Happy Birthday

"A disturbance of memory on the Acropolis" (1936) is actually a birthday greeting Freud sent to the seventy-year-old author Romain Rolland. It is a strangely beautiful gift. Freud could think of nothing else that would express his profound regard for Rolland and so sent him this personal piece of analysis on the problem of memory, not so much for the purposes of communication but rather to convey what it can be for the writer to touch upon a sense of memory's ineffable qualities. On the way to remembering, there will be difficulties, indirections, forgetting, and literary strains. And the writer will loosen his hold on intentions, even getting lost again in the labyrinth of childhood phantasy, a fun house of Oedipal wishes and regrets. Freud was eighty years old, believing he was long past his own wanderlust. Yet he met these desires again by way of a return of the repressed. Something unresolved remained from those long-gone years.

Freud found himself bothered by a memory of a trip he made with his brother forty years earlier. Taking some delight in the fact that his brother was ten years younger than himself, just as Freud was ten years older than Rolland, Freud writes the story of a summer visit they once made to the Acropolis. Only they did not originally mean to travel there. The trip was not without its own series of what, at first, seemed to be unrelated disturbances. The brothers intended to travel to Corfu but were advised because of the heat of that summer to travel instead to Athens. This change made for difficulty, perhaps a disturbance of nerves. Something was holding them back and the brothers almost gave up on making any plans at all. Freud notes they were somehow depressed by this confusion. Still, they managed to travel to Athens to visit the ruins: "When, finally, on the afternoon after our arrival, I stood on the Acropolis and cast my eyes around the landscape, a surprising thought suddenly entered my mind: 'So all this really *does* exist, just as we learnt at school!'" (Freud 1936, 241).

The rest of the birthday greeting puzzles over the meaning of this moment of incredulity, of *deja vu*, noting a certain split within the utterance. It is not that school knowledge is difficult to believe, or that seeing is believing. Was accepting or not accepting school knowledge really the problem? Freud thought the earlier depression that almost stopped their travels and his own incredulity made upon arrival was, in actuality, two dimensions of the same feeling, something he named as his "attempt to repudiate a piece of reality" (242). But why repudiate anything given how much pleasure occurred on visiting the Acropolis? Freud gives Rolland so many hints at the double displacements he would then reveal: As a child he doubted he would ever see the Acropolis and this doubt returned to him in distorted form. Here was Freud standing on its ground, doubting not his travels but the veracity of the Acropolis itself. There was a feeling of de-realization; something was strange.

Feelings of de-realization, or a denial of reality, are hints of the return of the repressed, and Freud describes a sense of his memory as being "doubly displaced . . . first, it was shifted back into the past, and secondly it was transposed from my relation to the Acropolis on to the very existence of the Acropolis" (243).

What was Freud's screen memory defending against? Freud comes to the view that his incredulity toward the reality of the Acropolis masked his sense of guilt that he had exceeded his father's life. There it was, so many years later, remnants of an earlier Oedipal conflict. After all, he did better than his father who never could travel to such far-off places. And yet, there is also, perhaps a question of who will do better than Freud? His letter ends poignantly, perhaps trading the father he left behind for the old man he had become: "And now you will no longer wonder that the recollection of this incident on the Acropolis should have troubled me so often since I myself have grown old and stand in need of forbearance and can travel no more" (248).

Repudiating a piece of reality and so transposing it—through displacements, condensations, and reversals—into new situations is how Freud described the transference, perhaps the beating heart of psychoanalytic interpretation. Transference is both an investigation and a resistance to the investigation (Freud 1912a). Our present occupations are filtered through and distorted by old conflicts, and this makes perception very difficult to distinguish from the passions and aggressions of projection. Freud's birthday greeting questions our loyalty to the past since its narration passes through screen memories that inhibit and distort a memory's significance. Here then is one piece of the difficulty for educators. Freud places the indelible signature of childhood onto adult impressions of their present. Then, he notes a reaction, a second move where the adult impressions are laid back down upon the childhood memory. So it is with teachers. Their emotional states may also transfer an unresolved conflict of childhood history onto the screen of current pedagogical desires. It will be difficult to see an actual student, just as it was difficult for Freud to see the Acropolis. The aesthetic conflict may then be animated when a turn toward one's history of learning is made not to repeat a remnant of childhood phantasy but to analyze its distortions. What fragments of this self return when the teacher makes a curriculum? If the transference is there between teachers and their texts, can students animate the teacher's new thinking on this old conflict?

## Call in the Monsters

As this chapter began to take shape, I found myself collecting monsters again, with all the manic zeal that I also now recognize as signaling aesthetic conflicts. Teachers must, I think, be magnificent collectors of literature, of social examples, and of curious events. It may take years to begin throwing these transitional objects away. It may take years for the teacher to forgive students for destroying the collection. The manic collection of objects may be a symptom of anxiety over the loss of the object. Robert Gardner (1994) described such excitement as "the furor to teach," where each and every furor is "goaded and guided by each teacher's theory of what is essential to teach. And each furor is heightened by conditions specific to the teacher's character, persuasion, and current preoccupations" (8). How can this be otherwise given the teacher's subjectivity? However one might try to disguise it, deny it, or even shed its more scaly qualities, the teacher's subjectivity is exaggerated, animated, and projected into these various objects that then become the teacher's proxy, made to communicate the teacher's desire. Mine happened to be monsters. There was no shortage of them.

One explanation for why I return to such an early teaching event whose topic happened to be monsters is that in our own time one can find the monstrous everywhere and because of this, its metaphorical qualities threaten to collapse into a terrible literalness where it can feel as if there is no difference between phantasy and reality. How easy it seems to become preoccupied with these scary creatures and see in them what is monstrous in the social. More difficult is to consider that one may also identify with the societal capacity to exorcize from itself what it considers as the monstrous: terrorism, poverty, hopelessness, depression. Or, one may identify with the monster. In Foucault's (1975/2003) lectures, "The Abnormal," the monster becomes a sort of conceptual hinge between discourses of the law and medicine. Three figures spring forth to be discerned: the human monster, the individual to be corrected, and the masturbating child. Education cannot be far behind. The furor to teach adds another dimension. The teacher may feel as if she must save the world that has already been destroyed. Then come the other monsters. They may stand in for and defend against an awareness of the emotional states that call them into being. Part of their appeal is that the monster is a creature of resistance. Something resists analyzing our emotional uses of monsters. After all, there are terrible events in the world, and in education we are obligated to speak of them. But we are also obligated to ask something intimate as we go about this work: What else do monsters signify for the self? How is the monster used and related to?

My first curriculum, I now understand, had a grandiose knowledge of monsters matched by a terrific ignorance of what is monstrous about our preoccupation with them. Students were missing, as was the teacher. Idealizations migrated to and defended against this empty place. I wished the course title "Monsters in Literature" would convey, in miniature, the whole story of what students could expect to learn. I would present to the class, whom I had never met, a series of literary monsters that would lead them by the hand to critique the monstrous in real life. The course title, so I thought, was a shortcut, a pedagogical telegraph, perhaps even a wish for pedagogical telepathy. Indeed, I was convinced that students who signed up for the course would already be interested in my ideal pedagogy. Certainly a young teacher's narcissism is required for this astounding confidence. But it may also be the case that the curriculum, too, was used as a terrific defense against not knowing what it will be to learn to teach as one is teaching monsters, I mean students. Idealization of the curriculum was a defense against my fear of losing control of everything, worrying the students would make me the monster. My idealization of the curriculum made me good, allowing the monsters to contain what was bad. In sequence, the curriculum began with the fantastic, but in my head these actual monsters would only set the stage for encountering something terribly real and literally terrible: the inhumanity of the state apparatus, class inequality, racism, and genocide.

Admittedly, this was a very depressing curriculum, one that I would meet again and again throughout the course of my teaching career. Little did I know how depressed it would make me. Only much later would I learn to become more attuned to the students' complaints, my own depression and even my role in their discomfort. When I began teaching, however, my rationalization for trading in such affect, that is, what I thought of as replacing their denial of false consciousness with my depressing truth only agitated my stubbornness. There were no aesthetic conflicts because there were no students to relate to, and no emotional states to explore. And I took all of this emptiness to literature. My ignorance was performed through a pedagogy that tried to insist that works of art are communications to be received and corrections to be made. It took me many years to see in this wish something manic, a teacher's defense against encountering both the literary and its excess and the students, all of whom had their own minds. The manic defense was a symptom of a kernel of the monstrous in my own teaching. And what now seems most monsterous was my incapacity to mourn the loss of omnipotence that I wished the teacher's role promised. This illusion, I now see, belongs to the child's view of the teacher/parent. The teacher requires disillusionment.

The idea that everything was political crowded my center stage. I used literary monsters to convey this truth. And because there was a truth, it never occurred to me that there would be an argument with students. The aesthetic conflict I would now place between me and the students emerged from the reasons they signed up for the course. These students simply wanted the excitement of monsters in the classroom. They liked scary stories, and they liked to scare adults by blurring the boundaries between reality and phantasy. They were adverse to using these creatures as a means to critique their society and to accepting my demand that everything, including the monster, is political. Simply put, they wanted to play, escape, and enjoy. Not only that. The students who found their way into this course did not like reading literature and were used to teachers not liking them. Their literacy skills were fragile, as was their individual sense of having to be a student in a place called school.

The shock of meeting the ninth-grade students that first day left me with my inappropriate curriculum. And while I held onto the hope that somehow my wish to raise their consciousness could still be preserved, I also worried that most of the literature I had chosen for the class would remain unread. But also, I worried I would be rejected. Today, when I think of monsters, I recall what Lyotard (1991) noted as something like "the inhuman," a kernel of madness belonging to the problem of both education and becoming a human. "We should remember," writes Lyotard, "that if the name of human can and must oscillate between native indetermination and instituted or self-instituting reason, it is the same for the name of inhuman. All education is inhuman because it does not happen without constraint and terror . . ." (4). The question remains in trying to situate this inhumanity: Whose terror and whose constraints? For after all, education is a relation and if constraint and terror are a part of learning, there is still the problem of who is doing what to whom. For the twenty-year-old that I once was, these psychological questions of significance and relation, indeed, the object relating and usage that are also the invisible work of the teacher—what it means to become human with other humans in the classroom—could not be recognized as the question *par excellence*. These significant doubts about the nature of humanity—my own and those of others—I now think, are the reasons we must even care for our monsters.

My ninth-grade students give me plenty of hints on their uses of monsters. Yet given my furor to teach, given the shock of inappropriate curriculum, a comedy of errors prevailed. I failed to understand anything about my students' interests and their literacy skills, but not in ways that I could learn from. After distributing Robert Louis Stevenson's *Dr. Jekyll and Mr. Hyde*, I worried that the novel was too difficult. I could not read the book through their eyes and, when preparing for the week's lesson, my misreading of their abilities and interests persisted. Stevenson's novel was to begin our social inquiry. Looking back, I realize that I must have thrown it into the curriculum only because there was an actual monster to encounter, only because there was some guilt with my false advertisement. And in that sense, I was right. After all, the course was called Monsters in Literature and not The Political in Literature and once I met the actual students, it dawned on me, in spite of my best defenses, that the students signed up for the Monster part, not the literature.

The weekend before our discussion of the novel's beginning, I panicked, imagining the students would hate it and would never be able to read it. I worried they would hate me as well. And I didn't quite know if I should just ask for the books back, acknowledge my pedagogical inexperience, probably apologize and then start all over with an easier novel. This agony was my weekend, as it is with so many young teachers who realize after the fact how utterly wrong their choice of text can become but then themselves become lost with what to do and who they can be. In this confused state we begin to wonder if the students then hate us. Then there is anger at the students who refuse to read. I turned feeling destroyed into destroying my students: They had become the monsters sent to ruin my curriculum. This is the teachers' defense against their anxieties of not knowing what they know—what Felman (1987) saw as the teacher's passion for ignorance. And in this passion, monsters thrive.

Yet there the students were that Monday morning. And, too, there was a sheepish student teacher to be greeted by their enthusiasm over the novel. In this difference between what I imagined and what occurred, the students began to be real because I could take no credit for their existence. They were mesmerized by split personalities and often felt like Dr. Jekyll and Mr. Hyde. They took great pleasure in narrating this monstrous change in parents and teachers and had a great deal to say about the insecurity of their own emotional states. And no matter how difficult the prose, how archaic the English, they read on, enjoying the suspense, identifying with what was monstrous in themselves and others, but not because they needed to change the world. Just the opposite, they wanted the world to take them in. Essentially, and like Shelley's Frankenstein, they wanted to be recognized, even adored, for all their foibles, phantasies, and desires. They may even have wanted teacher to like them. The twenty-year-old student teacher that I once was could now arrive at the Acropolis.

## Monsters in Teachers

I made the curriculum and so imagined the students. I gathered all the novels that had so affected my thinking and with a rather nascent theory of literature as capable of changing minds—literature as the royal road to political consciousness—I dove into the mysterious world of the student teacher. Much later I would describe through Dickensonian flavor the student teacher as the site of conflict (Britzman 2003b). The novel world of student teaching is a contradictory, conflictive, paradoxical world, where learning to teach is a strange admixture of childhood desires and adult fears and where student teachers would almost absorb the history of the profession's conflicts without even knowing them, feeling as if they created from their isolation, helplessness, and dependency a mythic, heroic, and so omnipotent self. It would be a world that is beyond the self, yet never so far from it. And in this gap the teacher shall suddenly spring forth, now to embody an identity: as expert, as self-made, and as single-handedly responsible for dragging students into learning. This omnipotent phantasy, the flipside of having to save the world, defends against the loss that learning also entails and ignores the working conditions Caper notes as key to the analysis: isolation within intimacy, aesthetic conflicts, and an awareness of one's own contribution to emotional states in self and other relations.

From the beginning of my student teaching, I was involved in two furors: the furor to teach and the furor to teach my politics. I was convinced that teaching is a political activity and that my work was to convince my students of their political obligations. At the time, teaching was called a subversive activity. That this desire sustains something conservative, what Gardner (1994) calls "the furor to teach," was not yet thinkable for me. I felt I had the answers without the thought of a terrific paradox: I railed against education as a banking method precisely as I banked on the message of consciousness raising. Many years later, I came across Gardner's curious warning: "What is the furor to teach? It is a menace. It's a menace to teachers, to students, and to innocent bystanders. Teachers possessed by that furor are in trouble. Teachers devoid of that furor—if such can be called teachers—are in more trouble" (3). We need our menaces if we are to be more than robots. And yet, what is the teacher's menace? I now think of the furor to teach as teaching against all odds, of teaching in spite of the students, even teaching to spite the students. Yet the furor is also made from being in love with the curriculum while hating the education system. Anxiety, defense, and symptom will be made from this divide. My anxiety was that the world (and my self) was in terrible shape. The defense was to render everything political, by which I meant that the ideology that blurred the judgments of everybody else must be destroyed. And the symptom of all this mess: monsters.

My university supervisor recognized some of my trouble although this took decades for me to accept. One supervisory session remains for memory. After a classroom observation, my supervisor took me for a walk. I recall being angry that I even had to be supervised although today, I consider my consternation to be symptomatic of a defense against having to learn to teach with others and so accepting the dependency this learning entails. Here is where the screen memory arrives. I recall one of those beautiful fall days in Cambridge, Massachusetts. There we are, me and my supervisor, walking arm and arm through the woods that suddenly gave way to Harvard Yard. Except there were no actual woods and I wasn't on my way to Harvard University. Did we even go for a walk?

How difficult it is to sort through these distortions, trading anger for the idealization of my education, imagining resolutions without problems, indeed, wishing for an education without having to learn. The memory of my surroundings is too dreamy, a screen memory that is also covering my embarrassment of not being in charge of any knowledge at all, even feeling as if I were lost in the woods. The supervisor's interpretation of my struggle with the class fell into one sentence: "Deborah, not all monsters are political." I had so many ways to argue with her. Years later I can return to that sentence and meet my supervisor again, now, to marvel at how she manages to survive my attacks. There is also in her observation another pull, reminding me that the students are separate from myself. They are people who did need to pass the course. If at first glance my aesthetic conflict was between loving the material and learning to attend to the students, a second thought followed: Would my teaching be as beautiful on the inside as I wished the outside to be? As long as everything was political, there were essentially no emotional states to understand. But also, I had difficulty using my supervisor's interpretation, an after-the-fact sign for the beginning of an aesthetic conflict, now literary, now pedagogical.

## Literary Beginnings

Questions of aesthetic conflict are best considered through Winnicott's (1969/1999) distinction between object relating and object usage. Pitt (2003) has described these relations through the student's use of the teacher and the teacher's capacity to survive that use. She notes that "Where object relating is an experience of the subject-in-isolation, object usage is an experience of the subject in relation to other subjects" (122). I want to suggest the other side: the teacher's relating and usage of students and curriculum. The term "object" refers both to a phantasy and a subject and "use of the object" has no relation to exploitation. It will be important to keep in mind that Winnicott was trying to see something in common in two different situations: one having to do with early development and relations between mother and infant and the other with relations between the analyst and analysand and how, in the analytic setting, interpretations may or may not be offered and used. It seems fitting to condense and relate these very different positions of analyst, analysand, mother and baby, particularly when thinking inside the pedagogical relation. There remains, after all, the infantile in the teacher, exaggerated in times of dependency upon students when trying to teach and learn. Here, then, is the childhood of teaching.

Object relating comes first and it is taken for granted when object usage develops. Winnicott describes the archaic emotional state of object relating as creative. It is the way in which the infant projects and so creates the mother who is already there. This is also the paradoxical quality of making a curriculum, still in the realm of object relating. The teacher projects the learners who are already there and does so by discovering the material of the curriculum which is also already there. Object usage, however, exceeds the baby's omnipotent projections, provided that there is another who facilitates with the infant a special appreciation of the object's separate existence. Its development, however, emerges from a negativity that can then be recognized and thought about provided that the Other does not retaliate through moralizing and correction. While close to Caper's emotional state of isolation within intimacy and with the sense of one's capacity to understand the contribution one can make to contexts already there, for Winnicott there is, in object usage, a quantity of needed aggression that paradoxically inaugurates both the relation and the isolation. Here is how Winnicott (1999) describes the two modes of being:

> This thing that there is between relating and use is the subject's placing of the object outside the area of the subject's omnipotent control; that is, the subject's perception of the object as an external phenomenon, not as a projective entity, in fact recognition of it as an entity in its own right. (89)

The movements from object relating to object usage involve an element of aggression that for Winnicott begins both phantasy and thinking: The object survives the subject's use. His description is elliptical: "after 'subject relates to object' comes 'subject destroys object' (as it becomes external); and then may come '*object survives* destruction by the subject.' . . . From now on, this stage having been reached, projective mechanisms assist in the act of *noticing what is there*, but are not *the reason why the object is there*" (90, emphasis original).

In object relating, there is only ruthless projection and anti-concern for there is no real Other. In this phantasy, the reason why the object is there is because baby made it. Baby will stretch this omnipotence to its furthest outpost, destroying the creation. (If I made you I can destroy you.) But the object will survive the destruction. Only then can there be the conditions needed to notice the tensions of emotional states, or what Caper sees as difference in relationality. The survival of the object is the key for Winnicott: Mother does not retaliate and so shows the baby that she has survived its omnipotence. But also in this survival, the omnipotence is disillusioned. That Monday morning and that supervisory session so long ago can now signify that the students and the supervisor had survived my destruction because I did not make them. But just as significantly, they did not retaliate, and in this, a reality beyond my projections can be found.

Winnicott's views allow new thinking on the teacher's aggression, or what Gardner has called "the furor to teach," as being somewhere in between object relating and object usage, for recall that Gardner also pities the poor teacher who does not possess furor. For any teaching to occur at all, there must be a measure of aggression and destruction. If the students can survive the teacher's object usage, by not being destroyed and not retaliating, then the teacher can begin to notice the students and her own isolation with them. The isolation with others, then, is not the sociological kind where the teacher is isolated from other adults, although this is certainly the case. The isolation of Winnicottian design touches the experience of being alone in the presence of others now to appreciate those others as separate but also as contributing to the self. The agony of dependency and the resistance to its helplessness may then give way to intersubjectivity. It also means that part of the work of analyzing the teacher's memories of learning includes its underside, the necessary aggression that also makes for our capacity to use the objects of teaching and learning and to create and find the reality that is already there.

One of the strangest footnotes I have ever read belongs to Winnicott's paper on the use of the object. It signals what is also difficult about his way of thinking. While discussing the paradox within the need to destroy the object as part of what allows the object to survive, Winnicott notices how difficult it is to think about these phantasies without conflating them with an intrusive reality. But also surviving phantasied attacks is quite difficult for the analyst. Then, the footnote reads: "When the analyst knows that the patient carries a revolver, then, it seems to me, this work cannot be done" (92, footnote 1). He is speaking about a significant difference between internal and external aggression but also suggesting that if internal aggression is met by moralism then it is impossible to achieve object usage: "It will be seen that, although destruction is the word I am using, this actual destruction belongs to the object's failure to survive" (93). For if the object fails to survive, if it can only be a fixed phantasy to defend, then there is no hope or reality at all. On this view, aggression is not so much a response to reality but a way to call reality forth. Can there be a comparable thought about the nature of the political and how the world is used in the classroom? After all, the curriculum is not the teacher's revolver.

The conditions for a working analysis of the teacher's memory entail the working through of untimely distortions and screen memories and reconstructions of the conceptual field upon which our work depends. For concepts such as the literary, the artistic, the political, and the subjective, for example, to be psychologically significant, each must be flexible enough to survive the teacher's aggression and to welcome the aesthetic conflicts of self/other relations. Then, education may become a potential space made from people who can narrate their experiences and survive the needed destruction of object relating and object usage. The developmental paradox is that remembering these beginnings as a part of the childhood of teaching comes after the fact. This is where narrative may then emerge.

Kristeva's (2001b) discussion of the politics and poetics of Hannah Arendt opens with the difference between the enacted story and the narrated story. The narrated story contains the literary events. It is a return to what the enacted story repressed. Like memory, narration may gather bits of distortion made from then and now. It also holds the potential to open what Kristeva identifies as a certain power: "to condense the action into an exemplary space, removing it from the general flow of events, and in drawing attention to a 'who'" (73). This "who" gives rise to interpretations and to their uses that are in excess of the interpreter's intentions. One can associate action with the dilemmas of its narration, with the uncertainty of what must come after the fact for there even to be a pedagogical fact. If narration begins with what is monstrous in learning to teach, a working analysis depends upon recognition of the emotional states that give rise to needing and using the monsters, to their object relating and object usage. What survives from all this furor, what does not retaliate through moralism or correction is the literary, a very different model for the teacher's beginnings and perhaps for extending psychoanalytic problems of learning to teach to the teacher's difficulty of remembering this novel learning.

# SEVEN

# Notes on the Teacher's Illness

## Note One: Points of Entry

How then to write of the teacher's illness when there are so many ways into this world? And how may narrative convey the incoherence of this narrative, a novel yet to be written?

## Note Two: Welcome Illness

Psychoanalytic training admits the candidate's illness as part of the program of study. The invitation is strange for while many may say that their education is driving them crazy, for those training to become analysts, the drive is the destination. No compatible home for illness awaits those studying the profession of education or teaching in schools and universities. The idea of the teacher's inner world, unless it becomes the specimen for a novel or a film script, is cause for suspicion. Indeed, the teacher's psychological world, including the teacher's capacity to contain what André Green (1986) calls our "private madness," is woefully ignored, until, that is, "it" seems to erupt out of nowhere, a destruction made to break relations with others. Quickly, the teacher's illness is isolated from the school and university, as if it should belong to nobody else. Then, the teacher comes to a deserted place. The collapsed teacher is another matter.

Compare the quickness of this expulsion to the psychological field of the psychoanalyst's world and with where the psychoanalyst's training is lost and found. Rosenfeld's (1999) formulation of psychoanalytic training will be our guide. Along with others, he is interested in the analyst's understanding of the analyst's own idiom or character as the fundamental resource under construction through the deconstruction.

> To function carefully and sensitively, and so to be therapeutic, an analyst depends to a crucial extent on the functioning of his personality as an important instrument or tool. For that reason we are trained not only clinically and theoretically through lectures and supervision, but also through personal analysis. . . . The analysis of the analyst's defensive structure must include his defenses against deep-seated early infantile anxieties, which often hide unconscious psychotic anxieties or problems. *Although our training forces us to be more sane, it must temporarily make us more disturbed and anxious in order to gain the knowledge and experience about ourselves for us to function.* (32–33, emphasis added)

To be sane, one works from within the awareness of one's own madness. Ostensibly, while experienced as belonging only to the self, it is the tie of madness and its work of untying that may be noticed by both the analyst and the analysand. Theirs will be the study of the vicissitudes of illness: where it belongs, to what it attaches, how it is used, and when it finds itself in the service of what Freud (1901, 115) notoriously named "the secondary gain of illness"—where, by way of its communication, the illness may be called upon to add needed protection from others. These bare essentials may be touched and put into the place of words. Somehow the ill relation that is illness itself becomes a resource.

The training makes the analyst ill and invites the illness already there for the purpose of self-knowledge and to understand the experience of being an analysand in dependency with an analyst. This experience of helplessness and dependency, allowing oneself to be placed in the other's hands, is not so far away from our earliest experiences as infants. And yet, for analysts-yet-to-become, this encounter with the inchoate, with the ambiguity of not knowing, with letting an unknown process design itself, and with finding the protests as part of the exploration, prepares new grounds to meet their illness. All these difficulties with helplessness, dependency, and uncertainty become the analysis. They surprise the experience of distress and its bodily symptoms with narrative turns. These difficulties meet others: resistance to narrative and to the Other who listens. But also, it is in this relation—through the transference and the counter-transference—that the uses and ruses of illness are felt profoundly. One experiences the surprise stirring, its terrifying force, and its inextricable flights to the rough edges of existence.

As for the counter-transference, Freud first felt it as the analysts' communication of their illness and so as a sign of the analysts' internal unanalyzed conflicts displaced into the analytic setting. Later, it came to be understood as a feature of the setting—as an unconscious relation—and as an obstacle, a compulsion, a technique, and communication caught in the service of resistance, memory, and desire. Counter-transference closes the distance between the words with the analyst's feelings, only to open the words again. To whom is the analyst relating? Which words bring which affects? Contemporary theories understand the analyst's counter-transference as a means for the analyst to reflect on the flutters of feelings. Here, too, not much can be settled. One may find the resistance because counter-transference is an experience to which one submits. This leads Pontalis (1981) to balance counter-transference with the same obscurity the transference carries: "One cannot talk about counter-transference in truth, but with tact it can be made perceptible" (171). With the concept's transformation of feelings into technique comes an unforgettable ethic: There are not a sane person and an insane person in the analytic setting but two people who may communicate and miss one another through both their respective illnesses and their respective sense of saneness (Etchegoyen 1991). This view has precedence in Nietzsche's philosophy. Karl Jaspers's (1936/1997) discussion of Nietzsche's illness concerns its interpretive use, posing a fundamental ambiguity: "Illness which derives from and serves true health—the health of *Existenz*—comes from within—is actually an indication of this health" (111). Here then begins a radical perspective: Health is incorporated into the field of illness. One cannot reference sanity without an index of madness (Phillips 2005).

Discussions of illness, even in the form of knowing one's own illness in order to be able to contain projections and displacements during practice can, however, feel like being saddled with an uninvited guest who not only refuses to leave but appears to take over the house and cause great consternation. It can seem as if discussions of illness cloud our clarity, but then we are likely to miss that illness itself contains its own obscurities. Where does one place the teacher's illness? In the teacher's brain or bodily chemistry? Within the depression that flowers upon returning to the place where one grew up? In the teacher's history? With the depressed society? Or, can we simply refer to the ordinary work of learning to become a subject who may come to be interested in understanding times when this metaphysical work of becoming a subject loses its object? Perhaps even when we contemplate these difficulties we are already under the sign of illness? When introducing Jacques Hassoun's essay on melancholy, Michael Miller (1997) considers the poles of illness through the question of timing: "The anxious person is tilted toward the future in a state of agitated waiting for some nameless but dreaded coming event. The depressives fix their gaze on misfortunes that have already happened" (vii).

To claim the disclaimed ill-at-ease self to be our research is one of our greatest challenges. And part of the challenge is to meet some objections to the psychoanalytic idea that not much separates, either in education or in analysis, illness from health. It is a strange intimacy made not from roles but from feelings. More objections follow, for what can it mean to understand illness and health as a relation? From the vantage of the psychoanalytic listening, what happens to feelings? The analyst's overhearing greets the indirection of the analysand's complaints with the relations heard in them. Roy Schafer (2003) places the analyst's listening on the borderline between what is said and the relation it may suppose:

> Even when the patient seems to be talking only about matters other than therapy itself . . . there is implied a particular stance toward the psychotherapist, an attitude or a set of expectations that shapes what is being told, how it is told, and when and why . . . it is often more important that the therapist attend to these details . . . [T]hey are more likely to indicate important transference fantasies and feelings and thereby open the way into available emotional intensity in the here-and-now-clinical situation. (76–77)

Listening narrows the distance between words, not because either knows what the other is doing but because in doing what they do together, a passionate relation may become therapeutic. Yet it must be stressed that there is no smooth translation here: The relation of an analyst to an analysand is not one of equality, and there is no technique that can prevent the analyst's failure to grasp what is being conveyed (Bollas 1992). Illness is a difficult, unruly discourse and meeting its events as a relation requires all that will make a new relation: sensitivity, openness, tact, and courage to experience negativity and the chaotic experience of not knowing what to do. The paradox illness presents is one that eludes and posits a truth. While it can be spoken of endlessly, its discourse of need, pain, and disappointment overwhelms a capacity to understand either the self or the Other. From whatever side, empathy, or an attempt to imagine the Other's experience, may go missing or be felt as intrusive. Yet still illness communicates a strange understanding.

Virginia Woolf's (1925/2002) essay "On Being Ill" holds the harshness of experiencing illness with difficulties of communicating the sense of loss. She insists the speaker is left defenseless: "There is, let us confess it (and illness is the great confessional), a childish outspokenness in illness; things are said, truths blurted out, which the cautious respectability of health conceals" (11). She also notices the particular defense mustered when listening to illness: "But in health the genial pretense must be kept up and the effort renewed—to communicate, to civilise, to share, to cultivate the desert, educate the native, to work together by day and by night to sport" (12). Illness is not persuaded: "In illness this make-believe ceases" (12). A terrible disruption of meaning and bodily experience estranges one from life. For Woolf, illness communicates the power of "incomprehensibility" (21): that the meanings which allowed one's life to proceed in life no longer console, that the defenses that keep time from taking on the terrible divisions of before and after, or good days and bad days, are fixated upon creating a claustrophobic now. As for the ill, Woolf imagines, "We ceased to be soldiers in the army of the upright; we become deserters" (12). How interesting that war imagery is so needed to describe the betrayals illness brings and to the feeling that one is betrayed by or may even betray one's illness. Illness as the ban on the discourse of illness may make deserters of us all.

To make a rough sketch of the teacher's illness we really should be outlining complex psychological states of unease, linking its myriad forms of conveyance to its history, reception, and interpretation. If illness repels and attracts, if its timing makes time meaningless, the loss of interaction isolates its signs. Indeed, affect exaggerates the sign beyond recognition.

Let us gather some bodily signs of distress that signal disturbances of thought: nervousness, yelling, helplessness, anxiety, despair, erotic wishes, stage fright, headaches, coughing, blowing up with small things or suffering from too many last straws, obsessive thoughts and paranoia, not wanting to go to school, inhibition, and manic elation and depression. There can be vague anticipations of waiting to fail and fear of being punished. There is disgust with others, threats of giving up, intrusive thoughts of revenge, fears of losing one's mind, and painful rashes, eye trouble, and headaches. And all these signs telegraph a story. It can be argued that all these symptoms are normal, typical expressions of the teacher's life. After all, this argument assures us, the work is stressful and the profession has a name for those who must exit or be sent away: teacher burnout. We should wonder why this disease is a typical expression, why burnout is an occupational hazard. If we consider teachers as suffering from a history of their teaching, can we locate a precipitating force made within that other typical situation, their own history of education? That is, teachers were once children who grew up in school and who, as students experienced their own army of teachers. As children they were already vulnerable to the dangers of a profession that they then joined as an adult. All this can sound tautological. And education itself can feel like its own teleology. Yet teaching is the only profession subject to this tautology. Does teacher burnout have a cause? Our inspirational literature may offer us ways to cope but say little about why. Certainly we are apt to find an avalanche of material on helping others, as if this activity in and of itself did not somehow animate the teacher's distress.

Many objections, then, will need to be aired when approaching this topic of the teacher's illness and when linking this illness to problems made from anxiety over loss of love, and the psychosis with its loss of reality.[1] There will be worries that the teacher will be a pathological subject and the defense that only other teachers exhibit distress. Some will say there is nothing specific about teaching per se that can or should be related to illness. A few won't mind the topic, so long as it remains safely ensconced in an interesting intellectual inquiry. A philosophical hesitation may bring us back to what is difficult: Our capacity for emotional extremes is not an illness but the human condition. This last objection takes us to the heart of the matter: If the human condition is a nervous condition, if we can be affected by that which we do not know, or something other than what we mean to know, and if "error," to use Canguilhem's (1991, 275) term, is our only form of life, then consciousness of life is also a consciousness of illness. That we have the capacity for anxiety, that being itself makes us nervous, raises special dilemmas in the human professions whose working paradox is anxiety's scene: That in our search for meaning, for what meaning our lives may compose, we also meet a void of meaninglessness, arbitrary events, and illness. Denial of this existential reality, or thinking this reality occurs only after hours, leaves us only the void and our neurotic avoidance.

What, then, becomes of diagnosis here? Verhaeghe (2004) distinguishes psychoanalytic diagnostics from medical models. In psychoanalytic views, a psychical symptom is an attempt at self-cure, recovery, and protection. One outcome of the idea that a symptom is a communication, a relation, and a compromise, is that there can be something like what Verhaeghe calls a "successful symptom" (16), solving the conflict in such a way that it is not noticed. One may venture that the successful symptom puts the conflict to sleep and so arrests it or even solves an underlying dilemma so that it is not in need of being noted. The symptom is unsuccessful when its losses overtake what was originally used for gain. The balance sheet proposed here is merely a scale: What tips the quota of affect is the symptom's attempts to turn against the illness, so to say.

A pervasive anxiety that finds work in education is the fear of failure. If this fear is seen as belonging solely to the individual, it is only because one suffers. Situating anxiety in the body, however, is not the same as understanding it. Verhaeghe considers fear of failure as a relation:

> This fear must always be understood from a structural perspective: one fails (or doesn't fail) in relation to someone else, as determined by the underlying context. The complement of this is the compulsion to succeed: one succeeds (or doesn't succeed) in relation to someone else. . . . The latter symptom is rarely presented for consultation, except in contemporary cases of burnout. (17)

How different would our understanding be if we were to stop using the term teacher burnout and instead speak of melancholia or depression? And would this then lead us to think differently about the institution where teachers feel they must comply? In his study of melancholia, Hassoun (1997) underlines the pressure of institutional life: "Anything that makes citizens passive inevitably entails the sort of withdrawal of object investments typical of melancholics" (7) and later he puts into words what his analysand has been asking all along: "Can social ills fail to leave their trace upon the subject?" (96). The emptiness of the teacher may mirror the vacuousness of institutional life, or perhaps the empty person enters the setting where emptiness is maintained as a defense against feeling too much?

There may be pervasive feelings that in schools, something is missing, that education feels empty. This is what Marion Milner (1957/1990) came to after analyzing her own inhibitions in painting. As an analyst, she had studied schools and children, called in to find out why children refused their school work. After completing a major study, she found herself left with feelings of emptiness but also a readiness to explore what she called her "own private misgivings" (xvii). Milner always wanted to paint but felt she did not know how. Her own instruction in schools demanded that she approach her painting with willful control and have in her mind a sense of the object prior to beginning. Unable to do this, she concluded that she had no talent. Privately, she continued to make drawings without these advanced plans and they were, for her, pleasurable. But she also felt this pleasure in her unwillful drawings as "disconcerting" since it meant that all she believed about herself and art would have to be rethought. Her education provided the elements of despair by failing to allow for her own misgivings to be followed. Perhaps she was always preparing for this rethinking. In her talks to teachers years earlier, Milner (1942/1996) pointed out what she believed to be the basis for believing in experience, what she called "the child's capacity for doubt." She could not paint until she made from her doubts a right to transfigure her world through illusion. This would be her contribution. Until Milner could encounter these thoughts, she could neither paint nor distinguish sanity from insanity.

## Note Three: Crazy Relations

From the childhood of my education I recall an army of crazy teachers. Some belonged to me, others I only imagined in fear or met in novels. Throughout my childhood, my parents contributed their crazy teachers to my catalogue. These composite fictions, memories, and ghost stories all had something in common: Crazy teachers were inexplicably mean and my family was always innocent. Some stepped on children, and others stabbed them with rulers, and still others took sadistic pleasure in the use of the paddle. A few devised rules that could not be followed and planned elaborate punishments without a crime. Some, in the middle of a lesson, would suddenly stop, turn blue, and yell as if this was how they could begin to breathe. Others ran out of the classroom in tears. The teachers stole our toys, or smashed them into pieces. Some would never leave their desks, as if they had no legs at all, and would send a poor student to run impossible errands, to fetch things that could not be found. Some put children in the corner until they languished or banished others to antiseptic hallways. They made them write their name ten thousand times. One put a circle on the chalkboard and had the child place his nose in it. These events seemed to justify why we felt compelled to drive the crazed teacher crazy. But it also meant that it was difficult to see who is doing what to whom, a confusion of desire and boundaries that made education, from whatever side, insane. My mythic stories have the ridiculous taste of a Wes Craven horror film; oddly, these crazy figures found their way into our childhood games of let's play school. Now they return for what I hope will be their last performance.

Perhaps it is not until one returns to that childhood place of torture, now as teacher, that one understands the unwieldy emotional qualities of this world. Yet even here, too rarely, do we speak of the teacher's depression and anxiety, preferring instead to diagnosis the learning problems of students and to idealize the statue of the teacher. We hope that private conflicts remain unanimated while teaching, that the choice of subject matter, the decisions within the pedagogical relation, the correction of student mistakes, and the endless grading of their papers neither carry our affective hostility nor mark our places of agony. We may even think that somehow, because we enter the classroom each day, we should have no conflict with stepping into a knowing role. Teachers, we often feel, must be adept at brushing off their private world like so much accrued lint. We may even feel we should read our students' minds even as ours might feel empty. Catastrophes in the world are something we may teach about but without the burden of agony, uncertainty, sadness, and pain that the catastrophes unleash. Crises belong to others. How different are these phantasies from my army of crazy teachers, except now, the teacher is unaffected, a robot.

That these defenses have a prehistory is not easily admitted. There is a denial of madness and a false view of sanity as its opposition. Adam

Phillips (2005) suggests, in his study of saneness, that this refusal of emotional turbulence takes its residence in prescriptions for childrearing relations: "The idealization of childhood, the pastoral myths of parenting, are complicit in their denial of the child's [and the parents'] emotional turbulence" (75). It is as if human development and maturity is a procedure for becoming unaffected.

If all of these views—the family mythology, prescriptions for childrearing, and the profession's defense—have a certain naivety, it is because they articulate that place of naivety: the childhood of teaching, what Jane Gallop (1999) has called "infantile pedagogy" (131). In a piece of self-analysis, Gallop coined this magnificent term to locate her childhood games of playing teacher and the strange reoccurrence of finding herself, now as a Professor of Literature, playing them again. In both places, then and now, love, hate, hostility, domination, and erotic phantasies fused into harsh lessons. There was the uncanny acting out of a sadistic persona: the teacher who is charged by her charges. Gallop begins her analysis with an admission: Teachers do not want to help and see their students as taking up their time. So, when forced to answer for the bad grade given to a student's (good) assignment, she decides to teach him a lesson. She would prove how wrong he is to question her judgment. No matter how much time this would take, she would make this sacrifice to reveal to him, error by error, the truth of his terrible writing. It is her secret game of punctuation. How different were her childhood games of playing teacher from what happens in this encounter, although now she brings the adult's rationalization to this lesson the infantile pedagogy devised so long ago. The child's helplessness is transformed into the adult who helps helpless others. But the affective force of having to teach someone else a lesson is what concerns Gallop. It is never easy to get rid of the hostility one once felt toward an authority. It is hard to forget having to accept harsh lessons. When one becomes this authority, old hostility is transferred, in the form of a retaliation, as if needing help itself must be punished. Here she hates the student so as to be a good teacher, except in Gallop's account, she falls in love with him and feels again like a bad student/teacher. If Gallop is now occupying all of the positions, she does so only because the lesson cannot be learned. Here, then, is a dramatic index of the transference-love: projections of one's infantile attitudes, demands for love, modes of loving, helplessness and disappointments with the self, and fears of punishment. Here, too, is the little return of a sadomasochist childhood game, itself provoking a nervous illness.

## Note Four: The Transference Headache

The analytic setting invites the transference, as does the classroom. All this means is that we bring our conflicts and demands for love with us to investigate the grounds for our relationship with others. They play promiscuously, without regard to their original relevance, leaving in their wake an impression on the demands for love. It is this impression, given free rein in the analytic setting, that marks the transference-love as what Freud (1914) catalogued as "an artificial illness" (154). In the transference, conflicts and wishes migrate to the Other, and while one may be pleased to receive them, mistaking these projections for clarity or adoration rather than the obstacles and *mésalliance* (or false connection) that they are may be the first mistake of the teacher or the analyst. Freud's (1915a) "Observations on Transference-Love" notes three of its characteristics: the transference is provoked by the analytic setting; it is intensified by resistance; and it lacks regard for reality (168–169). A piece of infantile phantasy is joined by the need for love. The paradox is that the combustible transference is required for analysis and for learning to proceed. This raises dangers for the analyst's narcissism, altruism, or hostility should the analyst gratify the analysand's demand for a love relationship rather than an analysis. More than this, the cure by love is directed at love's neurotic trends. Treat the transference "as something unreal" (166) advises Freud: Place it in the realm of phantasy. Everything depends, Freud (1915a) warns, on how the transference is handled.[2]

When things get difficult to handle, Stephen Appel (1999) writes, the teacher gets a headache. It has the qualities Freud noted in the transference in that a headache lacks regard for reality, is an intensified resistance, and is provoked by the setting. And usually, what the headache gets when one gets a headache is obscured by the nagging pain, itself a composite of destruction, revenge, and protection. Appel gets them both in his teaching and in his therapeutic practice. Sometimes his headaches begin when he feels he must be, for the sake of his students, positive and upbeat. His headache may express his hatred of having to be well. They appear when he feels compelled to assume responsibilities for student learning by taking on the persona of role model, as if he has no head of his own. But also, these headaches may be a communication of sympathy for the student, whose head must also hurt while learning new material. Appel's headaches may remind him of the ill fit between desire and responsibility; then the headache is intolerable. He is careful to state that his headaches are real but in treating them through the transference and the counter-transference, he begins to locate old hostilities and hatreds, seeing in the migraine a sign for the desire to destroy something, an internal drama of object relations. "Migraines," Appel concludes from his self-analysis, "are an eloquent and effective oblique expression of feelings *arising between me and someone else* that are denied direct or adequate expression in other ways" (140, emphasis original). Knowing this, however, may only mean that one may have a headache without losing one's head.

## Note Five: Typical Dreams

There is a category of dreams so usual that Freud (1900), in his *Interpretation of Dreams*, devoted a chapter to them under the title "Typical Dreams." The typical dream presented technical and existential problems to Freud. On one hand, he insisted on the uniqueness of dreams, that this piece of mental life was specific to each dreamer, especially created by the dreamer, and therefore whimsically unintelligible and worse, theoretically uninterpretable. But on the other hand, typical dreams—dreams that anyone has—seem to cancel out this idiosyncratic liberty and theoretical superficiality. Having noted that, Freud raises another problem. A second difficulty with typical dreams is their interpretation. Whereas untypical dreams invite the analysand's associations and so move into the dream thoughts, typical dreams resist associations. They can seem too obvious for comment. There is a problem of association. And besides, the meaning is transparent. A third difficulty may be a culmination of the previous ones since it resides with their nature. What makes them typical is that their content *dreams* the human condition: that we are born (which gives us the infantile), that we have parents (which gives us the Oedipus complex), that we learn (which gives us cultural authority).

Freud made three categories from the typical dream. The first kind are dreams of being naked, the second are dreams of a beloved parent dying, and the third kind concerns being given or taking examinations, mostly school examinations. Before I move to the last sort of typical dream, there are some commonalities that link these categories. Typical dreams are dreams of anxiety: The dreamer is ill at ease, sometimes immobilized, or not able to complete what one has accomplished in waking life. Then there is the population in the dream. The crowd we put there has a quality of being indifferent to the dreamer's plight, embarrassment, or panic made from the need for help. It is as if they do not see the trouble or act as if there is no trouble at all. It is almost as if these dreams carried the stamp of Kafka's approval, indexing the estranged conflation of affect and culture. There is an exaggeration, particularly in the first and third kinds of dreams, an existential ridiculousness. It is this third kind of typical dream—the examination dream—that plunges us into the underworld of education and repeats a history of passivity. What seems most interesting for Freud is that these examination dreams are usually the dreams of those who regularly pass their exams and also those long past having to take examinations. Given the distortions of the dream-work and its ill regard for representational logic, the issue is with the pressure of feeling examined, wishing to be examined, or wanting to examine.

These damned dreams always contain some vague educational purpose that no one can identify. The dreamer feels compelled to meet some imperative or fulfill without failing, a demand that cannot be met or, just as it is attempted, attention goes missing, the activity is somehow forgotten or, the directions cannot be followed. In these dreams there is some bodily distress made from forgetting what one already knows: sudden blindness, not being able to see letters, taking a test in a foreign language, being treated as a child while feeling grown-up, being given a test one has already passed, not being listened to or not being able to hear, and so on. In this category of examinations, there are also dreams of school. The obviousness of these typical dreams resists association since the dreamer has been to school and no doubt, did worry about failing. Yet the carnival of affects this typical dream represents—guilt, fear, hatred, love, humiliation, shame, loathing, excitement, for example—signal things far more archaic than the affective tie that schooling both obscures and animates. Freud argues that the examination dream is a remnant and residue of childhood, of having to grow up in a family and in a culture, of learning to live with beloved and hated others. From a child's perspective, ignoring a parent's demand creates a measure of guilt and the expectation of punishment. All of this is set into place by the fear of losing love. The examination dream links these elements together: helplessness, responsibility, punishment, and loss of love. Three conflicts coalesce for this affective world to begin again each night: the burden of responsibility, the worry of failing to meet this responsibility, and the expectation of and need for punishment. The dynamics are familiar. They also compose superego or moral anxiety. Significantly, the examination dream also holds Oedipal conflicts as well as traces of "infantile pedagogy" (Gallop 1999, 131).

## Note Six: Superego Anxiety

Psychoanalysis has a long history of critiquing education, holding to the idea that education makes one ill and psychoanalysis attempts to repair this harm. Teachers may be included in this crowd. Anna Freud's (1930/1974) talks to teachers follow this line of thought, but she also suggested to teachers that they act as "universal superegos" helping their students distinguish between right and wrong judgments and behaviors. Yet taking on the position of a universal superego may become the teacher's illness, pushing the teacher into the desire for an impossible success. Anna Freud, however, assumed that teachers could, with the help of their own analysis, contain their conflicts with authority, avoid projecting these onto their students, and somehow relieve themselves of their own superego anxiety. Without analysis, this is a dangerous proposition because superego anxiety easily becomes moral anxiety and, then a sadistic obsession with other people's (lack of) morality. I imagine Anna Freud wanted teachers to believe their superego could be a resource, as it is for all of us on better days. Yet, the problem of authority and what authorizes the teacher is a tension that can overwhelm. From where does authority come? Is there ever an original moment or a cause? Years later, in her Harvard talks to teachers, Anna Freud (1952/1992) backed away from her insistence upon the metaphor of the teacher as universal superego and addressed instead the need to understand the teacher's emotional life from the vantage of three great emotional dangers implicit in the work of teaching: not seeing the child's developmental trajectory over the life cycle and so having to respond to incomplete development; getting caught up in the lives of children and so losing one's adult world; and feeling as though the student was the teacher's own child or the child the teacher once was. Each danger destroyed difference but also the teachers' capacity to reflect upon their own representations. Notably, these are the transference dangers, the teacher's fatal attraction.

Ester Bick (1962/1996) also wrote of the contemporary dangers facing the child analyst: emotional overinvolvement and identification with the child; worries over one's effects upon the child; anxiety over relations with the child's parents; worries about the nature, reach, and ethics of one's responsibility to the child; becoming excessively attached to the child; overstrictness, rescue fantasies, and an incapacity to face painful experiences the child brings and projects. While many of these dangers have to do with counter-transference, or the ways the analyst is affected unconsciously by the analysand's material, there are also the analyst's unconscious identifications with the child the analyst once was, would have liked to be, or wanted to destroy. Further, the obscurity of the analyst's work stirs the analyst's helplessness. This, for Bick, is the compression of the psychoanalytic relation: "The intensity of the child's dependence, of his positive and negative transference, the primitive nature of his phantasies tends to arouse the analyst's own unconscious anxieties. . . . Also the child's suffering tends to evoke the analyst's potential feelings, which have to be controlled so that the proper analytic role can be maintained" (171).

The Other affects the teacher, animating the teacher's vulnerabilities, actions and phantasies. To be affected by one's emotional ties is not the illness. Rather, illness plays with their entanglements, these dangers in such a way that superego anxiety splits the self off from the relation of difference one must hold in mind. The teacher, too, suffers from a universal superego that takes form from professionalism and its moral qualms. What goes under the name of having to be a professional includes feeling one must submit to an authority that one must then carry out on others. It can include sacrificing the self without knowing or even missing what has been lost. But also, the pressure for perfection, itself a defense against fears of failure and fragmentation, may lead to fears of mistakes and losing one's mind. And so the teacher, too, has difficulty with dependency, so animated in pedagogical relations.

## Note Seven: Postmodern Neurosis

Being split off from one's feelings is quite common in everyday life and often goes under the name dissociation. When this split subject appears in theory, however, there can be a nervous response. In the middle of writing this chapter, a colleague who is preparing her own chapter for a book on teacher education sends an e-mail, asking for a few minutes of my time.

She hopes that her questions are not too complicated. She is trying to hold onto a particular tension, wanting to explore agency and voice in the poststructural era, so littered as it is with the notion of a split, nonunitary, performative subject. What can be left over? She asks, "How come we are all not complete, in my kids' words, 'wack jobs' when who we are is shifting, multiple, constructed, and contradictory? Is it stories that serve the purpose of making sense? But again, 'who' is it that makes that sense?" I print out the message and stick it in a book on psychoanalytic diagnosis which I have been assigned to read for a workshop. No, that can't be right. Questions linger: Can theory drive one crazy? How much self division, self difference can one tolerate? What splits the subject when the split subject is a teacher?

## Note Eight: Divided Loyalties

Around 1940, When Dr. Margaret Little (1901–1994) was training to be an analyst with the British Psychoanalytical Society, undergoing her own second analysis, she began analyzing Miss Alice M. Their relation would last over thirty-five years. When they first met, Miss M. described herself as suffering from divided loyalties. She felt torn between her sense of duty to parents, work, religion, and her own life. Her mother had chosen her career as a teacher and Miss M. felt miserable.

In the early work, and probably drawing upon her experience as analysand, Little's technique with Miss M. was classically Freudian. Miss M., a kindergarten teacher, age thirty-one, was on the couch for their first cycle, lasting about five years. Then, Little sat behind the couch, listening and interpreting. Years later she came to believe her interpretations of Miss M.'s symptoms were elementary. In the first cycle, Little interpreted defenses, Oedipal conflicts, and the transference. These classical techniques, Little came to believe, skirted the void of Miss M.'s despair and assumed solipsistic development. The techniques and her worries that the analyst would take over her mind may even have amplified the problem of Miss M.'s anxieties over what other people thought and how she used the thoughts of other people as a substitute for her own. Miss M. left this first cycle of analysis to care for ill parents. She returned to school to train as a teacher with a specialty in religion. This first analysis, however, may have prepared the ground for what would follow: a dramatic change in Little's analytic techniques and Miss M.'s foray into her own chaos through dream painting.

In the years that followed, Miss M. would return to Little as needed, usually during times of personal crisis. This use of psychoanalysis on demand was also true for Little herself, whose third analysis, beginning in 1945 was with Winnicott. That same year Miss M. returned to Little for more psychotherapy. For the next fifteen years, again with intermissions, Little continued to see Miss Alice M. Over their time together, Dr. Little's technique underwent significant transformations, as had the course of both their illnesses. Miss M.'s analysis, then, lasted twenty years, with fifteen additional years of collegial contact and the exchange of notes, with Little. In total, Little estimates they had some 553 sessions. Upon Miss Alice M.'s death, Little published an account in German. A year after Little's death, the English translation was published under the title *Miss Alice M. and Her Dragon: Recovery of a Hidden Talent* (1997). The book consists of Miss M.'s paintings, Little's discussion of sessions, and Miss M.'s notes on the paintings and on her analysis. As for Little's three personal analyses which spanned a comparable amount time from 1936–1957, Little (1990) also published her personal record of them, the largest section being with Winnicott. Little's memoir is titled *Psychotic Anxieties and Containment*.

Oddly, the analyst and the teacher shared the same complaint: divided loyalties. How, they seem to be asking, can one become a self when the self is loyal to that which fragments it? Both women had difficulty extricating themselves from the lives of others; each was attracted to the arts but frustrated early attempts to express this aspect of the self. In their respective analyses, both underwent deep regression to infantile states: there were tantrums, yelling matches, isolated withdrawals, and then, long periods of indecision with matters that terribly mattered. Their divided loyalties made for terrible geometry, exponential divisions of a fragmented self.

These two texts by Little belong together, not only because they share common years but also because together they narrate an unusual story of psychoanalysis, linking the illness of psychotic despair with the hope for creative technique. Little's commentaries on the devastating after-effects of education are subtle: One enters an object world littered by secrets, compliance, and angry headmasters, but also the making of what Winnicott called "a false self."

Their communication of the inner world occurs through the poetic license. Little presents Miss M.'s case by reproducing the latter's forty-seven paintings, what Little calls her "dream paintings." Both Little and Miss

M. come to think of these paintings as an index of Miss M.'s moods and battles. They convey as well Miss M.'s attitude to the analysis itself. Rather than say much about what actually happened in the analysis, though a few sessions are described, Little's comments are reserved for the paintings themselves and for her observations when Miss M. would paint during the analytic session. Little's own analysis with Winnicott may have been at midpoints when she, too, began to paint and write poetry. Just as Miss M. brought her work to Little, so, too, did Little bring her work to Winnicott. And Little learned that sharing her work did not require Winnicott's approval. He did not need to like them for a discussion to be made between them. In both analyses there is an unusual consideration toward living as containing elements of destruction and creativity: Painting will be used as a model of this.

Readers may find between these texts shared sentences, comparable passions in need of expression, and also a weird camaraderie that extends the identifications between the analyst and the analysand. Both studies are built from what Grotstein (1990), in his introduction to Little's own analysis, calls "the technical importance of reality" (6). The phrasing is exquisite for the question of where reality resides in psychoanalysis is either answered as missing or else as ignored. Grotstein, however, is interested in reality's impression on psychical life and its object relations and then in the analysands' impressions of reality. The reality, however, is something that must be constructed because it refers to what actually happened in early life. These events, particularly from the vantage of early care in infancy are considered through a paradox. Reality's technical importance cannot promise to explain the reason why an individual came to be the person now. Nor can its technical importance settle the symptom's vicissitudes. It can, however, work as a provision to investigate the early constructions of the first relation. For both Little and Miss M. there was the depressed mother whose life was also difficult. The technical importance of reality returns the analytic narrative to the conditions of being: the recognition of care taking in early life, when the infant is the least responsible for being because the infant is born into radical and irrevocable dependency. This can mean that what happens in early life may be so catastrophic that the self's development proceeds through fragmentation, despair, and psychotic anxiety. And this view of the technical importance of reality affects psychoanalytic treatment. Facile views of individuals responsible for their suffering, an unfortunate formulation found in some sectors of classical psychoanalysis, cannot be the *modus operandi.* The point of treatment is the experience of someone taking responsibility for the self that is missing.[3] This responsibility is what Winnicott called "the environmental provision," a scaffold made before need overwhelms the self's potential.

There is a quality of internal life that Little's two studies highlight, already hinted by Rosenfeld's description of the candidate's analysis as needing to reach into "unconscious psychotic anxieties." This term is frightening for unlike neurotic anxieties that have to do with relations with others and that, in some way, presuppose a self, psychotic anxieties occur before there is a sense of self or destroy the self's capacity to think. The predominating fear is of being annihilated by one's needs, of being stripped of the accoutrements of identity, and so of a being bereft of existence. These anxieties are reached only through deep regression and dependency. They are not to be understood in the sense of making insight from them but only as undergone and contained by the Other's reverie that will neither retaliate nor be destroyed. In analysis, as Little shows, it is a strange apprenticeship, playing again with the paradox and ambiguity that belong to the first relation of the caregiver and the baby: Care is needed but so, too, are experiences without being disturbed. The psychotic transference conveys this dependency as only broken, intrusive, and as disorienting. It may be carried through bodily actions such as tantrums, kicking, screaming, and breaking of objects; the saddest and most devastating expression is suicide.

Little's (1990) report of her analysis with D. W. Winnicott allows outsiders to understand an experience of his technique. Its other value belongs to her frank discussion of her own psychotic anxieties. She writes of both:

> In one early session with D. W. I felt in utter despair of ever getting him to understand anything. I wandered round his room trying to find a way. I contemplated throwing myself out of the window, but felt that he would stop me . . . finally I attacked and smashed a large vase filled with white lilac, and trampled on it. In a flash he was gone from the room, but he came back just before the end of the hour. Finding me clearing up the mess he said, "I might have expected you to do that [clear up? Or smash?] but later." The next day an exact replica had replaced the vase and the lilac, and a few days later he explained that I had destroyed something that

he valued. . . . Many years later, long after termination, when asking for advice about a very disturbed patient who hurt me knowingly and repeatedly, I spoke of having hurt him. He agreed that I had but added that it had been "useful." (43)

In other sessions, during times of painful fragmentation, crying, and bodily shaking, Little reported that Winnicott would hold her hands.

Hers was a severe illness: paranoid anxieties, sudden rage, incapacity to sustain love and feelings of profound despair and futility. But there coexisted with this illness, a sane part, an utterly normal life: work, success at school, a medical and therapeutic practice, and, by 1940, training as an analyst. Actually, her book reports three analyses: the first one occurring from 1936–1938 with Dr. X., with the presenting problem as not feeling like herself and being subject to a clingy friend who took over her life. The second analysis was with Ella Freeman Sharpe, from 1940 through to Sharpe's death in 1947. Her third analysis, between 1949–1955 and then again in 1957, was with Winnicott. She brought him depression, bouts of suicidal fears—what she would describe as "the wreckage" (61). With Winnicott's care, Little experienced deep regression to psychotic anxieties and describes how this rage, disappointment, and fear made their way into the transference. Except for one hospitalization around 1952, Little continued to see her own patients, one of whom was Miss M.

Let us turn now to Little's (1997) discussion of Miss M.'s analysis. In the third cycle of analysis, Miss M. began sessions by complaining about school, the children's misbehavior, and her disappointment with others. She was on the verge of terrible rage, only held back by her worry of what other people may think. Little would say, "Oh bother other people!" Slowly, Miss M. would vent her anger and a few months later, wanted to paint.

The first painting is titled "The Furious and Frightened Little Girl," and Little commented upon all of the boundaries in the paintings. It has a static quality, except for the small figure of a girl running from a house as a second girl placed on the roof of the house flaps her arms as if to take flight with the birds. The early paintings, however, were constrained and stereotypical; they both preserved and expressed an empty world. Miss M. holds herself back, seeming to agree with her mother that she had no talent. There are glimmers of deep despair. Another painting is titled

"The Chaotic World of Childhood." One must study it closely, for the drama is subtle yet devastating. A girl child leads her mother into the middle of the street just as a bus is coming toward them. It is as if the child brings the mother into the street to be run down. Behind the bus is a free-standing cross, as if a funeral was on its way into being. It is difficult to decide where the funeral begins since the painting itself may be a death march dream. Her seventh painting is titled "Divided Loyalties," which was Miss M.'s presenting complaint. It consists of isolation. There is a figure of the back of a girl sitting at a school desk watching other children playing and to the side, there is a religious procession. They all have their eyes on the girl. Compared to the others, the girl watching is small and alone.

The fifth and longest cycle of their analysis begins with Little asking Miss M. if she wants to finish the analysis. "As things had gone so far, we had spent fifteen years on and off and could go on like that, probably for the rest of our lives; otherwise we would have to tackle the underlying anxieties, possibly hidden behind her religion . . . she decided to go on" (22). More paintings were brought; the one that brought tears to Little is titled "The Burning (or Broken) Heart." The painting conveys anguish, a girl in a school uniform burrows her head and arms into a huge, black heart. Finally, Miss M. begins to experience her narrative rather than simply stating what happened. She cries as she remembers at age fifteen that her art teacher told her mother she was not talented enough to become an artist. The art lessons stopped and with this memory, Miss M. began to tell "the full story of her many failures" (23). There were also the mythologies of teaching that had to be worked through. Having to grow up in school leaves in its wake impressions in the teacher's body: no right to have a personality, worries that the teacher/mother will punish misbehavior, the manic desire to please authority, and sadness over abandoned and lost desires. Miss M. also feels anxiety over never having children of her own. Little reports a particular disillusionment: "Those she taught were no substitute, as she had been led to expect they would be" (10). But a substitute for what? And from where would such an expectation of fulfillment or trade come except from a child's fantasy of a teacher's power to always be happy and to always have happy children? It is almost as if Miss M. felt she had to make a terrible choice: Education or Life? Compliance in either, Miss M. was beginning to understand, is no substitute for her desire.

The next years are dramatic for Miss M. and Little. As Miss M. pours her body into painting, the paintings become larger. Little points out places of freedom. The rage and hostility were there as well:

> She poured out her full fury with her parents, and with me as, crouched on the floor, weeping and growling, she fairly attacked the paper, sweeping wildly across it with both hands and at one point tearing it. "You said '*Bother* other people,' but I think it's DAMN and BLAST other people," she screamed. "What about ME?" (27)

More sessions follow, now with discussions on existence and existential loneliness. The long analysis is ending and Little observes:

> She came to feel that she had a *right* to her own life, her own joys and sorrows. She would fail often and fall short of her ideals of herself. She was now joined to her heartbreak and her anger; and she no longer feared to lose the love of those on whom her being depended if she were loyal to her own self . . . she was ready to stop. (28)

Little's last remarks concern why the therapy worked. She attributes it to their therapeutic alliance and to the transference and counter-transference. Between them they made understanding and identification but also differences that made for the failure to understand and so for their separateness. In the counter-transference, Little saw in Miss M. her own mother and sister, both of whom were "driven to perfection and self-effacement" (35). These are also the stultifying qualities of a teacher Miss M. believed she had to embody; they are poor substitutes for the self. The character of Miss M.'s teaching also changed, and Little links this to the former's ability to grapple, in her paintings and life, with the nature of truth: "What is it? Is it absolute or literal (as she used to believe)? Is it imaginative? Psychic? Poetic?" (29).

## Note Nine: Novel Education

Without the containment of therapeutic action, the illness of the teacher is devastating. And literature knows this all too well. David Albahari's (2004) hauntingly bleak novel, *Götz and Meyer*, imagines paranoid/schizoid dimensions of the teacher's illness that lean upon paranoid/schizoid qualities of history. The novel recounts a teacher's research into World War II and the destruction of Serbian Jewry during those years. The teacher meets his terrible history in the archive when one day he tries to find out what happened to his family during the War. The silence surrounding the genocide of Jews in Belgrade is deafening, lonely, and maddening. But in the archive the teacher becomes fascinated with two SS men who gassed Jewish citizens in their roving truck. Their names, Götz and Meyer, are the title of the novel and its narrator, thinking that this is the way into understanding what happened to his family, tries to imagine these SS men. But they become too real and invade the narrator's inner world. Our nameless narrator's attempts lead to an obsession with details of their murderous travels, and in this process, the teacher's sanity is destroyed.

Albahari's novel is one long paragraph, running 160 pages. Its form mirrors the breathless tale but also its urgency and terror of needing to convey a traumatic past to those who have not experienced it. The teacher becomes a terrible messenger, obsessed with teaching a lesson. It is almost as if the narrator—a fifty-year-old high school poetry teacher living alone in Belgrade—barely tolerates what he is about to tell: his own story, itself a maze of dead ends, filled with paralyzing fragments that persecute him. "'My life,' I say aloud in the middle of a lecture on romanticism, 'is like a memory that doesn't know who is remembering it. . . . If Götz and Meyer were to knock at your door tomorrow,' I continue, 'What would you do?'" (103). The same details of transports, of gassing, of the destruction of the Jewish Serbian population in two short years, are shuffled and reshuffled, as if the sheer repetition of imagining these terrible events and reading the vast obsessions archived as details, evidence that is left behind, would somehow still the madness of their terrible meaning. Sense and closure belong elsewhere. Language and so imagination can only secure their own failure to understand. Our narrator cannot find his way back from the psychotic details he manically collects and then tries to bring to life through imagining their monstrosity. They affect him to such an extent that all he can do with pedagogy is enact the trauma.

One day in his poetry class he announces "a hands-on experience" (126). When the students ask him about the lesson, he summarizes the traumatic mess: "It was going to be about the difference between the tangible world and art, I explained, but also about the similarity between an instant of reality and a figment of the imagination" (127). The difference is where everyone loses a sense of self, becomes lost, bereft, and abandoned to their naked subjectivity. This experiment with fiction, with trying to know what such an unreal history might feel like in its naked force, was too much for everyone. The tangible world was already destroyed.

Near the novel's end, the teacher takes his students on a bus trip to the location of a former transport camp, a fairground situated on the outskirts of the city of Belgrade. As if a tour guide on some surreal educational trip, he demands that the students on the bus try to imagine being gassed. It is a pedagogy of "as ifs" and the students necessarily fail this experiment in the impossible. The ghosts of Götz and Meyer, the two SS men who drove the transport truck from 1941 to 1942 and whose ordinariness haunts the teacher since he first accidentally came across their names in an archive when trying to trace his family tree, these SS men who loaded the bus with Jews and drove the bus and who hooked up the exhaust pipe to asphyxiate the Serbian Jews trapped inside, now live in the narrator's mind which has become the bus. They watch his terrible pedagogical gamble. And the gamble is in asking the students who are now on a bus to imagine their own murder and to imagine the murders' ordinariness. The panic and despair of wanting to tell a story through the adhesions of identification, of wanting this story to prevent what has already happened, gradually becomes the failed story of trying to tell the story of moral failure and the story of the teacher's madness. There is the story of the failure of a world and the story of a failure of the teacher's mind. What made this teacher ill cannot be the topic. After all, the details of genocide and its haunting loss are disgusting, frightening, inconceivable. The ordinariness of the murderers is shocking. But in the teacher's desperation that became his material, where there was no difference between the past and the present, is where the illness flowered. That teachers become ill and that their material is on the side of illness make the transference particularly combustible, a transference psychosis.

I do not read Albahari's novel as a cautionary tale, as a warning of something to prevent, or as even an example of how the madness of history somehow transfigures the madness of the teacher. The novel makes an impossible request: What can it mean to become a historical subject when one teaches others? Ogden's (1986) discussion of the paranoid/schizoid and depressive position may be useful here. He suggests that with the paranoid/schizoid position the annihilating past is projected into the present and back to the past and so there cannot yet become a self.

But neither is there history. In the depressive position, one can make reparation but can neither rewrite the past nor ignore the remorse, sadness and pain left behind. In Ogden's view, "Feelings of loss, guilt, sadness, remorse, compassion, empathy, and loneliness are burdens that are unavoidable if one is to become a historical human being in the depressive position" (1986, 99). Ogden renames this position as the historical position. Albahari's novel may suggest the burden of becoming a historical human being but also, how this burden may crush second chances, called here the depressive position.

The violence that is pedagogy must also be referenced, however difficult this thought may be. For in the attempt to teach this "difficult knowledge," the teacher's difficult knowledge is touched and also conveyed. The urges to prevent what has already happened through the enactment of its violence, through shocking students into understanding, through forcing the others to undergo what the self cannot tolerate, indeed to punish the students with knowledge, all of these actions place the pedagogy in the paranoid/schizoid position. So the teacher suffers from reminiscences and the confusion of time. The present provides the imperative to learn from a destruction that had no lesson. The past—its helplessness and its amnesia, that is, its inability to know either itself as it unfolds or the social repression that accompanies the event—leaves the teacher helpless and adrift. And memory becomes this force of meaninglessness, this void, where details may only signify a terrible absence and where social repression aggravates the loss and the incapacity to mourn. The teacher's illness may telegraph fragments of this difficult problem and this ruined memory.

## Note Ten: "Shake Hands Please"

If one searches a thesaurus, the word *illness* will be distinguished from *health*, but it will also gather other groups of words, themselves ill with meaning. There will be words that give subjectivity over to fate, such as *misfortune*, *bad luck*, and *failure*. Other words designate confinement, such as *housebound* or *bedridden*. One will find fatal words as well, such as *wasting away*, *stricken*, and *bodily deficiencies*. Some words collapse boundaries, such as *contamination*, *plague*, *infectiousness*, and *trauma*. But nowhere will the word *illness* be associated with life itself. And it is this isolation, this "ill treatment" of the teacher's illness that may be associated with the illness of education.

In my personal analysis, education is often the stage for painful fights between my desire to be recognized and my need to be alone, for the urgency of wanting to learn and the defense of needing to already know. When my associations create this world of education, I waver between feeling too smart and going dumb and then, onto the vacillations of both wanting to destroy my education and wishing for its repair. And I wonder if this broken education may be a place that can contain fears of destruction and the need to repair, if there can be a depressive position for this affected education.

As for the teacher's illness, these are the threads of our existential condition, contained, in part through the gesture of taking of notes. To take a note is to try to impress one's impressions further, to welcome the incomplete and the yet to be formed. Without this peculiar effort, touches of meaning will escape notice. Taking notes may index what could have been dismissed; its wording may lend to reality technical importance. By their nature, notes hesitate; they are signals to the incomplete thought but also link things never associated. A number of disparate circumstances, accidents, and events may be juxtaposed or associated without the anchor of reason or the worry over success or failure. One may respect the loose connection, the dead end, the finding of relief. Perhaps they are a lost art, or serve as a place to wonder, to stumble in a thicket of ideas, or to mark places of loss. Taking notes itself references a nervous condition and a means for therapeutic action because these words make a form of life.

EIGHT

# What is a Pedagogical Fact? Notes from The Clinical Knowledge Project

Some years ago the American Educational Research Association convened a symposium titled "Yes, but Is It Research?"[1] There was strong anxiety as to how to account for what counts as research, how to decide whether new methods were permissible or useful, and whether educational research can borrow from the theoretical preoccupations of other disciplines, for instance, taking a narrative turn, and still recognize itself as both research and education. Our condensed problem of researchers trying to know their object through anticipation, belief, intelligibility, judgment, and implication is surely what all disciplines experience. Bringing these debates to oneself, however, made the researcher nervous. Given the frustration in the room, we may as well have asked of each other, "Yes, but is it a researcher?" because the boundaries we create to hold our objects, after all, also represent our subjectivity. The heart of the matter was reached during that symposium with the anxious question of whether writing a work of fiction might qualify as a dissertation or research report. There it was: research as reality, research as phantasy. But also, how does one represent the subjective experience of learning and not learning?

Our dilemma of whether a field of human practice is best thought through metaphors of science or literature is also shared with psychoanalysis. From the very beginning of his career, Freud noticed that his case studies read as fiction, even as he also desired to contribute to science. A thread of this ambivalence catches upon contemporary psychoanalytic debates, particularly with their question of "What is a clinical fact?" I turn to these debates, suggesting their relevance to our own conflicts in knowing education. By way of introduction my claim is that a pedagogical fact is a construction for thinking about the emotional work of practice. Ricoeur's (2004) discussion on history, memory, and forgetting influences the views I develop here because he is grappling with a philosophical problem in representing experience and historical reality. His consideration of Henri Bergson's idea of "a dynamic scheme" clarifies the conceptual tensions in my work. Like a clinical or pedagogical fact, a dynamic scheme is a representation of how ideas come to be memorable. In Bergson's (1920) words, "The idea does not contain images themselves so much as the indication of what we must do to reconstruct them" (160). While difficult to define, Bergson suggests that dynamic schemes are *feelings* useful for understanding the recollection of memories in professional contexts. His view is very close to the work of interpretations, and later in his essay Bergson states, "Interpretation, is therefore, in reality, a reconstruction" (170). A dynamic scheme represents reconstructive efforts that allow the idea its robust relations so that it can carry a commentary on the idea's history, its formulation, and on the efforts that lead to it. This discussion helped me to ask, can something like a pedagogical fact be used to reconstruct how we come to know ourselves in our pedagogical relationships?

I stay close to the problem of the emotional saliency ideas hold for us in education and in psychoanalysis to think about our efforts in thinking of others, a key dilemma when describing emotional qualities of learning made from trying to know in these two "impossible" professions.[2] Here, the question is no longer, "Yes, but is it research?" Paradoxically, however, we still require this question to comment upon how the very anxiety we create when trying to make our fields intelligible to ourselves and others signals both the danger of an original loss and its acting out and as urging the beginning work of new symbolization. We can think of anxiety over knowing as signaling what Freud (1914) called in one of his papers on psychoanalytic technique "working through." This work slowly reformulates old conflicts by interrupting unconscious repetitions. Working through requires patience as one considers how emotional states are made from and articulate the dilemma of trying to know the emotional geography and strange reach of one's narrative acts.

To draw out the conundrums of learning in both professions and consider the conceptual work that leans upon the emotional conditions of experiencing and commenting upon learning, I take a few detours through infancy and through institutional controversies. These thoughts are part of a larger study I call, "The Clinical Knowledge Project," which emerged from earlier research on the status of knowledge in learning and teaching undertaken with Alice Pitt. "The Difficult Knowledge Project" ended with a question of how to think about the differences between and confusion within obstacles to learning and obstacles to narrating learning. We speculated that these experiences of breakdown and repair in narrating learning could open awareness into the affective conflicts within narration and a glimmer of understanding into the subjective qualities of learning that are unrepresentable and felt as such (Pitt and Britzman 2003). In this chapter, I draw upon that narrative dilemma to suggest some ways to conceptualize the uses of emotional life in learning as the basis of constructing pedagogical facts that are other than an outcome of ideology or in the service of rules found in cognitive and neurological discussions. I stress the idea that tensions opened by pedagogical facts are literary and therefore call us to construct psychological significance in the process of coming to know. This orientation will take into account the institutional context of teaching and learning and thereby propose pedagogical facts as a needed paradox. Later I illustrate some critical dilemmas of training experienced in psychoanalytic institutes. I conclude with two examples in education on the emotional efforts in reconstructing learning relationships.

In the background of both fields of practice—that is, teaching and therapy—there is the double problem of how to represent its subjective force (including the subjectivity of its practitioners) and its therapeutic actions or mutative experience made from the work of representing and narrating learning. How do we characterize the significance of the emotional and intersubjective qualities carried by language and thinking? How might we grasp the immaterial meanings of a subjectivity which learns? Is describing an emotional experience comparable to knowing that experience? These phenomena of representing the representations of affect and idea can be called "clinical events."[3] The events are clinical in the sense that involved in the representation of learning is a description or diagnosis, an activity or therapy, and a theory or set of working assumptions on the nature, scope, efforts, and difficulties of change. The clinical also refers to an environment, or a transitional space, and so, a container made from some theory and belonging to those involved. I focus on clinical events from the perspective of their activity, which is to say, their activity of therapeutic representation and therapeutic action.[4] And, to read clinically, one learns how difficult it is to tolerate, from different sides, the problem of conveying emotional significance from this needed struggle.

How may we communicate through interpretations, observations, and speculations what we think is going on, what could have gone on, and what hasn't occurred but that still affects us because it is absent? Are there things we understand about the activity of learning and teaching that inform how we go about learning and teaching and then become useful to recognizing their vicissitudes and our work of transformations? These questions may also supply the framework of theory and impetus for practice. Our answers may be idiomatic but also thematic and theoretical, leading to good enough generalities. In education and psychoanalysis, a fact would then contain and communicate conceptualizations of how and why practice and theory may or may not work in a particular way, and it would also affect our efforts in reconceptualizing learning and teaching events. A pedagogical fact would not work as prolepsis; that is, a fact cannot assume the features of an already accomplished thing that is prior to the event's unfolding and that can anticipate its future. Rather, a fact would be a construction on the nature of the developing pedagogical relation. A fact would proceed from these clinical events and would be marked by an experience of latency and deferral. It would be an *after-fact* that may then found a subsequent story of origin or a narrative fiction of development. It would lead to further the work of clarification.

What a pedagogical fact is may be interpreted with great irony. Otto Kernberg (1996) took this approach in "Thirty Methods to Destroy the Creativity of Psychoanalytic Candidates." He was pointing to institutionally induced learning inhibitions, or the ways institutional design forecloses, from whatever side, creative efforts and autonomy. The irony is that what Kernberg noticed is true, namely, that schools have a way of inhibiting creativity in learning and that if teachers themselves are inhibited through institutional design, this helplessness will be passed on to their students.[5] Here we have another quality of a pedagogical fact: It can be used to identify the fault lines or vulnerable grounds of learning and teaching and then aid in understanding how conflicts are passed around from teacher to student and then back to the teacher.

## Freudian Slips, Science, and Infants

"What is a pedagogical fact?" began with a Freudian slip. I first typed: "What is a pedagogical feat?" Perhaps I really did wonder if it is a feat, when the topic is pedagogy, to make a fact. Psychoanalysis teaches us to love beginnings, mistakes, and our accidents so much so that we try to discern their emotional geography and their logic, wishes, object relations, anxieties, and defenses. This dynamic scheme of the Freudian slip can only be approached through the play of interpretation.

My slip allows me to suggest three related dilemmas pedagogical facts contain, all under the psychoanalytic idea that a pedagogical fact will be affected by what it tries to influence and will repeat, through variation, the very problem it attempts to think. These dilemmas are anxiety, epistemological uncertainty, and the transference. Samuel Weber (2000) characterizes these conflictive processes well in his study of Freud. Weber analyzed "how Freud's writing and thinking become progressively caught up in what they set out primarily to describe and elucidate. Such involvement of the observer and the observed contrasts with the efforts of most scientific or scholarly texts to keep their subject matter at a safe distance" (1). Except in psychoanalytic inquiry, there is no safe distance because safety depends upon intersubjective and intrapsychic dynamics. Indeed, a curiosity is maintained toward the question of why boundaries are so fragile and may need defense. It can then comment on how narration itself, on its way to emotional significance, is subject to repeating, to resistance, to defense, and to unconscious wishes.

Before discussing the anxieties that underlie my Freudian slip, it is worth saying a bit more about Weber's sense that most science and scholarly texts wish for a safe distance from its object by trying to think with the infant's thoughts, or with a premature dating of how objectivity is even established. My punch line is that within the desire for the objective, something infantile remains. I may be skipping ahead here, but it occurs to me that if I am to say something about a pedagogical fact, I must acknowledge a set of pressures from pedagogical science and its insistence upon "the safe distance" of objectivity though measurement. Along with many child analysts, I want to point out that objectivity is an existential and emotional problem for the infant, the child, the adolescent, the adult, and the elder—everyone—because it has to do with trying to know "reality as such" or all that exists without us. The philosopher Kant (1787/1965) warned us about the thing-in-itself: We cannot know it directly, even as we can think its existence. This knowledge may know its own limits. But it cannot overcome them.

Winnicott (1945/1992) dates the infant's beginning sense of objectivity to around six months of age, and this objectivity is made from the caregiver's actions with the infant. By sense of objectivity he means the infant may sense its own integration, be aware of other people and objects, and begin to grasp the qualities of time and space. Winnicott is also interested in what he calls "primitive emotional development" before the age of six months and knows the difficulty of trying to convey in theory the infant's mind in psychological terms. He considers the development of understanding both objectivity and subjectivity an emotional achievement. And while Winnicott sees external reality as "putting a brake" on phantasy, he also sees that if subjectivity has tremendous value "it is so alarming and magical that it cannot be enjoyed except as a parallel to the objective" (153). I think he means that in our beginnings, in our infancy, we sense, very mistakenly but with deep commitment that we do in fact create the objects that appear before us, that those hallucinations actually work. This is magical thinking, or omnipotence that contributes to a sense of confidence. It is a gift that the Other bestows. The mother calls forth and addresses the infant's illusions. And the good enough mother sustains this paradox of illusion for a while in order for infants to create the world they will find. Notably, Winnicott also links this illusion to the beginning of becoming a self who may then be interested in something like science when he writes:

> . . . it is a mother's job to protect the infant from complications that cannot yet be understood by the infant and to go on steadily providing the simplified bit of the world which the infant, through her, comes to know. Only on such a foundation can objectivity or scientific attitude be built. (153)

There is a sense that the good enough mother will not mind spoon-feeding the infant bit by bit. Winnicott suggests that reality, in the form of interpretations, can only be taken in by small doses. And this sustains the view that because learning, like interpretation, involves both illusion and disillusion, the activities of learning are slow and developmental, requiring both frustration and creativity and illusion and disillusion.

Few of us may try to trace the question of objectivity to our infantile origins, and I'm not sure that Weber had this in mind when he suggested how psychoanalytic thinking breeched the boundaries of science as safe distance. Yet Winnicott's sense of where science emerges—between the mother and infant—and sense that what is first established between them is a transitional space of play, of illusion, and of gradual disillusion brings us to the conditions and intimate relations that make up subjectivity and objectivity. Our arguments over what usually constitute science do not include, within its ground of possibilities, emotional needs (as opposed to just emotions) that must be accepted and understood for something like reality to be established. Nor do we typically understand how the early meeting of these emotional needs for omnipotence and the sustenance of illusion, at least for a little while, become the basis for thinking objectively. To keep something at a distance means that it must have, at first, been very close. This wavering proximity is another dilemma for the pedagogical fact.

While Winnicott sketches the three dilemmas of anxiety, epistemological uncertainty, and the transference in our earliest beginnings, these conundrums belong to pedagogical facts. The dilemma of my anxiety is used as a shortcut to describe a terrible anticipation of danger that invokes yet another difficulty of determining from where the danger emanates and what the loss may entail. Even to raise the question of a pedagogical fact is to become caught in some sticky institutional pressures, some obsessional mandates and views of accountability that usually defend empirical proof as the measure of truth and the worthiness of research. There is an expectation that one can produce from our efforts, observable, stable, and repeated results in others. The wish is that they show us what we did through their improvement of test scores. Now this rather bald statement must eschew the first pedagogical fact that, while intersubjectivity, dependency, and phantasy are the conditions for learning, the psychical consequences of having to be human are defended against with efforts to control, isolate, and measure our separateness. This may be why requirements for accountability feel so heavy handed, unimaginative, authoritarian, constraining, inhibiting, and prosecutory. This is how anxiety feels.

In the language of psychoanalysis, institutional discourse of accountability comes from the profession's superego and its demands (Reeder 2004). Superego anxiety exacts the ego defenses of idealization and disparagement; the professional superego demands perfection and guilt, thereby foreclosing the problem that makes these requirements so harsh, namely, that learning occurs through dependency and the slow work of finding and creating significance in that learning relation.

The dilemma of anxiety is also associated with the distinctively uncertain features or qualities of a "fact" in both education and psychoanalysis. An epistemological uncertainty emerges from our current preoccupation with differences between history and representation, theory and practice, and with determinism and hermeneutics (Ricoeur 2004). Is a fact something that is found or made? Does it come from theory or practice? Relatedly, and for some time, we have been trying to situate the significance and work of modernity and postmodernity in education and in psychoanalysis, where relativism, pluralism, culture, and democracy conflict with one another and where, when trying to characterize knowledge, identity, and events in the world, we now confront the incitements of discourse, indeterminacy, incompleteness, and overdetermination that cause us to doubt the veracity of our claims and that give us the gift of skepticism. Within these differences, there may be no such thing as a fact unencumbered by the debates that negate its existence and to which it must then respond. In this way, and akin to Winnicott's (1952/1992) surprising utterance *"There is no such thing as a baby"* (99) because a baby always involves a world of object relations, actual people, and material goods, there is no such thing as a fact, because it requires an apparatus that provides a set of relations and meeting points needed for further contact. A fact requires and calls forth a thinker. Otherwise, an isolated fact can appear disembodied, as in what Bion (1994) called "a thought without a thinker" (83).[6]

A third dilemma that pedagogical facts contain concerns the problem of emotional relations that sustain our attachment to others. In psychoanalysis, the emotional basis of relations to the world of others is organized through "the transference" which simply refers to how we see ourselves in others and the wishes and conflicts this projected commonality entails. I use the transference in two ways. First, the transference highlights how parts of the self or aspects of old experience are projected into the meanings of new events. Here, the transference works in the service of continuity and sameness and represents the interaction of the past in conceptualizations of the present. Any pedagogical fact must pass through and accommodate the teacher's education on three historical planes: the teacher's childhood where learning and teaching are first experienced; the teacher's tertiary education where hopes and fears of practice are made; and the teacher's understanding of the relation between these two experiences while teaching others. There will be arguments over the status of practice and theory but also general conundrums on what knowing something is founded upon, experiencing the displacements of projections and identifications, and glimpsing uncanny feelings of repetition of conflicts. A second meaning of the transference focuses on the presence of current affects such as love, hate, and envy exchanged between people. The transference carries the vicissitudes of love and hate in our current affective states that are a part of present conflicts. A pedagogical fact, then, is also a commentary on an object relation made from the transference of experience into conceptual investments. Put slightly differently, these subjective thoughts require a thinker.

I think I can accommodate these dilemmas of anxiety, epistemological uncertainty, and the transference with the idea that a pedagogical fact is not something that one teaches to others. Nor is it a preventive measure that can protect us from pedagogical meltdowns, teaching accidents, teacher-inspired failure, or curricular disappointments. A pedagogical fact can be the means to notice breakdowns in meanings, repetitions, missed experiences, and learners and teachers missing in action. As a construction, these pedagogical facts as such cannot fix things, but they can affect how experience is interpreted, analyzed and repaired. As I am using it here, a fact is not a foundation for the building blocks of action but an experiment to be used for thinking about what is occurring or has already happened. By keeping in mind some good enough understandings of the context of learning and teaching, a pedagogical fact, however mythic and speculative, may provide a container for thinking about problems of "difficulty," "resistance," "not learning," and "impossibility." A pedagogical fact is a work involving and being transformed by "unknowable" and "elusive" qualities of subjectivity and intersubjectivity. My approach to constructing a pedagogical fact tries to respect the indeterminacy of knowledge and its ethical failings, the problem of loss and not learning, the question of anxiety in learning and teaching, and the possibility that this emotional experience of knowing the limits of knowledge and of intersubjectivity matters to how we carry on. Perhaps this, too, is a feat.

## Pedagogical Facts, Clinical Events

An archive of pedagogical facts can be found in the work of Felman (1992) who brings into conceptual tension traumatic history and the pedagogy of learning from this trauma. Felman is interested in what it means to learn from history through literature, poetry, and testimonials, all genres that are composed from subjective and speculative worlds and are needed to say something significant about understanding experiences of being in the world with others. In her teaching of testimonial texts on historical catastrophes to students at Yale University she says explicitly (which I read as a paradox that always lives within any pedagogical fact) that there can be no learning without a crisis, but it is not the crisis that ushers in any learning. A third term is needed. Someone must be there to understand what is going on in the class. Felman hopes this someone can be a teacher provided that the teacher assumes authority, by which she means the authority of a signification, the capacity to digest the indigestible and return in smaller doses, the conditions that may allow thinkers to think their thoughts. This delicate undertaking for constructing meaning does not supply what is to be understood but only new conditions that then lead to the work of signification. Felman's questions startle. She begins with the problem of not learning and not wanting to know, each a clinical event. She asks:

> Is there a relation between crisis and the very enterprise of education? . . . To put the question even more audaciously and sharply: Is there a relation between trauma and pedagogy? In a posttraumatic century, a century that has survived unthinkable historical catastrophes, is there anything that we have learned or that we should learn about education, that we did not know before? Can trauma *instruct* pedagogy, and can pedagogy shed light on the mystery of trauma? Can the task of teaching be instructed by clinical experience, and can the clinical experience be instructed, on the other hand by the task of teaching? (1)

When Felman raises the question of clinical experience, I think she may assume its background: That from the experience of the clinic, clinical knowledge is made and found. In a recent paper coauthored with Pitt (Britzman and Pitt 2004) on the qualities of clinical knowledge, we wrote: "Clinical knowledge is not an apparatus but the thinking of it" (357). Clinical knowledge is both an object and the means to affect its own qualities of experience and understanding. It is not something to be applied to another, but rather the case study of clinical practice from which clinical knowledge is constructed, presents a mode of relationality—the analyst's practices and thoughts on her work as she goes about trying to encounter the particular facts of clinical work. I want to suggest here that these efforts also characterize the work of the teacher. There are many ideas to consider, but generally to read clinically one learns how difficult it is to tolerate, from different sides, the problem of having to learn by conveying emotional significance needed to digest psychological knowledge. This clinical view highlights a literary knowing that reaches the recesses of one's emotional world of learning for the purpose of representing emotional reality to the self and Other.

Representing emotional meaning, of course, occupies and creates the psychoanalytic setting. Yet articulating the particular sense of emotional knowing in terms of its underlying structures by way of the question "What is a clinical fact?" is deeply debated. It carries trepidation, conflict, and conviction; for many psychoanalysts it is counterintuitive to claim something like a fact when the exploration of a working analysis is one of subjectivity and filled with such immaterial objects as phantasies, mishearing, dreams, and symptoms. Even here there would be something like a common agreement to the following fact of Jean Laplanche (1999): "The work of the analysand in the analysis is both determined and free" (164). This clinical fact as a dynamic scheme—that others are there, that the analysand brings a history that is conscious and unconscious, that the analyst listens and points to the smallest thing, that there will be resistance and defense, that dreams will be narrated and associated with—will be subject to further interpretation. Laplanche anticipates the tension with his view of psychoanalysis: "Analysis is, first and foremost," he writes, "a method of deconstruction (ana-lysis), with the aim of clearing the way for a new construction, which is the task of the analysand" (165).

Whereas Laplanche focuses on the aim of analysis, Edna O'Shaughnessy's (1994/1997) descriptive language considers the "here and now" of the analysis or the relation that inaugurates, finds, or creates, a clinical fact. She suggests three of its qualities: "plurality, subjectivity and the immateriality of psychological phenomenon" (33). This last aspect, immateriality, holds two different ideas. One idea comes from Freud's plea about the peculiar nature of listening to unconscious wishes and phantasies. Freud (1911) can barely get this into a sentence: "We must never allow oneself to be misled into applying the standards of reality to repressed psychical structures, and on that account, perhaps, into undervaluing the importance of phantasies in the formation of symptoms on the grounds that they are not actualities . . ." (225). In other words, psychical reality has its own logic, and to try to understand this particular reality with criteria from external reality will be of no help. One can, however, use psychical reality as a means for understanding. A second idea on the qualities of immateriality focuses upon the intimate nature of the analytic encounter: There are only words, and the exploration of psychical life is not an action in the world but a reflective effort of inquiry, research, and emotional relating. Words, however, will carry misunderstanding, mishearing, and be subject to bad timing. There is also, O'Shaughnessy points out, "an anxiety of knowing with its inbuilt risk of being wrong" (36). Fallibility leads me to suppose a clinical fact may allow for the fact of mistakenness and that the fact itself may be mistaken.

How these mistaken facts come about is constitutive of the conditions from which something like a fact may be noticed to become the grounds for a working analysis. A mistaken fact is one that cannot be used, and not being able to use a fact is also a dilemma. Robert Caper (1999) identified three qualities of emotional states that compose a clinical fact: a sense of isolation in intimate relations, or an awareness of the separateness of individuals when working together; an aesthetic conflict, where an interpretation electrifies both the sublime and a conflict within its significance and use; and an awareness of one's role in creating emotional states. However, in both education and in psychoanalysis, recognition of these intersubjective conditions is neither automatic nor apparent. Indeed, much will occur to ignore and forget them. There will be resistance to implication, a desire to be unencumbered by the unknowable Other, a passion for ignorance, and censorship, repression, or resistance to the erotic ties these emotional states depend upon and animate.

The intersubjective and intrapsychic qualities of emotional states pose intimate difficulties. Because emotional states repeat in and can be an obstacle to their narration, there is no agreement how clinical facts may even exist. Just two small examples will help move my discussion along, both of which have to do with the nature of relationality in the analytic couple. Jurgen Reeder (2004, 32) has argued that new knowledge may allow for new phantasies, but the only fact relevant to psychoanalysis is the paradox that the Other is always beyond the reach of the analyst's knowledge. From this mystery there can be made "a faith in the Other" (33) so that, over time, meaningful relations can be constructed from this faith. And while Freud (1900) is not directly referenced, I am reminded of his thoughts on what he called "the navel" of the dream, a spot that cannot be touched by interpretation and understanding and where the dream "reaches down into the unknown" (525). Indeed, the limit of knowledge is that we cannot have absolute meaning. There will be literary excess, so at times, interpretation will turn against itself, resist insight, and be incapable of any therapeutic action. Allowing for this aporia may also be why Reeder distinguishes knowledge, which he places in the realm of facts and content, from knowing, which refers to the realm of dispositions or "a capacity for saying and doing" (251). Knowing is an act of faith. And much of this faith depends upon a desire to tolerate conflictive aspects of knowledge, points of ontological insecurity made into epistemological insecurity. This idea may be traced back to Freud's (1911) discussion on thinking, where he called thinking "an experimental form of acting" (221), able to contain, as opposed to acting out, internal conflicts as material for thinking. Reeder, however, does not move to thinking but to another effort—acts of faith which are also experimental. One does not know what will happen with an act of faith between people.

A second example of relationality that affects the composition of a clinical fact has to do with the transference. Most analysts will agree about the fact of the transference as the grounds of therapy—that the analysand will communicate a history of communication in the form of free associations and that the analyst will listen to parts of that communication as a commentary upon the present analytic relationship. There are so many detours to take into account when trying to exchange meaning with, as Freud (1911, 225) put it, the "neurotic currency" of psychical reality. The fact of transference, however, does not foreclose the disputes as to what the transference actually carries. These are the obstacles in learning and the obstacles to narrating learning. What exactly is transferred? Debates are ongoing, and Laplanche's (1999) idea contains some of the difficulty of knowing the transference: "Psychoanalysis is a method of free association polarized by the transference" (162). Freedom and need charge the efforts of communication and association, and this polarization catches upon libidinal wishes and defenses that communication also carries.

Even with my tentative approaches to the terms of a clinical fact, there still must be objections made if we only think of a fact from the vantage of empirical methods that represent facts as stable entities where idea is adequate to object and can be repeated by others. Or if we think of a clinical fact only through positivism or realism, other intimate difficulties emerge with the idea of a clinical fact. A clinical fact is made from what O'Shaughnessy (1997, 44) considers an "amalgam" of many subjective categories such as the analysand's private world, the analyst's emotional experience in the analytic setting, observable data, and the discourse of the unconscious. Poetically, a clinical fact will be "a view from some-where" (44). Because this amalgam is also conflictive and poetic, it will hold, from the private world, much that is also unknown, speculative, fan-tastic, and mythic. These facts have also been termed "immaterial facts" by Caper (1988), "theoretical understandings" by Ruth Riesenberg-Mal-colm (1997), and "selective facts" by Bion (1994, 72). Bion's understand-ings of "selected facts" stress their emotional qualities used to lend coher-ence to confusing scenes: "The selected fact is the name of an emotional experience, or a feeling of discovery, of coherence . . ." (Grinberg et al. 1975, 40). Riesenberg-Malcolm (1997) distinguishes an analytic fact from a pseudofact: "In my opinion, a clinical fact happens in the session and is expressed in the relationship between patient and analyst. It is the ana-lyst's theoretical understanding of aspects of this relationship at any given moment, when the analyst believes it to be reasonably correct . . ." (51). There is, in this view, a timing to the creation of clinical fact but also deep conceptualization when feelings of being understood meet with feelings of understanding. Such containment also holds qualities of the unknown, in-cluding doubts of one's own authority. To raise the question, "What makes psychoanalysis psychoanalytic?" is also to confront, more intimately, an anxious authority: "What right do I have to interpret another?"

We can ask of education, "What makes pedagogy pedagogical?" Here we are interested in reconstructing qualities of relations and their condi-tions that allow for interpretations, for characterizations of experiences that allow for insight, and for clarification of the dilemmas made from rec-ognizing and understanding pedagogical relations. Pedagogy may become pedagogical when it conveys both the conditions of learning and a theory of learning that can then provide the means for new relations with knowl-edge and other people. Yet this view also touches upon the practitioner's dilemma: "How do I know what I am doing and when do I know this?" A clinical fact, as Roy Schafer (1997) suggests, contains the importance of the practitioner's questions in order to convey the idea that one is working well. And by this he means only that one is aware that such clinical facts are story lines, still subject to conflict, to interpretative debates, and to the unconscious wish. In this way, a clinical fact may be flexible enough to take on its irony and then move thinking closer to literary truths, or the complexity of affective narratives.

Caper (1999), whom I introduced earlier, takes a different approach by linking clinical facts to the achievement of having one's own mind. His interest is in what makes for a working analysis and what is the basis for interpretation of emotional states when emotional states—conveyed through the transference and counter-transference—are the means for an interpretation. The fact may be simple but constructing it is not, and this leads Caper to suggest "a simple clinical psychoanalytic fact is a creature of a complex apparatus and a lot of theory" (47). Even then, Caper concludes, there is so much indeterminacy, insecurity, and anxiety over putting into words what a psychoanalyst does and what words do to a psychoanalyst. Caper's idea, however, is that a clinical fact made in the analytic setting emerges from the analyst and the analysand becoming aware of two dimensions of emotional states—that they care about something and that there are states of mind which convey more than one knows. These understandings begin with recognizing the contribution and role each person plays for there to be a mind at all. A clinical fact, then, is a responsibility that ushers in a new responsibility: A clinical fact must be subject to interpretation which subjects itself to the renewal of the work of signification.

## Some Pedagogical Facts

I have questions about how to listen to the unconscious—my own and that of the Other—and what this listening means in relation to the transference and its interpretation. How does one learn to speak in that language when there are so many disputes in the field of psychoanalytic writing and when its Freudian beginnings are so criticized by the field itself? These questions belong to the realm of technique and its theories but also to experiences with one's own personal analysis, clinical supervision, therapeutic practices, and discussions with others interested in these matters. And in much of what I read, there is a large anxiety over the basis of psychoanalytic practice and what is actually important to believe in the analytic setting. These debates are also found in education where we wonder and argue over the relation between technical knowledge and its theoretical framework. Another commonality is how easy it is to forget that acts of faith are also the grounds of learning how one learns. And, while there has been much discussion in the field on the status of theory in the analytic practice, there has not been much debate on what theory means to the analyst. This is also the case in education. Lear (2003) understands the dilemma of psychoanalysts this way: "So, how could a communication *about* therapeutic action be part *of* the therapeutic action?" (17). Here then is a new meeting of education and psychoanalysis, not just as two separate fields but as sharing a problem of representing education itself.

In the field of a psychoanalysis, as soon as teaching and learning become the topic, avalanches of childhood anxieties return as do phantasies of how learning occurs. Freud (1919) did not settle the matter of learning within psychoanalytic education, except to point out two kinds of learning: learning from a psychoanalysis and learning about a psychoanalysis. He felt the best insight into one's education for the analyst was one's own analysis, and, while he did write technique papers that are still being read today, Freud left it to others to grapple with the building of psychoanalytic learning institutes. During World War II, the British Psychoanalytical Society almost split apart over "The Controversial Discussions" between the Anna Freudians and the Kleinians (King and Steiner 1991). It turns out that within the question of psychoanalytic technique, a key difficulty was in specifying the nature of education for the analysts and what learning psychoanalytically can mean (Britzman 2003a).

In a different context, after World War II, French psychoanalytic training institutes were continually at war over the nature of the analyst's education and when one can say that one is, indeed, an analyst. Jacqueline Rose's introduction to Moustapha Safouan's (2000) critique and proposal for psychoanalytic training begins with a key dilemma: Psychoanalytic institutes, Rose points out, may not tolerate their own psychoanalysis. Working within a Lacanian frame, Safouan offers a radical deconstruction of institutional life:

> The analytic act is something else. *In principio*, in the beginning was the act. It is born, not of a form of power to be actualized, but of nothing, *ex nihilo*. It is an act which founds itself on nothing whatsoever; it is its own foundation. It rests on, comes with, and brings no guarantee. (Cited in Rose 2000, 44)

So here is the foundationless act of being where all the identifications that secure the ego to give us purpose and the figure of the subject-sup-posed-to-know cannot justify our existence. What's left is nothing, the only way to begin anew. Similarly, Bion (1975) links the question of new beginnings to the analyst's "capacity . . . to tolerate (respect) his own discoveries without having to believe they are of general significance or interest" (1). In both cases, there is a call to relinquish identifications with institutions, with professional superegos, and with narcissistic sat-isfactions made from having omnipotent timeless facts. We are left with the question of uncertain being and meeting the unknown without hav-ing to secure institutional authority.

For anyone interested in the unconscious, then, new problems emerge because psychical reality may not be judged by ordinary measures of con-sciousness and logic. This love of the unconscious really does something unexpected to the institutional education of psychoanalysts. Rose (2000) has put it marvelously: "the unconscious . . . repeatedly empties all ut-terances of their authority. No one 'can give the reasons for their reasons' (they do not know whether the reasons they give constitute all their rea-sons, and there is no ultimate reason for their reasons, or whether known or unknown)" (42). In other words, if the unconscious is its own reason and cannot know its own grounds, just as representation cannot know its own activity of metabolization, then an education that centers this paradox must also be prepared to engage displacement and connotation in terms of its psychical consequences, its defenses, and its resistance to insight. And this approach renders education interminable.

Many clinical and pedagogical facts follow if one tries to empty out institutional authority and its professional superego demands and engage and be affected by the authority of signification, or a respect for the force of meaning made from the work of making insight into one's desire to work with others. Below is a summary of some clinical/pedagogical facts made from the arguments of this book. They are formulated, although not in any particular order, to support exploration into and sustain curios-ity for the emotional workings of learning and not learning.

—Knowledge will carry a wish for knowledge and a phantasy as to how it will be learned. A pedagogical fact will try to "communicate what cannot be shown" (Reeder 2004, 131).

—A pedagogical fact will be caught up in the very dynamic it com-poses. It will be "a view from somewhere" (O'Shaughnessy 1997, 44). The fact may be a rule or an exception to itself and therefore will reach into the poetic.

—There is no learning without the transference, but the transference is an obstacle to and act of faith within learning.

—The teacher/the analyst is the "keeper of the analytic [or pedagogical] setting" (Reeder 2004, 139).

—A pedagogical fact will sustain the desire for free association.

—A pedagogical fact will affect the teacher just as a clinical fact affects the analyst. It is not to be used on others and so will invite only the teacher's experimental actions or thinking that may link affect and idea to conception and realization.

—A pedagogical fact will be affected by the very experience it tries to grasp. It will pass through the transference and, at times, stall right there, leaving no safe distance between obstacles to learning and obstacles to narrating learning.

—A pedagogical fact will emerge from analytic progress and so will help in reapproaching with greater creativity and freedom the sources of difficulty. It will open, what Loewald (1960/2000) called, "the new discovery of objects" (225).

## Two Clinical Examples of Learning Pedagogical Facts

The immaterial pedagogical facts noted above can now be used to magnify and interpret the emotional worlds that compose learning and not learning. I use two examples that blur the boundaries between not knowing and knowing and between teaching and learning. These examples emphasize a problem in my presentation, namely application, or what happens to ideas in practice and why demands to apply learning may also be a defense against learning and not learning. This also means that practitioners must be able to study the various meanings of our demands for knowledge to settle epistemological uncertainty, anxiety and the transference. The first example is drawn from Winnicott's (1950/1996) discussion on trying to learn the field of psychology. The other example comes from an unexpected conversation with a student teacher that occurred after a talk I gave. While I did not know this student, except for this exchange, I have come to consider this example as supervision on demand. What strikes me about these examples is their capacity to illustrate how a history of learning both repeats with each new endeavor and provokes the means for working through the emotional qualities animated when trying to know the Other as one bumps up against the otherness of one's knowing. Here, "the Other" refers to both an encounter with new knowledge and understanding other people trying to learn knowledge. Understanding these two relations—knowledge as Other and people as Other—composes the dilemmas of the teacher's work. And this encounter with the double unknown animates defenses of not wanting to know and, perhaps, a curiosity toward the unknown in the self. There will be, then, epistemological uncertainty, anxiety, and the transference.

In a paper on teaching psychology in universities, Winnicott (1950/1996) identifies what can be thought of as two pedagogical facts: Students will pass through some stages of learning, which is to say, their relation to new material will be in flux, and they may move from their subjective experience of the material to wonder, too soon, about an idea's application on others. Winnicott observes that in first learning psychology, students will see it as useful only if it confirms their experience. So they will ask of the material, "Yes, but is it true?" Later, the question will transform to "Yes, but is it research?" These questions are not yet an act of faith but the testing of preconceptions. Then, they will try to apply it to others. If the psychology survives this ruthlessness, it will then be deemed worthy for learning. This is only their first sense; it is just the beginning of their relation to something new. And Winnicott will then see learning as beginning in anti-concern for the object. This view is difficult for all teachers who love their teaching objects.

The second pedagogical fact proceeds from the first idea that knowledge will be destroyed before it can be created. Rather than present the experiences of the stages of learning one carries out on the way to knowing, this second fact magnifies the existential problem of knowing psychology and the epistemological uncertainty, anxiety, and the transference this entails. The existential problem pertains to an emotional experience of confronting the limits of this knowledge and the position of the subject-supposed-to-know. In other words, understanding something about the mind's working does not help us with what to do with knowledge. Nor can it authorize our actions. Our second pedagogical fact contains the idea for recognizing self-contribution to the limits of the knowledge. Paradoxically, the self experiences a transformation because the knowledge learned is incomplete. Winnicott writes: "You can be taught how to proceed in a Juvenile Court case, but you cannot be taught how to cope with a child who is unhappy in a foster-home" (14). Procedures cannot help us with our feelings, and our feelings reference the incompleteness of procedures. Winnicott does help us out of this dilemma when he joins our two pedagogical facts: "Psychology does not try to teach you what to do when your friend needs your help. It can do a lot, however, toward enabling you to be more sure of yourself, to understand what is going on, to grow on experiences, to see where mistakes might have been made, to prevent distress and disasters" (15).

In a harried exchange with an undergraduate student in education, I was reminded of the depth of Winnicott's warning of the difficulty of learning when encountering new material; that is, of needing to doubt it before it can be used and of the emotional relations revitalized by and transformed within the taking in of new ideas. Anti-concern, splitting, and even hatred will begin this learning adventure. But this means that when we think of learning new material, we are speaking of selves learning something about the emotional relations that both make objects and are made by objects. This student of education was involved in her student teaching in an elementary classroom and had a burning question although, in much of the interaction, the question seemed burnt by anxious feelings and some guilt. She excitedly referred to our Education Faculty's insistence that student teachers provide their students with "rubrics." And she saw this as a demand for certainty: Student teachers were to give these rubrics to their students so that both would be clear on their learning responsibilities and carry them out without difficulty.

But she had a problem with handing over this rubric. She explained that when she was a child, she never had a rubric, didn't need one, and still knew what was expected of her. Now, she was expected to give one to each of her students. And she felt she was babying them by doing so. She said, "Giving them a rubric is treating them like babies." I said I was sorry and that while I knew that in our Faculty some believed rubrics were important, I had managed to avoid them and did not know what they were. But rather than explain them to me, I continued, why not give me an example of what is bothering you so much? The example she gave was her frustration with having to hear a child repeatedly ask her, "Do we have to check our spelling?" This question bothered her because on the rubric she gave her students it demanded explicitly that students check their spelling. So not only was she angry at having to answer a question she already thought was settled, she was angry at even having to offer a rubric that reminded students to check their spelling. I could see there was little elbow room in how she was feeling. Both students and rubrics were persecuting her.

So far there are no acts of faith, only a persecutor superego. Her presentation of events underscores two different yet related dilemmas. One concerned the transference, posited as her memory, although it was difficult to see whose memory was the problem. As a child, no one ever had to remind this student teacher to check her spelling, and so in this logic there was something very wrong if others had to be reminded of something she always knew! Yet her thinking should be kept separate from her students' thinking. The problem was there were not separate minds and so, experiences she never had. The other dilemma emerges with the question of what it can mean to help others, even if that help includes reminding others about their work as learners. She felt she was babying the students by having to remind them to check their spelling. I thought it must have felt like spoonfeeding babies, although we both probably knew that babies do not care about spelling. Perhaps she felt they did not care or maybe she felt like a helpless baby because she was helpless in having to give them a rubric they could not use or even believe and because even the rules of the rubric were useless to her own sense of learning. I also wondered if this student noticed how there were others in the room with her, a room where her phantasies of a pristine childhood were being ruined, where her own keen desires to have a magical learning free of dependency and conflict were uncovered, and where her beliefs that one could know perfectly without having to learn were exposed. And there was still the thorny rubric which ruined a wish for knowledge without a teacher.

These are my interpretations, made from trying to understand the emotional reach of her distress, the ways epistemological uncertainty, anxiety and the transference may have unfolded. To clear the way for a new construction, to newly discover (old) objects, I said, "Well, I have a theory about spelling and you tell me what you think of it. I think that the only students who ask if spelling must be checked are students who already have trouble spelling correctly." With some surprise, she agreed. I then asked her what she might think now of their question given that she could consider there were students in her class with spelling troubles. She could not use that question at all. So I said, "I think that if students have trouble spelling they probably have trouble checking their spelling and to be reminded of checking their spelling is actually reminding them that they cannot spell, which they already know." She said, "Oh, they need my help." I said, "Yes. They are not babies you are spoiling by spoonfeeding them rubrics. You are their teacher and you will have to tolerate their struggle to learn, particularly during times when they say to you, 'Look here. You give me a rubric that you yourself do not need or believe in, or didn't need as a child. Can you help me without the rubric?'" We both seemed relieved.

This second example condenses a great deal about what I have been trying to suggest about a pedagogical fact as clearing the way for the reconstruction of our emotional efforts and the emotional significance that can then be made. Pedagogical facts are not rubrics but closer to Bergson's notion of dynamic schemes that allow for the recollection of practices in such a way that new efforts can be made. This student struck me as passionately concerned for what to do but caught between gratification and frustration, a common space of learning that Winnicott also noticed in his teaching of psychology. The tension was that this student had not yet thought about why she was so frantic and disappointed with her efforts, except to think that the students were failing babies, that she was not good enough as a teacher, and that even her faculty had betrayed her by demanding that she use something she could not tolerate. The rubric came to symbolize all these tensions, and her phantasy of the rubric transformed a good teacher to a bad teacher and then to a bad student. The conflict was passed around, took a detour through an idealized childhood, then stalled with the baby. I think this emotional complex needed to be sorted out for this student to begin to learn that the teacher, not the rubric, is the keeper of the pedagogical setting.

As Winnicott suggested, infancy is never so far away as one might hope and worrying about the failing baby is one clue. If infancy stands in for adult helplessness, animating the infantile side of the adult, the infant can also be a sign of new beginnings, provided that there is another since there is no such thing as only a baby. This student presented a question on the difference between obstacles in student learning and obstacles to narrating her learning as a new teacher. Until this difference could be explored, there could be no understanding of the teacher's emotional states needed for the development of a pedagogical fact. It was not until she was asked to think with another person that she could begin to glimpse how her idealized childhood defended against her present helplessness in learning a profession and in how needing help came to be viewed as a sign of weakness. Here is the transference, where the teacher's imagined childhood is projected into current events, usually when the teacher becomes nervous about what to do next. But also, until this student noticed that her own students' learning difficulties were not meant to throw her into epistemological uncertainty—were not meant to ruin her teaching self—but were meant to care about something, she could not understand just what her students were actually doing with that terrible question, "Do we have to check our spelling?"

These, of course, are my interpretations of the reconstruction of our interaction. Other views are welcome. However, I suspect that a pedagogical fact should give us some relief from anxiety in learning and teaching by sorting through the emotional congealment in educational relations. If a pedagogical fact cannot explain what happened in our teaching events, if it is not something to apply to others, constructing them may allow thinkers new approaches to familiar conflicts. In this way, a pedagogical fact may perform the work of a dynamic scheme, reminding us that practice also entails the recollecting of events in a way that may clarify understanding. I use the term clarification in the sense of containing the anxiety that is also a part of learning and so conceptualizing a pedagogical fact as lending some coherence to the work of trying to know. In the emotional clinic of education, a pedagogical fact might help teachers to tolerate and respect, without repeating the agony, the urgency of learning either psychology or listening to a needed question from a distraught student. Indeed, then a pedagogical fact can sustain the literary events of a novel education and contain some aesthetic conflicts that education must also encounter in order to affect its own procedures. In so doing, we might then conceptualize emotions in education as relational, as acts of faith, and as a resource that carries both complex and contradictory instructions, themselves the immaterial material for interpretative, literary claims.

# Notes

## Chapter One

1. This formulation of learning, from our difficult knowledge project, is discussed in Pitt and Britzman (2003).
2. The example of trying to write without writing is found in Marcel Bénabou's (1996) amusing text, *Why I have not written any of my books*. He writes of having trouble with language, paper, blank pages, childhood, lost sentences, jumbled drafts, flawed thinking, deadlines, not being able to stop reading, and the desire to write imaginary books. Readers are presented with a story of negation: of not writing books that he has continued to write.
3. Alan Bass's (1984) essay on psychoanalysis and Derrida begins with an autobiographical note that illustrates what lies beneath sublimation and what sublimation cannot sublimate. He speaks of his uneven development as professor of literature, as analysand and as learning to become an analyst. He asks and then parenthetically answers: "Will the practice of analysis be at all affected by the deconstructive readings of analytic theory? (You are accrediting the metaphysical opposition of theory and practice, of "text" and "reality," all the values they imply, the deconstructive reader says here) . . ." (66). His parenthetical answer is incomplete, repeating only what is left out, a story of his own unhappiness masked by a manic defense of

theory. Bass tells his readers that as a undergraduate he studied in France. Before leaving, his advisor warned him not to go crazy with structuralism. Bass sought therapy as well because he was unhappy. His therapist recommended an analysis and instead he went to France, losing himself in the euphoria of study and, in retrospect, "to a powerful transference" (68) with Derrida.

4. The title of Freud's essay "Analysis Terminable and Interminable" has been translated by Harald Leupold-Löwenthal (1991) as "Analysis Finite and Infinite." This translation stresses Freud's alliance with German romanticism and philosophy, and its association with Goethe's quatraim from *Sprüche in Reimen:*

> If thou wilt step into the infinite,
> Just explore every path in the finite.
> If thou will feast on the whole,
> Thought must seek the whole in the smallest.
> (cited in Leupold-Löwenthal 1991, 69)

5. There are so many ways to think about Freud's (1937) essay: from the vantage of Freud's illness and his despair over National Socialism; as a means to intervene the rigidity of analyst's formulations; as a defense of the life and death drives; as a call against developmental and adaptation goals; as a reminder of the need to understand psychoanalytic failures; as a reply to Ferenczi's complaints on his incomplete analysis with Freud; and as a critique of therapeutic ambitions. For a rich discussion of this essay from different views, see the edited volume by Sandler (1991).

## Chapter Two

1. Freud's (1912a) take on listening to analysands begins with the practical observation that analysts' memories are too limited to master all that is told to them. Listening, then, " . . . consists simply in not directing one's notice to anything in particular and in maintaining the same 'evenly-suspended attention' . . . in the face of all that one hears. In this way we spare ourselves a strain on our attention which could not in any case be kept up for several hours daily . . ." (111–112). The analyst's concentration, then, is the culprit for as soon as one focuses on something, it may only confirm what the analyst expects to find. But also, meaning is not coincident to the act of listening and listening then trails behind the speech.

2. Adorno's (1959/2001) lectures on Kant's *Critique of Pure Reason* continually repeat this Kantian mantra of the 'I think that accompanies all of my representations.' It is a phrase that advertises a constitutive problem of reason, what Adorno called "a mania for foundations" (52), where think-

ing proceeds by unifying itself with its concept and so produces the illusion of thinking as self-identical to the thought. Consciousness in this view is thought to give to its experience its unity. This raises the problem of where knowledge originates, a question reason can ask but cannot finally answer in any way that sustains the unity of the "I think." Adorno (1965/2000) continues this problem in his lectures on metaphysics where he argues that after Auschwitz the affirmative character of metaphysics is no longer possible and where the ethics of thinking begin when thinking can think against itself.

3. Freud's six papers on technique were written between 1911–1915, and comprise a series of recommendations to practitioners of psychoanalysis. Originally, Freud planned to write a total of twelve. The six, however, include: dream interpretation, thinking about the transference, beginning psychoanalysis, the difficulties of working through, and then further recommendations on the transference. The complex personal issues that precipitated Freud's discussions on these techniques can be found in his vast correspondence. While it is beyond the scope of this chapter to detail the psychoanalytic breakdowns that give rise to Freud's (1912a, 1912b) recommendations, it is worth noting that Freud hints at the personal conflicts the psychoanalytic practice stirs for the analyst in his correspondence with Ferenczi who seemed to be breaking all the rules, except, of course, the fundamental one.

The difficulty of holding to these recommendations can be observed in Freud's case studies and also in Ferder's (2004) discussion of Freud and his walk with Mahler. Ferder describes Freud's analysis of Princess Marie Bonaparte in 1925. Their relationship was one of colleagues and according to Bonaparte, Freud would speak about his worries to her. We know about Mahler's four-hour walk with Freud in 1910 from her notes recalling Freud's description of this walk and from some reminiscences of analysts who attended Freud's Wednesday night meetings (Sterba 1982).

4. Klein (1930) gives this term over to unconscious phantasy and how omnipotence allows phantasy its imposing qualities and the need for something like reality to be made:

> I pointed out that the object of sadism at its height, and of the desire for knowledge arising simultaneously with sadism, in the mother's body with its phantasied content. The sadistic phantasies directed against the inside of her body constitute the first and basic relation to the outside world and to reality. . . . As the ego develops, a true relation to reality is gradually established out of this unreal reality. . . . A sufficient quantity of anxiety is the necessary basis for an abundance of symbol-formation and of phantasy; an adequate

capacity on the part of the ego to tolerate anxiety is essential if anxiety is to be satisfactorily worked over (221).

5. Wilfred Bion (1997) begins with wild thoughts when he comments:
   If a thought without a thinker comes along, it may be what is a 'stray thought,' or it could be a thought with the wonder's name and address upon it, or it could be a 'wild thought.' The problem, should such a thought come along, is what to do with it. (27)

6. The Freud/Ferenczi correspondence spans three volumes of over 1,200 letters and telegrams. See Brabant et al. (1994), Falzeder and Brabant (1996), and Falzeder and Brabant (2000).

7. Ferenczi believed that mutual analysis would destroy the asymmetry of the analytic relation and so the analyst's authority. In his *Clinical Diary* he made this entry: "Certain phases of mutual analysis represent the complete renunciation of all compulsion and of all authority on both sides: they give the impression of two equally terrified children who compare their experiences, and because of their common fate understand each other completely and instinctively try to comfort each other. Awareness of this shared fate allows the partner to appear completely harmless, therefore as someone whom one can trust with confidence" (quoted in Hoffer 1996, 115).

8. For discussions of Ferenczi's life and his work, see Rachman (1997) and the edited volume of Rudnytsky et al. (1996).

9. Sigmund Freud had a rather uneven professional relationship with Havelock Ellis. In 1934, when Freud was seventy-eight, one of Ellis's graduate students, a twenty-eight-year-old Joseph Wortis entered a short analysis with Freud. Wortis wrote a description of his analysis with Freud and at times, the description reads like a battle of the titans, where Wortis seems caught between Freud and Ellis, specifically on the question of whether psychoanalysis is a science or art. See Wortis (1994).

## Chapter Three

1. Freud (1926) distinguished between realistic anxiety and neurotic anxiety, but posited the latter as "an unknown danger," a signal designating "a lack of an object" (165). Anxiety is animated by an expectation of a repetition of an earlier scene of helplessness. Its central feature as a relationship belongs to infancy: "Thus, the first determinant of anxiety, which the ego itself introduces, is loss of perception of the object (which is equated with loss of the object itself). . . . Pain is thus the actual reaction to loss of object, while anxiety is the reaction to the danger which that loss entails and, by a further displacement, a reaction to the danger of the loss of the object itself" (170). See also Freud (1933[1932]).

2.  The term "phantasy" connotes unconscious mental processes, pertaining to phantasies with or of a world of objects. The "ph" spelling is used to distinguish itself from "fantasy" that is associated with daydreams or literary genres. Moreover, in the work of Melanie Klein, phantasies are the beginning of thinking over instinctual conflict and so they are not viewed as a binary with reality.

3.  Laplanche (1989) describes self-representation as a creative act where, "the representative is 'not constrained by the restrictive demands of the real,' and that its 'essential quality is to bring about the possible' . . . [this] concerns the human being's capacity for self-symbolization" (84).

4.  While the concept of "third space" can be found in the postcolonial work of Homi Bhabha, it is also a term in object relations theory. It refers to the analytic area created between subjects but also to the analytic setting and the knowledge made there.

5.  In everyday language, the term "object" is often conflated with objectification. However, psychoanalytic vocabulary uses it as a technical term to associate a representation of the instinct (or a phantasy) with a representation of one's feelings toward actual others. Objects then, are not "the Other," although in phantasy they may take on the qualities of others. Objects are internal relationships of self and other. Felt within the self, these are called internal objects. If felt as outside, they are external objects. Originally, the object is bestowed by the self with a motivation before it is known.

6.  For a discussion on internalization that highlights subjection, see Butler (1997).

7.  See R. D. Hinshelwood's (1991) entry "Symbols in the Depressive Position" where he overviews the phases of recognizing a symbol as separate from the original object. This division, indeed, the qualities of difference, is necessary in Kleinian views because in the beginning, phantasy made from anxiety renders meaning terrifying and persecuting. Defenses against this profound helplessness include omnipotence, idealization, splitting, and projective identification. Klein (1946) called this early position "the paranoid-schizoid position." If these feelings are to be contained and worked through, the damaging phantasies incur some guilt and then lead to the urge to repair, what Klein saw as the "depressive position."

8.  Fanon's (1952/1986) view of psychoanalysis is notoriously difficult in that as a psychiatrist he was more than aware of its techniques and practices. Yet in his passionate exploration of the existential painfulness of racism in colonial contexts and the ways in which the figure of "the Black man" functioned as a phobic object, Fanon also argued passionately against any psychoanalytic generalization on subject formation and sexuality

for understanding the predicament of race, even as he himself depended upon some of its concepts. It is only in his discussions of his own clinical practices that one senses his gifts as a psychiatric clinician. See, for example, the chapter "Colonial War and Mental Disorders" in Fanon (1961/1991). For diverse views on the ambivalent status of the psychoanalytic in Fanon and the uses of ambivalence in cultural expression, see Read (1996), Fuss (1995), and Young-Bruehl (1996).

9. For a rich discussion on Du Bois's "double consciousness" and one that traces the ambivalence of split identifications, see Gilroy (1993).

10. The Oedipus complex refers to a phantasy relation children make to their parents, where one parent is loved while the other is considered a rival. Freud believed Oedipal feelings begin around the ages of 3–5 and the feelings are the emotional logic of the child. The resolution, if there is one, is that the child introjects the parents, accepting their prohibitions and their love. Freud called this resolution, the super-ego. Now internal, the parents form its nucleus. The identification with the more powerful parent comes under the category of identification with the aggressor.

11. For a psychoanalytic orientation to working with youth, see Aichhorn (1964).

## Chapter Four

1. The concept of "object," refers to one's feelings for things, people, and relationships. It may refer to a whole object or part objects. Klein derived this view from her observations of children playing with toys. She saw their passionate relation to these objects, where the toys became personified, had feelings for the child and were used as if they were alive with as many complex feelings as the child may project onto them. From these observations, Klein speculated that these projected feelings lived as objects in the mind of the child: These objects lived, died, and had the capacity to haunt and persecute. They could also be cared for. Paradoxically, objects contain concealed motivations, secrets, and minds of their own. There are, for Klein, good and bad objects, the first object being the mother's breast. And these objects are given life by or expressed through phantasy. Object relations refers to the to and fro projections and identifications, the love, hate, and ambivalence that phantasies carry. For further discussion, see Hinshelwood (1991).

2. I am using the term "archive" in two ways. The first references a storage place where the documents of life are cataloged and housed. The second meaning is psychical and existential in that it references the phenomena of our own mind as both memory trace and as affected by its impressions.

This archive has the capacity to register, be affected by, and metabolize impressions of the world, creating and altering memory and its workings. (See Bion 1961/1996). In this second dynamic meaning, the archive affects and is affected by its holdings. It also an economy dedicated to the drive to repeat (See Derrida 1996).

3.  Object relations theory begins with the view that from the beginning of our lives, the human is object seeking and object making and requires, for development, relations with others. Klein's idea is that from the beginning of life, the infant has an emergent psychological knowledge constituted from the anxiety of dependency and primal helplessness. This is not a knowledge that has words but rather is carried through feeling states that are projected into the world and identified with. One of the interesting paradoxes that Klein presents us with concerns the idea that while the human is object seeking, the objects carry the burden of the self's phantasies of good and bad.

4.  The drives (*tribe*) are a psychoanalytic metaphor used to speculate upon human motivations for life and death. Sometimes, the drives are spoken of as instincts, biological entities that attach to representations. When the drive finds a psychical representative, it becomes a psychological event. Drives are inner excitations that have a source, an aim, and an object and that seek release or bind excitations. Freud placed the drives somewhere between psyche and soma, and he saw the term as a frontier concept. The drives demand both notice and meaning, and Freud tried to use them as a way to characterize how psychical life drew its force, its motives, its susceptibility to the world, its capacity for representation, and its vicissitudes or transformations. Indeed, the drives are carried by psychical representations. In an important sense, the drives would be thought of as a speculation, as Freud only assumed their existence. Here is how Freud (1933) announced the conceptual problem of describing interior forces: "The theory of the instincts is so to say our mythology. Instincts are mythical entities, magnificent in their indefiniteness" (95).

## Chapter Seven

1.  These objections are not new when considering the teacher's illness. In fact they structure Jersild's (1955) study of the teacher's emotional life where he emphasized the centrality of anxiety and meaninglessness in education. Indeed, Jersild reads the history of educational theory as a history of anxiety.

    While Jersild reports on a study of anomie in teaching, Salzberger-Wittenberg et al. (1992) discuss issues in conceptualizing the teacher's emotional world. These authors invite reflection on emotional rhythm and its disruptions in teaching. They speak of missing students and lost opportunities, of overexcitement and boredom, and the teacher's rage, jealousy, envy. Theirs is a compendium of emotions, filling the situation of teachers as being a part of their emotional world. They also speak of typical experiences: rescue fantasies, over-helping, idealizing, loneliness, feelings of vengefulness and then guilt for carrying out a plan of revenge, outrage at one thing or another, and worries as to how they may be remembered. They write of painful disillusionment over not having what the profession seemed to promise: endless fulfilment. What teachers have lost, they suggest, is as significant as what teachers feel they have found.

2.  Here is where the work becomes difficult. Freud's (1915a) term for the symptom's displacement is the transference-neurosis: "an intermediate region between illness and real life through which the transition from one to the other is made. The new condition has taken over all the features of an illness, but it represents an artificial illness . . . [but also] . . . it is a piece of real experience . . . it is of a provisional nature" (154). The transference-neurosis is real because it feels real and to treat it as unreal is to place the transference-love into the work of phantasy. Its nature is provisional because the transference-neurosis is an analytic relation: past and present commingle without apparent reason, but also there is the analytic relation which calls these projections as commentaries on the relationship and addresses them. Because the self is also interested in change, more anxiety develops, and this new anxiety is what Freud may have had in mind when he noted it as "an artificial illness" which must be treated as it feels, that is, treated as real.

3.  The analyst taking responsibility for the analysand is also something Freud accepted. The responsibility is a lifting of blame but also a way to assure analysands that that someone will care for their distress. In his biography of Mahler, Feder (2004) recounts the story of Bruno Walter's consultations with Freud, which Walter relives in his autobiography. Walter was a composer and conductor with the Court Opera in Vienna. He was also Mahler's assistant and friend. In 1906, Walter developed arm paralysis and went to see Freud since no physical cause could be ascertained. Walter was afraid that he could no longer conduct. Freud advised him to forget about his arm and go on a vacation. The vacation relaxed Walter, but his arm was not cured. On the next visit Freud told Walter to continue conducting and that nothing bad would happen. But Walter was worried that he would freeze as he conducted. When Walter asked, "Can I take upon myself the responsibility of possibly upsetting a performance?" Freud replied, "I'll take the responsibility" (225). While as Feder notes, Freud's

cure was not miraculous, the issue of his willingness to relieve Walter of responsibility was. Walter was also impressed with Freud's humanity and recommended that his friend, Mahler, see Freud for a consultation. Given Walter's idea that psychoanalysis was the art of memory, what struck him most strangely was Freud's insistence that he try to forget his arm. What Walter did not forget was Freud's willingness to accept a responsibility that could never really be taken: "So by dint of much effort and confidence [in Freud], by learning and forgetting, I finally succeeded in finding my way back to my profession" (225).

## Chapter Eight

1. I now think of this 1996 American Educational Research Association panel as an echo of Winnicott's (1950/1996) paper on the problem of learning to teach psychology, "Yes, but How Do We Know It's True?" I'll have more to say on the uses of doubt in learning later. For purposes of full disclosure, I should also add that I was a member of this panel, invited to present poststructuralist views on research.

2. The idea of the impossible professions belongs to Sigmund Freud (1937): "It almost looks as if analysis were the third of those "impossible" professions in which one can be sure beforehand of achieving unsatisfying results. The other two, which have been known much longer, are education and government" (248).

3. Typically, the idea of "the clinic" has been limited to medical discourse and its capacity for normalization, a direction critiqued by Foucault (1975/2003). There is also a literary sense of the clinical, concerned with the question of therapeutic action found in literary studies such as Felman (1992), discussed later in this chapter. From another vantage, this literary direction composes the essays of Deleuze (1997) whose "critique et clinique" project begins with the supposition that writers may be read as proffering a diagnosis of the society's symptoms of disease and a therapeutic model for its curiosity toward founding new modes of existence. And finally, in education, supervision has a history of being conceptualized as "clinical supervision."

4. Throughout this chapter, I will be using psychoanalytic descriptions for immaterial phenomena. Therapeutic action is one example, although I cannot think of a comparable concept in education to connote the changes and transformations of the relationship itself that do occur in learning unless we stretch the concept of learning to include internal transformations. Loewald (1960/2000) describes therapeutic action as a "new discovery of objects": "I say new discovery of objects, and not discovery of new objects,

because the essence of such new object-relationships is the opportunity they offer for rediscovery of the early paths of the development of object relations, leading to a new way of relating to objects as well as of being and relating to oneself" (225). Such discoveries are made from a relation to new objects, like the analyst.

5. As an example, here is Kernberg's (1996) method number 28: "Fortunately, long experience has taught us that the hierarchical extension of the educational process into the social structure of the psychoanalytic society is easily achieved and can be most effective" (1038).

6. Bion's (1961/1996) theory of thinking begins with the understanding that phantasies comes before knowledge: "It is convenient to regard thinking as dependent on the successful outcome of two main mental developments. The first is the development of thoughts. They require an apparatus to cope with them. The second development, therefore, is of this apparatus that I shall provisionally call thinking. I repeat—thinking has to be called into existence to cope with thoughts" (179).

# Bibliography

Abadi, Sonia. (2001). "Explorations: Losing and Finding Oneself in the Potential Space." In *Squiggles and Spaces, Volume 1: Revisiting the Work of D. W. Winnicott*. Edited by Mario Bertolini, Andreas Giannakoulas, and Max Hernandez in collaboration with Anthony Molino. London: Whurr Publishers, pp. 79–87.

Adorno, Theodor. (1959/2001). *Kant's Critique of Pure Reason*. Edited by Rolf Tiedeman. Translated by Rodney Livingstone. Stanford, CA: Stanford University Press.

———. (1965/2000). *Metaphysics: Concepts and Problems*. Edited by Rolf Tiedeman. Translated by Edmund Jephcott. Stanford, CA: Stanford University Press.

Aichhorn, August. (1964). *Delinquency and Child Guidance: Selected Papers*. Edited by Otto Fleischmann, Paul Kramer and Helen Ross. New York: International Universities Press.

Albahari, David. (2004). *Götz and Meyer*. Translated by Ellen Elias-Bursa. London: Random House.

Appel, Stephen. (1999). "The Teacher's Headache." In *Psychoanalysis and Pedagogy*. Edited by Stephen Appel. Westport, CT: Bergin and Garvey, pp. 133–146.

Balint, Alice. (1954). *The Early Years of Life*. New York: Basic Books.

Bass, Alan. (1984). "The Double Game: An Introduction." In *Chances. Derrida, Psychoanalysis, and Literature*. Edited by Joseph H. Smith and William Kerrigan. Baltimore, MD: Johns Hopkins University Press, pp. 66–85.

———. (1998). "Sigmund Freud: The Question of *Weltanschauung* and of Defense." *Psychoanalytic Versions of the Human Condition: Philosophies of Life and Their Impact on Practice.* Edited by Paul Marcus and Alan Rosenberg. New York: New York University Press, pp. 412–446.

Bénabou, Marcel. (1996). *Why I Have not Written Any of My Books.* Translated by David Kornacker. Lincoln, NE: University of Nebraska Press.

Bergson, Henri. (1920). "Intellectual Effort." In *Mind-Energy: Lectures and Essays.* Translated by H. Wildon Carr. London: Macmillan and Co., pp. 152–188.

Bersani, Leo. (1986). *The Freudian Body: Psychoanalysis and Art.* New York: Columbia University Press.

Bick, Ester. (1962/1996). "Child Analysis Today." In *Melanie Klein Today: Developments in Theory and Practice, Volume 2: Mainly Practice.* Edited by Elisabeth Bott Spillius. London: Routledge, pp. 169–176.

Bion, Wilfred. (1961/1996). "A Theory of Thinking." In *Melanie Klein Today: Developments in Theory and Practice, Volume 1: Mainly Theory.* Edited by Elisabeth Bott Spillius. London: Routledge, pp. 178–186.

———. (1975). "Foreword." In *Introduction to the Work of Bion: Groups, Knowledge, Psychosis, Thought, Transformations, Psychoanalytic Practice.* By Leon Grinberg, Sor Dario, and Elizabeth Tabak de Bianchedi. Translated by Alberto Hahn. Perthshire, UK: Roland Harris Educational Trust.

———. (1994). *Learning from Experience.* Northvale, NJ: Jason Aronson Inc.

———. (1997). *Taming Wild Thoughts.* Edited by Francesca Bion. London: Karnac Books.

Blanchot, Maurice. (1982). *The Space of Literature.* Translated by Ann Smock. Lincoln, NE: University of Nebraska Press.

Bollas, Christopher. (1992). *Being a Character: Psychoanalysis and Self Experience.* New York: Hill and Wang.

———. (1999). *The Mystery of Things.* London: Routledge.

———. (2000). *Hysteria.* London: Routledge.

———. (2002). *Free Association.* London: Icon Books.

Brabant, Eva, Falzeder, Ernst, and Giampieri-Deutsch, Patrizia, eds. (1994). *The Correspondence of Sigmund Freud and Sándor Ferenczi, Vol. I, 1908–1914.* Translated by Peter Hoffer. Cambridge, MA: Harvard University Press.

Britzman, Deborah P. (2000). "If the Story Cannot End: Deferred Action, Ambivalence, and Difficult Knowledge." In *Between Hope and Despair: Pedagogy and the Remembrance of Historical Trauma.* Edited by Roger Simon, Sharon Rosenberg, and Claudia Eppert. Lanham: Rowman and Littlefield Publishers, pp. 27–57.

———. (2003a). *After-Education: Anna Freud, Melanie Klein and Psychoanalytic Histories of Learning.* Albany, NY: State University of New York Press.

———. (2003b). *Practice Makes Practice: A Critical Study of Learning to Teach*, revised edition. Albany, NY: State University of New York Press.

Britzman, Deborah P. and Pitt, Alice J. (2004). "Pedagogy and Clinical Knowledge: Some Psychoanalytic Observations on Losing and Re-finding Significance." *JAC: A Quarterly Journal for the Interdisciplinary Study of Rhetoric, Literacy, Culture, and Politics* 2(24): 353–375.

Butler, Judith. (1997). *The Psychic Life of Power: Theories in Subjection*. Stanford, CA: Stanford University Press.

Canguilhem, Georges. (1966/1991). *The Normal and the Pathological*. Translated by Carolyn R. Fawcett in collaboration with Robert S. Cohen. New York: Zone Books.

Caper, Robert. (1988). *Immaterial Facts: Freud's Discovery of Psychic Reality and Klein's Development of His Work*. Northvale, NJ: Jason Aronson Inc.

———. (1999). *A Mind of One's Own: A Kleinian View of Self and Object*. London: Routledge.

Cavell, Marcia. (1993). *The Psychoanalytic Mind: From Freud to Philosophy*. Cambridge, MA: Harvard University Press.

Cheng, Anne. (2001). *The Melancholy of Race: Psychoanalysis, Assimilation and Hidden Grief*. Oxford: Oxford University Press.

de Certeau, Michel. (1988). *The Writing of History*. Translated by Tom Conley. New York: Columbia University Press.

———. (1993). *Heterologies: Discourse on the Other*. Translated by Brian Massumi. Minneapolis, MN: University of Minnesota Press.

Deleuze, Gilles. (1997). *Essays: Critical and Clinical*. Translated by Daniel W. Smith and Michael A. Greco. Minneapolis, MN: University of Minnesota Press.

Derrida, Jacques. (1996). *Archive Fever: A Freudian Impression*. Translated by Eric Prenowitz. Chicago: University of Chicago Press.

Du Bois, W. E. B. (1903/1989). *The Souls of Black Folk*. New York: Bantam.

Etchegoyen, R. H. (1991). *The Fundamentals of Psychoanalytic Technique*. London: Karnac Books.

Falzeder, Ernst and Brabant, Eva, eds. (1996). *The Correspondence of Sigmund Freud and Sándor Ferenczi, Volume 2, 1914–1919*. Translated by Peter T. Hoffer. Cambridge, MA: Harvard University Press.

———. (2000). *The Correspondence of Sigmund Freud and Sándor Ferenczi, Volume 3, 1920–1933*. Translated by Peter T. Hoffer. Cambridge, MA: Harvard University Press.

Fanon, Frantz. (1952/1986). *Black Skin, White Masks*. Translated by Charles Lam Markmann. London: Pluto Press.

———. (1961/1991). *The Wretched of the Earth*. Translated by Constance Farrington. New York: Grove Weidenfeld.

Feder, Stuart. (2004). *Mahler: A Life in Crisis.* New Haven, CT: Yale University Press.

Felman, Shoshana. (1985/2003). *Writing and Madness: Literature/Philosophy/Psychoanalysis.* Translated by Martha Noel Evans and Shoshana Felman with assistance by Brian Massumi. Stanford, CA: Stanford University Press.

———. (1987). *Jacques Lacan and the Adventure of Insight: Psychoanalysis in Contemporary Culture.* Cambridge, MA: Harvard University Press.

———. (1992). "Education and Crisis, or the Vicissitudes of Teaching." In *Testimony: Crises of Witnessing in Literature, Psychoanalysis and History.* Edited by Shoshana Felman and Dori Laub. New York: Routledge Press, pp. 1–56.

Ferenczi, Sándor. (1933/1988). "Confusion of Tongues between Adults and the Child: The Language of Tenderness and Passion." *Contemporary Psychoanalysis* 24(2):196–206.

Foucault, Michel. (1975/2003). *Abnormal: Lectures at the Collége de France 1974–1975.* Edited by Valerio Marchetti and Antonella Salomoni. Translated by Graham Burchell. New York: Picador.

Freud, Anna. (1930/1974). "Four Lectures on Psychoanalysis." In *The Writings of Anna Freud, Vol. 1.* Madison, CT: International Universities Press, pp. 73–136.

———. (1936/1995). *The Ego and Its Mechanisms of Defense: Revised Edition.* In *The Writings of Anna Freud, Vol. II, 1936.* Madison, CT: International Universities Press.

———. (1952/1992). *The Harvard Lectures.* Edited and annotated by Joseph Sandler. Madison, CT: International Universities Press.

Freud, Sigmund. (1953–1974). *The Standard Edition of the Complete Psychological Works of Sigmund Freud.* Edited and translated by James Strachey in collaboration with Anna Freud, assisted by Alix Strachey and Alan Tyson. 24 vols. London: Hogarth Press and Institute for Psychoanalysis.

———. (1893–1895). *Studies in Hysteria* (with Joseph Breuer). *SE* 2: 3–319.

———. (1899). "Screen Memories." *SE* 3: 301–322.

———. (1900). *The Interpretation of Dreams (Second Part). SE* 5: 339–751.

———. (1901). *The Psychopathology of Everyday Life. SE* 6: 1–310.

———. (1905). "Three Essays on Sexuality." *SE* 7: 125–243.

———. (1909). "Analysis of a Phobia in a Five-Year-Old Boy." *SE* 10: 5–149.

———. (1911). "Formulations on the Two Principles of Mental Functioning." *SE* 12: 215–226.

———. (1912a). "The Dynamics of Transference." *SE* 12: 97–108.

———. (1912b). "Recommendations to Physicians Practising Psycho-Analysis." *SE* 12: 111–120.

———. (1913a). "On Beginning the Treatment. (Further Recommendations on the Technique of Psycho-analysis, I)." *SE* 12: 123–144.

———. (1913b [1911]). "On Psycho-Analysis." *SE* 12: 205–212.

———. (1914). "Remembering, Repeating and Working Through. (Further Recommendations on the Technique of Psycho-analysis, II.)" *SE* 12: 145–156.

———. (1915a [1914]). "Observations on Transference-Love. (Further Recommendations on the Techniques of Psycho-analysis, III.)" *SE* 12: 157–171.

———. (1915b). "Papers on Meta-psychology." *SE* 14: 105–216.

———. (1916). "Some Character-Types Met with in Psychoanalytic Work." *SE* 14: 311–333.

———. (1919 [1918]). "On the Teaching of Psycho-analysis in Universities." *SE* 17: 159–74.

———. (1920). "A Note on the Prehistory of the Technique of Analysis." *SE* 17: 263–265.

———. (1923). "The Ego and the Id." *SE* 19: 3–68.

———. (1926). "Inhibitions, Symptoms and Anxiety." *SE* 20: 77–178.

———. (1933 [1932]). "New Introductory Lectures on Psychoanalysis." *SE* 22: 3–184.

———. (1936). "A Disturbance of Memory on the Acropolis." *SE* 22: 239–248.

———. (1940[1938]a). "An Outline of Psycho-Analysis. *SE* 23:141–207.

———. (1937). "Analysis Terminable and Interminable." *SE* 23: 209–54.

———. (1940 [1938]b). "Some Elementary Lessons in Psycho-Analysis." *SE* 23: 279–287.

Fuss, Diana. (1995). *The Identification Papers.* New York: Routledge.

Gallop, Jane. (1999). "Knot a love story." In *Psychoanalysis and Pedagogy.* Edited by Stephen Appel. Westport, CT: Bergin and Garvey, pp. 125–132.

Gardner, M. Robert. (1994). *On Trying to Teach: The Mind in Correspondence.* Hillsdale, NJ: The Analytic Press.

Gilroy, Paul. (1993). *The Black Atlantic: Modernity and Double Consciousness.* Cambridge, MA: Harvard University Press.

Green, André. (1986). *On Private Madness.* Madison, CT: International Universities Press.

Grinberg, L., Sor, D., and Tabak de Bianchedi, E. (1975). *Introduction to the Work of Bion.* Translated by Alberto Hahn. Perthshire, UK: Roland Harris Educational Trust.

Grosskurth, Phyllis. (1987). *Melanie Klein: Her World and Her Work.* Cambridge, MA: Harvard University Press.

Grotstein, James. (1990). "Introduction." In *Psychotic Anxieties and Containment: A Personal Record of an Analysis with Winnicott.* By Margaret I. Little. Northvale, New Jersey: Jason Aronson Inc.

Guyer, Paul. (2005). *Values of Beauty: Historical Essays in Aesthetics.* New York: Cambridge University Press.

Hassoun, Jacques. (1997). *The Cruelty of Depression: On Melancholy.* Translated by David Jacobson. Reading, MA: Addison-Wesley.

Hinshelwood, R. D. (1991). *A Dictionary of Kleinian Thought.* London: Free Association Books.

Hoffer, Axel. (1996). "Asymmetry and Mutuality in the Analytic Relationship: Contemporary Lessons from the Freud-Ferenczi Dialogue." In *Ferenczi's Turn in Psychoanalysis.* Edited by Peter Rudnytsky, Antal Bókay, and Patrizia Giampieri-Deutsch. New York: New York University Press, pp. 107–119.

Horney, Karen. (1942). *Self-Analysis.* New York: W. W. Norton and Company.

———. (1991). *Final Lectures.* New York: W. W. Norton and Company.

Isaacs, Susan. (1952). "The Nature and Function of Phantasy." In *Developments in Psychoanalysis.* Edited by Joan Riviere. London: Hogarth Press, pp. 67–121.

Jaspers, Karl. (1936/1997). *Nietzsche: An Introduction to the Understanding of His Philosophical Activity.* Translated by Charles F. Wallraff and Frederick J. Schmitz. Baltimore, MD: Johns Hopkins University Press.

Jersild, Arthur. (1955). *When Teachers Face Themselves.* New York: Teachers College Press.

Kant, Immanuel. (1784/1999). "An Answer to the Question: 'What Is Enlightenment?'" In *Political Writings.* Edited by Hans Reiss. Cambridge: Cambridge University Press, pp. 54–60.

———. (1787/1965). *Critique of Pure Reason.* Translated by Norman Kemp Smith. New York: St. Martin's Press.

———. (1803/2003). *On Education.* Translated by Annette Chuton. New York: Dover Publications.

Kernberg, Otto. (1996). "Thirty Methods to Destroy the Creativity of Psychoanalytic Candidates." *International Journal of Psychoanalysis* 77: 1032–1040.

King, Pearl and Steiner, Piccardo, eds. (1991). *The Freud-Klein Controversies, 1941–1945.* London: Tavistock/Routledge.

Klein, Melanie. (1921/1975). "Development of a Child." In *Love, Guilt and Reparation and Other Works, 1921–1945.* London: Delacorte Press/Seymour Lawrence, pp. 1–53.

———. (1928/1975). "Early Stages of the Oedipus Conflict." In *Love, Guilt and Reparation and Other Works, 1921–1945.* London: Delacorte Press/Seymour Lawrence, pp. 186–189.

———. (1930/1975). "The Importance of Symbol-Formation in the Development of the Ego." In *Love, Guilt, and Reparation and Other Works, 1921–1945.* London: Delacorte Press/Seymour Lawrence, pp. 219–232.

———. (1937/1975). "Love, Guilt, and Reparation." In *Love, Guilt and Reparation and Other Works, 1921–1945.* London: Delacorte Press/Seymour Lawrence, pp. 344–369.

———. (1940/1975). "Mourning and Its Relation to Manic-Depressive States." In *Love, Guilt and Reparation and Other Words, 1921–1945*. London: Delacorte Press/Seymour Lawrence, pp. 344–369.

———. (1946/1975). "Notes on Some Schizoid Mechanisms." In *Envy and Gratitude and Other Works, 1946–1963*. London: Delacorte Press/Seymour Lawrence, pp. 1–26.

———. (1957/1975). "Envy and Gratitude." In *Envy and Gratitude and Other Works, 1946–1963*. London: Delacorte Press/Seymour Lawrence, pp. 176–235.

———. (1961). *Narrative of a Child Analysis: The Conduct of the Psycho-Analysis of Children as Seen in the Treatment of a Ten-Year-Old Boy*. New York: Basic Books.

Kofman, Sarah. (1988). *The Childhood of Art: An Interpretation of Freud's Aesthetics*. Translated by Winifred Woodhull. New York: Columbia University Press.

Kohon, Gregorio. (1999). *No Lost Certainties to Be Recovered*. London: Karnac Books.

Kristeva, Julia. (1995). *New Maladies of the Soul*. Translated by Ross Guberman. New York: Columbia University Press.

———. (2000). *The Sense and Non-Sense of Revolt: The Powers and Limits of Psychoanalysis, Vol. I*. Translated by Jeanine Herman. New York: Columbia University Press.

———. (2001a). *Melanie Klein*. Translated by Ross Guberman. New York: Columbia University Press.

———. (2001b). *Hannah Arendt*. Translated by Ross Guberman. New York: Columbia University Press.

———. (2002). *Intimate Revolt: The Powers and Limits of Psychoanalysis, Vol. II*. Translated by Jeanine Herman. New York: Columbia University Press.

Lane, Christopher, ed. (1998). *The Psychoanalysis of Race*. New York: Columbia University Press.

Laplanche, Jean. (1989). *New Foundations for Psychoanalysis*. Translated by David Macey. Oxford: Blackwell.

———. (1999). *Essays on Otherness*. Edited by John Fletcher. London: Routledge.

Lear, Jonathan. (2003). *Therapeutic Action: An Ernest Plea for Irony*. New York: Other Press.

Leupold-Löwenthal, Harald. (1991). "Analysis Finite and Infinite." In *On Freud's "Analysis Terminable and Interminable."* Edited by Joseph Sandler. New Haven, CT: Yale University Press, pp. 56–75.

Likierman, Meira. (2001). *Melanie Klein: Her Work in Context*. New York: Continuum Books.

Little, Margaret. (1990). *Psychotic Anxieties and Containment: A Personal Record of an Analysis with Winnicott*. Northvale, NJ: Jason Aronson Inc.

———. (1997). *Miss Alice M. and Her Dragon: Recovery of a Hidden Talent*. Binghamton: *Esf* Publishers.

Loewald, Hans. (1960/2000). "On the Therapeutic Action of Psychoanalysis." In *The Essential Loewald: Collected Papers and Monographs.* Hagerstown, MD: University Publishing Group, pp. 221–256.

Lyotard, Jean-François. (1988). *Peregrinations: Law, Form, Event.* New York: Columbia University Press.

———. (1991). *The Inhuman: Reflections on Time.* Translated by Geoffrey Bennington and Rachel Bowlby. Stanford, CA: Stanford University Press.

———. (1994). *Lessons on the Analytic Sublime.* Translated by Elizabeth Rottenberg. Stanford, CA: Stanford University Press.

Meltzer, Donald. (1998). *The Kleinian Development.* London: Karnac Books.

———. (2004). "New Considerations on the Concept of the Aesthetic Conflict." In *Psychoanalysis and Art: Kleinian Perspectives.* Edited by Sandra Gosso. London: Karnac Books, pp. 211–218.

Miller, Michael Vincent. (1997). "Foreword." In *The Cruelty of Depression: On Melancholy.* By Hassoun, Jacques. Translated by David Jacobson. Reading, MA: Addison-Wesley, pp. vii–xxix.

Milner, Marion. (1942/1996). "The Child's Capacity for Doubt." In *The Suppressed Madness of Sane Men: Forty-Four Years of Exploring Psychoanalysis.* London: Routledge, pp. 12–15.

———. (1957/1990). *On Not Being Able to Paint.* Madison, CT: International Universities Press.

———. (1977/1996). "Winnicott and Overlapping Circles." In *The Suppressed Madness of Sane Men: Forty-Four Years of Exploring Psychoanalysis.* London: Routledge, pp. 279–86.

Ogbu, John. (1974). *The Next Generation: An Ethnography of Education in an Urban Neighborhood.* New York: Academic Press.

Ogden, Thomas. (1986). *The Matrix of the Mind: Object Relations and the Psychoanalytic Dialogue.* Northvale, NJ: Jason Aronson Inc.

O'Shaughnessy, Edna. (1994/1997). "What Is a Clinical Fact?" In *The Contemporary Kleinians of London.* Edited by Roy Schafer. Madison, CT: International Universities Press, pp. 30–46.

Petot, Jacques. (1990). *Melanie Klein: First Discoveries and First System 1919–1932, Volume I.* Translated by Christine Trollop. Madison, CT: International Universities Press.

Phillips, Adam. (1996). *Terrors and Experts.* Cambridge, MA: Harvard University Press.

———. (1998). *The Beast in the Nursery: On Curiosity and Other Appetites.* New York: Pantheon Books.

———. (2000). "Bombs Away." In *Promises, Promises: Essays on Literature and Psychoanalysis.* London: Farber Press, pp. 35–58.

———. (2002). *Equals.* New York: Basic Books.

———. (2005). *Going Sane: Maps of Happiness*. New York: HarperCollins Publishers.

Phillips, John. (1998). "The Fissure of Authority: Violence and the Acquisition of Knowledge." In *Reading Melanie Klein*. Edited by Lyndsey Stonebridge and John Phillips. London: Routledge, pp. 160–78.

Pitt, Alice. (2003). *The Play of the Personal: Psychoanalytic Narratives of Feminist Education*. New York: Peter Lang Publishing.

Pitt, Alice and Britzman, Deborah. (2003). "Speculations on the Qualities of Difficult Knowledge: A Psychoanalytic Experiment in Research." *International Journal of Qualitative Studies in Education* 16(6): 755–777.

Pontalis, J.-B. (1981). *Frontiers in Psychoanalysis: Between the Dream and Psychic Pain*. Translated by Catherine Cullen and Philip Cullen. New York: International Universities Press.

———. (2003). *Windows*. Translated by Anne Quinney. Lincoln, NE: University of Nebraska Press.

Rachman, Arnold William. (1997). *Sándor Ferenczi: The Psychotherapist of Tenderness and Passion*. Northvale, NJ: Jason Aronson Inc.

Read, Alan, ed. (1996). *The Fact of Blackness: Frantz Fanon and Visual Representation*. Seattle, WA: Bay Press.

Reeder, Jurgen. (2004). *Hate and Love in Psychoanalytic Institutions: The Dilemma of a Profession*. New York: The Other Press.

Ricoeur, Paul. (1970). *Freud and Philosophy: An Essay on Interpretation*. Translated by Denis Savage. New Haven, CT: Yale University Press.

———. (2004). *Memory, History, and Forgetting*. Translated by Kathleen Blumery and David Dellauer. Chicago: University of Chicago Press.

Riesenberg-Malcolm, Ruth. (1997). "Conceptualization of Clinical Facts." In *The Contemporary Kleinians of London*. Edited by Roy Schafer. Madison, CT: International Universities Press, pp. 51–70.

Rose, Jacqueline. (1993). *Why War? Psychoanalysis, Politics, and the Return to Melanie Klein*. London: Blackwell Press.

———. (2000). "Introduction." In *Jacques Lacan and the Question of Psychoanalytic Training*. By Moustapha Safouan. Translated by Jacqueline Rose. London: Macmillan Press, pp. 1–48.

Rosenfeld, Herbert. (1999). *Impasse and Interpretation: Therapeutic and Anti-therapeutic Factors in the Psychoanalytic Treatment of Psychotic, Borderline, and Neurotic Patients*. London: Routledge.

Roudinesco, Elisabeth. (2001). *Why Psychoanalysis?* Translated by Rachel Bowlby. New York: Columbia University Press.

Roustang, François. (2000). *How to Make a Paranoid Laugh: Or, What Is Psychoanalysis?* Translated by Anne C. Vila. Philadelphia: University of Pennsylvania Press.

Rudnytsky, P., Bókay, A., and Giampieri-Deutch, P., eds. (1996). *Ferenczi's Turn in Psychoanalysis*. New York: New York University Press.

Safouan, Moustapha. (2000). *Jacques Lacan and the Question of Psychoanalytic Training*. Translated by Jacqueline Rose. London: Macmillan Press.

Salzberger-Wittenberg, I., Henry, G., and Osborne, E. (1992). *The Emotional Experience of Learning and Teaching*. New York: Routledge.

Sandler, Joseph, ed. (1991). *On Freud's "Analysis Terminable and Interminable."* New Haven, CT: Yale University Press.

Schafer, Roy. (1997). "Introduction: The Contemporary Kleinians of London." *The Contemporary Kleinians of London*. Edited by Roy Schafer. Madison, CT: International Universities Press, pp. 1–25.

———. (2003). *Bad Feelings: Selected Psychoanalytic Essays*. New York: Other Press.

Schmidt, James, ed. (1996). *What Is Enlightenment?: Eighteenth-Century Answers and Twentieth-Century Questions*. Berkeley, CA: University of California Press.

Segal, Hannah. (1952/2004). "A Psycho-analytical Approach to Aesthetics." In *Psychoanalysis and Art: Kleinian Perspectives*. Edited by Sandra Gosso. London: Karnac Books, pp. 42–61.

Simon, Roger I. (2000). "The Paradoxical Practice of *Zakhor*: Memories of 'What has never been my fault or my deed.'" In *Between Hope and Despair: Pedagogy and the Remembrance of Historical Trauma*. Edited by Roger Simon, Sharon Rosenberg, and Claudia Eppert. New York: Rowman and Littlefield Publishers, pp. 9–26.

Smock, Ann. (1982). "Translator's Introduction." In *The Space of Literature*. By Maurice Blanchot. Translated by Ann Smock. Lincoln, NE: University of Nebraska Press, pp. 1–18.

Sterba, Richard. (1982). *Reminiscences of a Viennese Psychoanalyst*. Detroit, MI: Wayne State University Press.

Steuerman, Emilia. (2000). *The Bounds of Reason: Habermas, Lyotard and Melanie Klein on Rationality*. London: Routledge.

Todorov, Tzvetan. (2001). *Frail Happiness: An Essay on Rousseau*. Translated by John T. Scott and Robert D. Zaretsky. University Park, PA: Penn State Press.

———. (2002). *Imperfect Garden: The Legacy of Humanism*. Translated by Carol Cosman. Princeton, NJ: Princeton University Press.

Verhaeghe, Paul. (1999). *Love in a Time of Loneliness*. Translated by Plym Peters and Tony Langham. New York: The Other Press.

———. (2001). *Beyond Gender: From Subject to Drive*. New York: Other Press.

———. (2004). *On Being Normal and Other Disorders: A Manual for Clinical Psychodiagnostics*. Translated by Sigi Jottkandt. New York: Other Press.

Weber, Samuel. (2000). *The Legend of Freud, Expanded Edition*. Stanford: Stanford University Press.

Winnicott, D. W. (1945/1992). "Primitive Emotional Development." In *Through Paediatrics to Psycho-Analysis: Collected Papers*. New York: Brunner/Mazel, pp. 145–156.

———. (1950/1996). "Yes, but How Do We Know It's True?" In *Thinking About Children*. Edited by Ray Shepherd, Jennifer Johns, and Helen Taylor Robinson. Reading, MA: Addison-Wesley Press, pp. 13–20.

———. (1952/1992). "Anxiety Associated with Insecurity." In *Through Paediatrics to Psycho-Analysis: Collected Papers*. New York: Brunner/Mazel, pp. 97–100.

———. (1969/1999). "The Use of an Object and Relating through Identifications." In *Playing and Reality*. Philadelphia: Brunner-Routledge, pp. 86–94.

Woolf, Virginia. (1925/2002). *On Being Ill*. Ashfield, MA: Paris Press.

Wortis, Joseph. (1994). *My Analysis with Freud*. London: Jason Aronson Inc.

Young-Bruehl, Elizabeth. (1996). *The Anatomy of Prejudice*. Cambridge, MA: Harvard University Press.

# Index

## Studies in the Postmodern Theory of Education

*General Editors*
*Joe L. Kincheloe & Shirley R. Steinberg*

Counterpoints publishes the most compelling and imaginative books being written in education today. Grounded on the theoretical advances in criticalism, feminism, and postmodernism in the last two decades of the twentieth century, Counterpoints engages the meaning of these innovations in various forms of educational expression. Committed to the proposition that theoretical literature should be accessible to a variety of audiences, the series insists that its authors avoid esoteric and jargonistic languages that transform educational scholarship into an elite discourse for the initiated. Scholarly work matters only to the degree it affects consciousness and practice at multiple sites. Counterpoints' editorial policy is based on these principles and the ability of scholars to break new ground, to open new conversations, to go where educators have never gone before.

For additional information about this series or for the submission of manuscripts, please contact:

Joe L. Kincheloe & Shirley R. Steinberg
c/o Peter Lang Publishing, Inc.
275 Seventh Avenue, 28th floor
New York, New York 10001

To order other books in this series, please contact our Customer Service Department:

(800) 770-LANG (within the U.S.)
(212) 647-7706 (outside the U.S.)
(212) 647-7707 FAX

Or browse online by series:

www.peterlangusa.com